THE OVERCOMER'S MANDATE

THE OVERCOMER'S MANDATE

In Training for Reigning

R.C. SMITH

XULON PRESS

Xulon Press
2301 Lucien Way #415
Maitland, FL 32751
407.339.4217
www.xulonpress.com

Unless otherwise indicated, Scripture quotations taken from the
New American Standard Bible (NASB). Copyright © 1960, 1962,
1963, 1968, 1971, 1972, 1973, 1975, 1977, 1995 by The Lockman
Foundation. Used by permission. All rights reserved.

Scripture quotations taken from the Modern English Version (MEV).
Copyright © 2014 by Military Bible Association. Published and
distributed by Charisma House. All rights reserved.

Scripture quotations taken from the King James Version
(KJV)–public domain.

Scripture quotations taken from the The Amplified Bible Classic Edition
© 1987 The Lockman Foundation and Zondervan Publishing House.
Used by permission. All rights reserved.

Paperback ISBN-13: 978-1-6312-9776-2
Ebook ISBN-13: 978-1-6312-9777-9

Table of contents

INTRODUCTION. ix

Chapter one. The Three Tenses of our
                  Salvation. 1

Chapter two. Apostasy: The End of the
                  Church Age. 31

Chapter three. God's Appointed Times. 43

Chapter four. The Feasts of the Lord. 60

Chapter five. God's Prophetic Time Clock. . 102

Chapter six. The Harpazo of the Faithful. . 137

Chapter seven. In Training for Reigning. . 164

Chapter eight. Christ is our Plumb Line. . . 182

Chapter nine. Prophetic Patterns of
                  Overcomers: Abraham. 207

Chapter ten. Prophetic Patterns of
                  Overcomers: Joshua. 227

Chapter eleven. Overcomers: Zacharias,
                  Elisabeth, & John. 261

Chapter twelve. God is Good and Just. . . . 297

Chapter thirteen. Enter or Possess and
                  Inherit. 335

Chapter fourteen. God's Plan for Earth
                  and Man. 363

EPILOGUE 393

Introduction

This volume of work is our second book and we will build upon the Foundational stones of Truth established in: *The Believer's Mandate – Why are we here?*

The primary objective of this discourse is to preach the genuine Gospel of the Kingdom and answer the questions that should naturally follow our discovery of why we are here on this planet, and to be a continued reference resource or an overcomer's field manual as we make ourselves ready.

Questions such as: Who are these overcomers that Jesus speaks of, and is it the Father's will that all His children would be overcomers? What must I do to be an overcomer, and why is it important for me to become an overcomer now? How do we live the victorious overcoming lifestyle? There must be something to overcome if we are to be called overcomers? And when exactly do we become an official overcomer? And what do the overcomers do once they become one?

Heaven and hell are very real places and every individual soul will in-fact spend all of eternity in one of these two final destinations, and as believer's we all must know that we know that heaven is our eternal home.

However, what most people do not seem to understand is that heaven and hell have different levels and heaven and hell will not be the same for all that go to their chosen respective final destinations. Yes, we said "chosen destination" because we are the one who ultimately decides our eternal terminus.

Therefore, hell has different levels of eternal torment based on the persons behavior while here on earth, and likewise even heaven too will not be the same for everyone that believes in Jesus. Believes what?

We must believe that Jesus is the Son of God and believe He died to pay the ransom price for our sins, and after three days rose from the grave, and is now at the right hand of God interceding for those that believe in Him and have ask Jesus into their hearts and lives, thus becoming our personal Savior and Lord.

However, before any believer arrives at their ultimate and eternal destination, which is New Jerusalem as described in Revelation chapters twenty-one and twenty-two; there is the soon coming Kingdom age here on earth as recorded in Revelation chapter twenty when King Jesus will rule and reign for one thousand years here on this earth.

The Kingdom age will begin at the end of the current Church age when Jesus returns to this earth on that great and terrible day of the Lord, more commonly known as Judgement Day. That enormously important Day will be great for some and terrible for others when Jesus takes His throne in Jerusalem as King of kings and Lord of lords to rule and reign with the overcomers.

We are in the last of the last days of the age of grace and within this study, we provide a summation of God's prophetic time clock, His appointed times, and His plan for the restoration of all things from the fall in the Garden of Eden until the end of the Kingdom age. Our opportunity to impact our eternity is quickly closing because at the conclusion of the Church age the opportunity to affect our place and position in the soon coming Kingdom age shall end as well.

What you have in your hands, *The Overcomer's Mandate*; is a synopsis of the Master's plan for the redemption of man and the restoration of all things and the Father's desired destiny for every one of His children that is etched in His heart.

All genuine believers are now *in training for reigning* with King Jesus in the swiftly coming Kingdom age, and it really matters how we elect to live now because our choices will affect our place and position in the Kingdom age and our rewards and inheritance forevermore. There is a lot at stake for every believer, truly far more than most realize or comprehend. The King and His Kingdom are at the door.

Our soon coming Savior, Lord, Judge, and King said to John the Revelator:

Behold, I am coming soon, and I shall bring My wages and rewards with Me, to repay and render to each one just what his own actions and his own work merit. Revelation 22:12 AMPC

Folks please take heed. We are truly living in a critical hour and the current Church age is quickly consummating and the coronation of our King is very near, and it is a lot better to live ready than trying to get ready.

Are you ready to meet your King?

CHAPTER ONE

The three Tenses of our Salvation.

Foundational Truth: Salvation has three tenses–past, present, and future tense; and our comprehension and subsequent action based on our faith of this Truth will determine our place in the Kingdom age and our eternal inheritance.

Yes, our salvation is found in One name only. In Hebrew it is pronounced *Yeshua HaMashiach*, and in English it is transliterated Jesus the Christ; and we know according to Acts chapter four and verse twelve that salvation is found in no other name: *There is no salvation in any other, for there is no other name under heaven given among men by which we must be saved.* And just as we see in the book of Hebrews chapter thirteen and verse eight: *Jesus Christ is the same yesterday, and today, and forever;* this Truth shall never change. Amen.

Past tense is separation from the *penalty* of sin, which was our justification.

Present tense is separation from the *power* of sin, is the process of sanctification.

Future tense is separation from the *presence* of sin, will be our glorification.

Justification means that we have been justified: *Just as if I'd never sinned.* We are forgiven and washed clean of all our past sins and iniquities. We are declared righteous by our heavenly Father the moment we accept by faith the atoning sacrifice of Jesus the Son of God made for us on the cross. (Romans 3:21-26) We believe by grace we have been saved. Jesus came to this earth and took our place and paid in full the ransom price with His own blood, that we might be set free from the sin-debt that we simply could not pay. This is the incredibly *good news* of the Gospel.

What? Do you not know that your body in the temple of the Holy Spirit, who is in you, whom you have received from God, and that you are not your own? You were bought with a price, Therefore glorify

God in your body and in your spirit, which are God's. I Corinthians 6:19-20 MEV

For by grace you have been saved through faith, and this is not of yourselves. It is the gift of God, not works, so that no one should boast. For we are His workmanship, created in Christ Jesus for good works, which God prepared beforehand, so that we should walk in them. Ephesians 2:8-10 MEV

We also were once foolish, disobedient, deceived, serving various desires and pleasures, living in evil and envy, filled with hatred and hating each other. But when the kindness and the love of God our Savior toward mankind appeared, not by works of righteousness which we have done, but according to His mercy He saved us, through the washing of rebirth and the renewal of the Holy Spirit, whom He poured out on us abundantly through Jesus Christ our Savior, so that, being justified by His grace, we might become heirs according to the hope of eternal life. Titus 3:3-5 MEV

We are all born into this world with a sin-nature that we inherited from our progenitors Adam and Eve. Every individual is born into this present world a sinner in need of a Savior and we cannot do anything to save ourselves, thus we are saved by grace and grace alone, and through faith and faith alone in Jesus Christ the Son of the living God.

Sanctification is a life-long dynamic process. We all are a work in progress and should be throughout our lives as devoted followers and bond-servants of Jesus. This renewal process is not in our own strength, but; is the result of an act of our will to desire and *yield* to the work of the Holy Spirit in us, and this ongoing transfiguring work should continue until we leave this earth through natural death, or Jesus returns; and we are caught-up to meet Him in the air. With the help of the Holy Spirit, as we faithfully commit ourselves to the study of the Word and the practical application of the revealed Truth to our lives; we will continue to grow in wisdom and mature spiritually as we continue to walk in the light with our Lord, as Holy Spirit leads, guides, and perfects us.

I urge you therefore, brothers, by the mercies of God, that you present your bodies as a living sacrifice, holy, and acceptable to God, which is your reasonable service of worship. Do not be conformed to this world, but be transformed by the renewing of your mind, that you may prove what is the good and acceptable and perfect will of God. Romans 12:1-2 MEV

I am confident of this very thing, that He who began a good work in you will perfect it until the day of Jesus Christ. Philippians 1:6 MEV

Therefore, my beloved, as you have always obeyed, not only in my presence, but so much more in my absence, work out your own salvation with fear and trembling. For God is the One working in you, both to will and to do His good pleasure. Philippians 2:12-13 MEV

But grow in the grace and knowledge of our Lord and Savior Jesus Christ. To Him be glory, both now and forever. Amen. II Peter 3:18 MEV

Glorification shall occur when every believer receives their resurrected and glorified bodies. At the precise moment of our natural physical death, or at the catching away of the overcomers, whichever event comes first for the believer; our spirit and souls are liberated from this earthly temporary tent of flesh that our spirit and soul has been sojourning in here on earth.

If our earthly house fails and dies naturally before Christ's return, our flesh, blood, and bone bodies decompose and return to the earth from which we were formed by Father God (Genesis 2:7) to wait until the day of the first resurrection (Revelation

20:1-6), and at our natural death our spirit and soul are escorted by angels to be with our Lord Jesus.

It came to pass that the beggar died and was carried by the angels to Abraham's presence. The rich man died and was buried. Luke 16:22 MEV

Are they not all ministering spirits sent out to minister to those who will inherit salvation? Hebrews 1:14 MEV

This is the will of Him who sent Me, I should lose nothing, but should raise it up at the last day. This is the will of Him who sent Me, that everyone who sees the Son and believes in Him may have eternal life, and I will raise him up on the last day. John 6:39-40 MEV

We know that if our earthly house, this tent, were to be destroyed, we have an eternal building of God in the heavens, a house not made with hands. Therefore we are always confident, knowing that while we are at home in the body, we are absent from the Lord. For we walk by faith and not by sight. Instead, I say that we are confident and willing to be absent from the body and to be present with the Lord. II Corinthians 5:1,6-8 MEV

I am in a difficult position between the two, having a desire to depart and to be with Christ, which is far better. Philippians 1:23 MEV

The overcoming saints that are still naturally alive when King Jesus returns, shall be caught-up (raptured) to meet Him in the clouds; we will then receive our new, incorruptible, and glorified body shortly after those saints that have physically died in Christ before us receive their resurrected and glorified bodies.

But now is Christ risen from the dead and become the first fruits of those who have fallen asleep. For since death came by man, by man came also the resurrection of the dead. For as in Adam all die, even so in Christ shall all be made alive. But every man in his own order: Christ the first fruits; afterward, those who are Christ's at His coming. I Corinthians 15:20-23 MEV

Now this I say, brothers, that flesh and blood cannot inherit the kingdom of God, nor does corruption inherit incorruption. Listen, I tell you a mystery: We shall not all sleep, but we shall all be changed. In a moment, in the twinkling of an eye, at the last trumpet, for the trumpet will sound, the dead will be raised incorruptible, and we shall be changed. For this corruptible will put on immortality. When this corruptible will have put on incorruption, and this mortal will have put on immortality, then the saying that is written shall come to pass: Death is swallowed up in victory. O death, where is your sting? O grave, where is your victory? I Corinthians 15:50-55 MEV

If you then were raised with Christ, desire those things which are above, where Christ sits at the right hand of God. Set your affection on things above, not on things on earth. For you are dead, and your life is hidden with Christ in God, When Christ who is our life shall appear, then you also shall appear with Him in glory. Colossians 3:1-4 MEV

The Spirit Himself bears witness with our spirits that we are children of God, and if children, then heirs: heirs of God and joint heirs with Christ, if in deed we suffer with Him, that we may also be glorified with Him. For I consider that the sufferings of this present time are not worthy to be compared with the glory which shall be revealed to us. Romans 8:16-18 MEV

For this we say to you by the word of the Lord, that we who are alive and remain until the coming of the Lord will not precede those who are asleep. For the Lord Himself will descend from heaven with a shout, with the voice of the archangel, and with the trumpet call of God. And the dead in Christ will rise first. Then we who are alive and remain shall be caught up together with them in the clouds to meet the Lord in the air. And so we shall be forever with the Lord. Therefore comfort one another with these words. I Thessalonians 4:15-18 MEV

Thus, to summarize the three tenses of our salvation we see that when our spirit-man is born-again, we have become (past tense) justified in Christ. Please take note of the fact that we have absolutely nothing to do with this supernatural miracle except to simply receive freely the grace of Jesus Christ as our Savior through faith in His finished work on the cross, thus; no one can earn justification.

And likewise, when our physical life here in our earth suit of flesh has come to an end through natural death, or at the future harpazo of the overcoming believers, we will at that (future tense) moment receive our immortal, incorruptible, and glorified bodies. And just like our justification, we have absolutely nothing to do with the supernatural glorification of our future eternal bodies.

The overcomers – Who are they?

Now we have arrived at the central precept and focus of this teaching, which is the (present tense)

dynamic portion of our salvation. We must comprehend that our Sovereign heavenly Fathers' excellent purpose in creation and His complete divine plan of redemption has ultimately one objective, and that supreme goal is to have a large family of volunteer lovers that have been willingly and enthusiastically transfigured into the express image of His Son and our Lord Jesus the Christ. These are the overcomers.

This leads us to every believer's mandate and the principal issue of our life in Christ, which is our progressive sanctification and becoming overcomers. We all desperately need to accurately understand and receive revelation of this process, and accordingly; make this our supreme focus of our life here and now. Why?

Because the absolute measure of our willingness to surrender and submit to this on-going development and spiritual maturing process shall directly affect our position, our place, our rewards, and our inheritance as we rule with Christ during the one-thousand-year millennial reign, which is the Kingdom age.

Our level of sanctification will also impact our place and our inheritance for all of eternity in our future home in the Holy City–the New Jerusalem. (Revelation 21:1-8) We must clearly understand that this progressive course of action is an act of our sovereign will as we continue to choose daily to submit to the Lordship of Jesus Christ, and thus He will fulfil His plan and purpose for our lives.

Behold saints, we are now literally *in training for reigning* with King Jesus. However, it will be only those faithful believers that truly desire and choose to live surrendered lives totally submitted to the Lordship of Jesus Christ. These are the true overcomers that will rule and reign with our soon coming King.

This active present tense portion of our salvation, and the clarion call to sanctification, consecration, sacrifice, and holiness; is exactly what our Lord Jesus was teaching us about, along with His clear instructions regarding the present tense realities and the genuine cost and sacrifice required of true discipleship in this contemporary age; when He said:

You, therefore, must be perfect [growing into complete maturity of godliness in mind and character, having reached the proper height of virtue and integrity], as your heavenly Father is perfect. Matthew 5:48 AMPC

Why do you call Me, Lord, Lord, and not do what I say? Luke 6:46 MEV

That is indeed a really, really good question Jesus.

Then He said to them all, If anyone will come after Me, let him deny himself, and take up his cross daily, and follow Me. For whoever will save his life will lose it, but whoever loses his life for My sake will save it. Luke 9:23-24 MEV

If anyone comes to Me and does not hate his father and mother and wife and children and brothers and sisters, yes, and even his own life, he cannot be My disciple. And whoever does not bear his cross and follow me cannot be My disciple. So likewise, any of you who does not forsake all that he has cannot be My disciple. Luke 14:26-27,33 MEV

And this same sanctification, transformation, spiritually maturing, and perfecting process is exactly what apostle Paul was writing about in the Holy Spirit inspired epistles to the churches and to all of us whom the end of the age has come.

We are assured and know that [God being a partner in their labor] all things work together and are [fitting into a plan] for good to and for those who love God and are called according to [His] design and purpose. For those He foreknew [of whom He was aware and loved beforehand], He also destined from the beginning [foreordaining them] to be molded into the image of His Son [and share inwardly His likeness], that He might become the firstborn among many brethren. And those whom He thus foreordained, He also called; and those whom He called, He also justified (acquitted, made righteous, putting them into right standing with Himself). And those whom He justified, He also glorified [raising them to a heavenly dignity and condition or state of being]. Romans 8:28-30 AMPC

Now the Lord is the Spirit, and where the Spirit of the Lord is, there is liberty (emancipation from bondage, freedom). And all of us, as with unveiled face, [because we] continued to behold [in the Word of God] as in a mirror the glory of the Lord, are constantly being transfigured into His very own image in ever increasing splendor and from one degree of glory to another; [for this comes] from the Lord [Who is] the Spirit. II Corinthians 3:17-18 AMPC

But whatever former things I had that might have been gains to me, I have come to consider as [one combined] loss for Christ's sake. Yes, furthermore, I count everything as loss compared to the possession of the priceless privilege (the overwhelming preciousness, the surpassing worth, and supreme advantage) of knowing Christ Jesus my Lord and of progressively becoming more deeply and intimately acquainted with Him [of perceiving and recognizing and under-standing Him more fully and clearly]. For His sake I have lost everything and consider it all to be mere rubbish (refuse, dregs), in order that I may win (gain) Christ (the Anointed One), And that I may [actu-ally] be found and known as in Him, not having any [self-achieved] righteousness that can be called my own, based on my obedience to the Law's demands (ritualistic uprightness and supposed right standing with God thus acquired), but possessing that [gen-uine righteousness] which comes through faith in Christ (the Anointed One), the [truly] right standing with God, which comes from God by [saving] faith. [For my determined purpose is] that I may know Him [that I may progressively become more deeply and intimately acquainted with Him, perceiving and recognizing and understanding the wonders of His Person more strongly and more clearly], and that I may in that same way come to know the power out-flowing from His resurrection [which it exerts over believers], and that I may share His sufferings as to be continually transformed [in spirit into His likeness even] to His death, [in the hope] that if possible I may attain to the [spiritual and moral] resurrection [that lifts me] out from among the dead [even while in the body]. Not that I have now attained [this ideal], or have already been made perfect, but I press on to lay hold of (grasp) and make my own, that for which Christ Jesus (the Messiah) has laid hold of me and made me His own. I do not consider, brethren, that I have captured and made it my own [yet]; but this one thing I do [it is my one aspiration]: forgetting what lies behind and straining forward to what lies ahead, I press on toward the goal to win the [supreme and heavenly] prize to which God in Christ Jesus is calling us upward. **So let those [of us] who are spiritually mature and full-grown have this mind and hold these convictions**; and if in any respect you have a different attitude of mind, God will make that clear to you also. Only let us hold true to what we have already attained and walk and order our lives by that. Brethren, together follow my example and observe those who live after the pattern we have set for you. Philippians 3:7-17 AMPC

[Even] now I rejoice in the midst of my sufferings on your behalf. And in my own person I am making up whatever is still lacking and remains to be completed [on our part] of Christ's afflictions, for the sake of His body, which is the church. In it I became a minister in accordance with the divine stewardship which was entrusted to me for you [as its object and for your benefit], to make the Word of God fully known [among you] – The mystery of which was hidden for ages and generations [from angels and men], but is now revealed to His holy people (the saints), to whom God was pleased to make known how great for the Gentiles are the riches of the glory of this mystery, which is Christ within and among you, the Hope of [realizing the] glory. Him we preach and proclaim, warning and admonishing everyone and instructing everyone in all wisdom (comprehensive insight into the ways and purposes of God), **that we may present every person mature (full-grown, fully initiated, complete, and perfect) in Christ (the Anointed One)**. For this I labor [unto weariness], striving with all the superhuman energy which He so mightily enkindles and works within me. Colossians 1:24-29 AMPC

And for the sake of any individuals among us that might still be wavering in their faith a bit and are still pondering if this call to surrender, sacrifice, and to holiness really applies to you and your present life as a fully devoted bond-servant of Jesus Christ, please prayerfully consider the following Truths from the living Word of God.

I do not write this to shame you, but to warn and counsel you as my beloved children. After all, though you should have ten thousand teachers (guides to direct you) in Christ, yet you do not have many fathers. For I became your father in Christ Jesus through the glad tidings (the Gospel). So I urge and implore you, be imitators of me. I Corinthians 4:14-16 AMPC

Pattern yourselves after me [follow my example], as I imitate and follow Christ (the Messiah). I Corinthians 11:1 AMPC

And you [set yourselves to] become imitators of us and [through us] of the Lord Himself, for you welcomed our message in [spite of] much per-secution, with joy [inspired] by the Holy Spirit; I Thessalonians 1:6 AMPC

This letter is from Paul, a slave of God and an apostle of Jesus Christ. I have been sent to proclaim faith to those God has chosen and to teach them to know the truth that shows them how to live godly lives. Titus 1:1 NLT

Who may ascend the hill of the Lord? Who may stand in His holy place? He who has clean hands and a pure heart; who has not lifted up his soul unto vanity, nor sworn deceitfully. Psalm 24:3-4 MEV

Blessed are the pure in heart, for they will see God. Blessed are the peacemakers, for they shall be called the sons of God. Matthew 5:8-9 MEV

Strive to live in peace with everybody and pursue that consecration and holiness without which no one will [ever] see the Lord. Hebrews 12:14 AMPC

James, a bond-servant of God and of the Lord Jesus Christ, To the twelve tribes who are dispersed abroad: Greetings. Consider it all joy, my brethren, when you encounter various trials, knowing that the testing of your faith produces endurance. And let endurance have its perfect result, so that you may be perfect and complete, lacking in nothing. James 1:1-4 NASB

So, how are we doing thus far folks? Are you a genuine bond-servant of Jesus? Are you actively emulating Paul just as he was following and imitating Christ? Only the true genuine bond-servants of Jesus Christ are the overcomers.

The sad reality is that many so-called Church leaders and pastors today are not proclaiming the full Gospel of the Kingdom. Many of these doctrinally unsound and compromising preachers and deceived teachers shy away from preaching and teaching about sin and repentance, and certainly not about sacrifice and holiness. Thus, the people are not learning the Truth, which is learning the sincere cost of genuine discipleship.

However, these gatherings do have relevant pastors and leaders, and they have super-cool smoke and light shows to enhance their so-called Christian praise and worship sing-along concerts, which transitions into a maximum of a thirty-minute pep talk sermonette about the six steps on how you can live the blessed life now! These high energy super-hipsters draw big crowds, so; they must be righteous and doing this thing called church correctly, right?

Well, here is what Jesus Christ said about the super-popular church leaders: *What sorrow awaits you who are praised by the crowds, for their ancestors also praised the false prophets.* Luke 6:26 NLT

For this is a rebellious people, faithless and lying sons, children who will not hear the law and instruction of the Lord! Who [virtually] say to the seers [by their conduct], See not! And to the prophets, Prophesy not to us what is right! *Speak to us smooth things,* prophesy deceitful illusions. Isaiah 30:9-10 AMPC

An appalling and horrible thing [bringing desolation and destruction] has come to pass in the land: The prophets prophesy falsely, and the priests exercise rule at their own hands and by means of the prophets. *And My people love to have it so!* But what will you do when the end comes? Jeremiah 5:30-31 AMPC

The consequences of this over-consumption of the sugar-coated gospel has been emotionally stimulating meetings, but; very few changed lives. All of this has resulted in weak and powerless church gatherings full of spiritual infants focused on self-ambitions and their own prosperity and blessings.

The net result has been in many denominational and non-denominational churches being virtually barren of the presence and power and the glory of the great I AM, and thus resulting in very, very few radically changed and transformed believers and followers of Jesus Christ. Hey, do we not know that you can't feed an Army just one meal a week of cake and ice-cream and expect that Army to be victorious on any battlefield, and certainly not win the war.

Behold, what the real bottom line is here: The Church at large is simply *not* making genuine disciples of Jesus Christ!

We do not change the Truth; the Truth changes us. So, what is the answer?

Herald and preach the Word! Keep your sense of urgency [stand by, be at hand and ready], whether the opportunity seems to be favorable or unfavorable. [Whether it is convenient or inconvenient, whether it is welcome or unwelcome, you as preacher of the Word are to show people in what way their lives are wrong.] And convince them, rebuking and correcting, warning and urging and encouraging them, being unflagging and inexhaustible in patience and teaching. For the time is coming when [people] will not tolerate (endure) sound and wholesome instruction, but, having ears itching [for something pleasing and gratifying], they will gather to themselves one teacher after another to a considerable number, chosen to satisfy their own liking and to foster the errors they hold, and will turn aside from hearing the truth and wander off into myths and man-made fictions. II Timothy 4:2-4 AMPC

These seeker-friendly *"Christian lite"* gatherings and the dead denominational and religious churches are deceived churches full of individuals still in their spiritual pampers. There motto is *"All the salvation with half the guilt!"* and the last thing they want to hear about is obedience and repentance, or self-denial and holiness; and they certainly do not want to hear anything about self-sacrifice!

What they want to hear again and again is a pleasant, ear tickling, and inspirational message about how blessed and highly favored they are regardless of their lifestyle. Of course, this is assuming that they are truly born-again and thus bearing the spiritual fruit of repentance.

Every one of us were newly-born babies once, but; our parents did not expect us to stay infants. No, our caregivers expected us to grow-up and quit pooping in our britches and learn to feed ourselves. Likewise, we all were spiritual babies once, nevertheless; we must now grow-up physically, emotionally, and mature spiritually. We must learn to feed ourselves spiritually and then teach others too.

Bring forth fruit that is consistent with repentance [let your lives prove your change of heart]. Matthew 3:8 AMPC

For once you were darkness, but now you are light in the Lord; walk as children of Light [lead the lives of those native-born to the Light]. For the fruit (the effect, the product) of the Light or the Spirit [consists]

in every form of kindly goodness, uprightness of heart, and trueness of life. Ephesians 5:8-9 AMPC

Many of these Holy Spiritless gatherings and institutions have focus groups committed to finding out what it takes to attract the carnally minded to their services, and then discover what things, programs, or features that will appeal to their flesh and make them comfy and coming back.

Now if the marketing department has done a really good job, then some of these super-cool churches will have two or even three services on Sunday. Hurry now, let's get them in and get them out! We must make room for the next performance; the show must go on! Of course, at Passover they will have the Easter bunny flopping around and around Christmas time some of these worldly infested churches will even have their very own Santa in the lobby, and maybe some elves too!

But, these still have some catching-up to do to arrive at the backslidden level of one church in California that has a micro-brewery in the basement of the church, but; not to worry because they boast that all the profits from beer sales go directly to the local Planned Parenthood to murder some more babies.

We can't help but wonder when is Holy Spirit scheduled to show-up during these professionally choreographed performances? Please remember and do not forget that big crowds and popularity do not necessarily mean good success in the Kingdom of God because this is exactly how the world thinks and operates.

We must awaken to the fact that "church" is not about you! Instead of these works of the carnally minded and all of this worldly madness, we need to be seeking the face of God and His presence while endeavoring to create an environment that is welcoming and pleasing to Holy Spirit to come and have His way among His people and His church service. If Holy Spirit hasn't come in your mist, then you have <u>not</u> had a true Jesus Christ centered gathering of God's sanctified people, and absolutely everyone will go home just like they came to the meeting. How sad is that.

The late man of God, Kenneth E. Hagin (1917-2003) would say just about now: *I think some preachers, even Full Gospel, Pentecostal preachers wouldn't know the Holy Spirit if they saw Him coming down the street with a red hat on! He will start to move in their services, and they just keep on with their little programs.*

This is the Laodicean church, which was the seventh of the seven churches of Asia minor that Jesus prophesied would manifest in the last of the last days of the Church age.

The word Lao in Greek means *laity* and the Greek word Dice means *rule* thus the new compounded name of this church means *ruled by the laity*, or the compromising, self-confident, conceited, deceived, utterly nauseating, and Spirit-devoid church; and consequently; this church obviously is not ruled or approved or attended by the Lord Jesus Christ or the Holy Spirit.

And to the angel (messenger) of the assembly (church) in Laodicea write: These are the words of the Amen, the trusty and faithful and true Witness, the Origin and Beginning and Author of God's creation: I know your [record of] works and what you are doing; you are neither cold nor hot. Would that you were cold or hot! So, because you are lukewarm and neither cold nor hot, I will spew you out of My mouth! For you say, I am rich; I have prospered and grown wealthy, and I am in need of nothing; and you do not realize and understand that you are wretched, pitiable, poor, blind, and naked. Therefore I counsel you to purchase from Me gold refined and tested by fire, that you may be [truly] wealthy, and white clothes to clothe you and to keep the shame of your nudity from being seen, and salve to put on your eyes, that you may see. Those whom I [dearly and tenderly] love, I tell their faults and convict and convince and reprove and chasten [I discipline and instruct them]. So be enthusiastic and in earnest and burning with zeal and repent [changing your mind and attitude]. Behold, I stand at the door and knock; if anyone hears and listens to and heeds My voice and opens the door, I will come in to him and will eat with him, and he [will eat] with Me. He who overcomes (is victorious), I will grant him to sit beside Me on My throne, as I Myself overcame (was victorious) and sat down beside MY Father on His throne. He who is able to hear, let him listen to and heed what the [Holy] Spirit says to the assemblies (churches). Revelation 3:14-22 AMPC

Jesus clearly says that He is standing <u>outside</u> this compromised and apostate church and He is knocking to see if anyone will invite Him in. Jesus is the Head and the Cornerstone of the Church, however; He is not welcome in this backslidden assembly where the people are doing things their own way. This is not good, because the church is supposed to be all about Jesus.

He is also the head of the body, the church; and He is the beginning, the firstborn from the dead, so that He Himself will come to have first place in every-thing. Colossians 1:18 NASB

You are built upon the foundation of the apos-tles and prophets with Christ Jesus Himself the chief Cornerstone. In Him the whole structure is joined (bound, welded) together harmoniously, and it con-tinues to rise (grow, increase) into a holy temple in the Lord [a sanctuary dedicated, consecrated, and sacred to the presence of the Lord]. In Him [and in fellowship with one another] you yourselves also are being built up [into this structure] with the rest, to form a fixed abode (dwelling place) of God in (by, through) the Spirit. Ephesians 1:20-22 AMPC

If you find yourself attending or supporting such a local church, we would like to ask you a simple question: Why would you attend a church that Jesus doesn't?

Selah – Carefully meditate on this precept as if your place and position in eternity hangs in the bal-ance, because it absolutely does.

The *narrow* gate and the *broad* way.

Jesus taught us that there would be *few* over-comers in His coming Kingdom.

Enter through the narrow gate; for wide is the gate and spacious and broad is the way that leads away to destruction, and many are those who are entering through it. But the gate is narrow (con-tracted by pressure) and the way is straightened and compressed that leads away to life, and *few* are those who find it. Matthew 7:13-14 AMPC

Not everyone who says to Me, Lord, Lord, will enter the kingdom of heaven, but he who does the will of My Father Who is in heaven. Many will say to Me on that day, Lord, Lord, have we not prophesied in Your name and driven out demons in Your name and done many mighty works in Your name? And then I will say to them openly (publicly), I never knew you; depart from Me, you who act wickedly [disregarding My commands]. Matthew 7:21-23 AMPC

[Jesus] journeyed on through towns and villages, teaching, and making His way towards Jerusalem. And someone asked Him, Lord, will only a *few* be saved (rescued, delivered from the penalties of the last judgement, and made partakers of the salvation by Christ)? And He said to them, **Strive to enter by the narrow door** [force yourselves through it], **for many, I tell you, will try to enter and will not be able.** When once the Master of the house gets up and closes the door, and you begin to stand outside and knock at the door [again and again], saying, Lord, open to us! He will answer you, I do not know where [what household – certainly not Mine] you come from. Then you will begin to say, We ate and drank in Your presence, and You taught in our streets. But He will say, I tell you, I do not know where [what household – certainly not Mine] you come from; depart from Me, all you wrongdoers! There will be weeping and grinding of teeth when you see Abraham and Isaac and Jacob and all the prophets in the kingdom of God, but you yourselves being cast forth (banished, driven away). And [people] will come from east and west, and from north and south, and sit down (feast at table) in the kingdom of God. And behold, there are some [now] last who will be first [then], and there are some [now] first who will be last [then]. Luke 13:22-30 AMPC

Whoa now, what is this all about? Who are the many that are doing these mighty works in His name? Who specifically are the few that are striving to enter through the narrow gate? Is Jesus teaching that these preachers are going to hell?

No, that is not the revelation Jesus is teaching here. These many that are on the broad way that leads to destruction are these very same popular, cosmopolitan, and self-assured pastors, teachers, leaders, pew-warmers, and church member-spectators that all are part of this deceived end time Laodicean apostate church, that are doing things their own way, and not the way of the Master.

Sometimes the best way to understand and identify something is to show you exactly what it is not. Therefore, we must be abundantly clear on this point: These broad way walkers and self-centered individuals are *not* overcomers.

Jesus commanded you and me to walk the narrow path and strive to enter the narrow door.

This is the overcomer's mandate.

CHAPTER TWO

Apostasy: The End of the Church Age.

Foundational Truth: The end of the Church age cannot conclude until the great falling away comes first, and then the lawless antichrist is revealed.

The *apostasy* is the abandonment of the Truth, and the *Church age* is the present dispensation of grace that began on the day of Pentecost (fourth Feast) and will continue until the harpazo or rapture (fifth Feast) of the faithful bride of Christ, which are the overcomers.

But relative to the coming of our Lord Jesus Christ (the Messiah) and our gathering together to [meet] Him, we beg you, brethren, not to allow your minds to be quickly unsettled or disturbed or kept excited or alarmed, whether it be by some [pretended] revelation of [the] Spirit or by word or by letter [alleged to be] from us, to the effect that the day of the Lord has [already] arrived and is here. Let no one deceive you or beguile you in any way, for that day will not come except the apostasy comes first [unless the predicted great falling away of those who have professed to be Christians has come], and the man of lawlessness (sin) is revealed, who is the son of doom (of perdition), who opposes and exalts himself so proudly and insolently against and over all that is called God or that is worshiped, [even to his actually] taking his seat in the temple of God, proclaiming he himself is God. II Thessalonians 2:1-4 AMPC

Three bond-servants of Christ, namely Paul, Peter, and Jude; all received revelation of the latter days and wrote extensively about these coming days within the Church. These revelations were received by Peter and Paul at the most somber time of their ministries because these inspired teachings came at the very end of their natural lives.

These overcoming servants of Jesus Christ prophesied about a slow but an ever-increasing corruption and fading away from the Truth throughout the entire Church age, ultimately leading to the end of the age and the rapture (fifth Feast), followed by the seven years of tribulation (seven days of awe), thus leading to the Day of Judgement (sixth Feast), which is the end of the sixth prophetic day and the completion of man's six thousand years. Then what? (seventh Feast) The seventh day – the Kingdom age.

In the following three chapters we shall fully expound on Father God's prophetic time signals, His appointed dates and events, and the Lord's complete plan of redemption encoded within His seven Feasts which we have eluded to here. We shall endeavor to answer any question that might be lingering about how all of these things fit together as one continual flowing plan that Father God is revealing to His people.

The following Scriptures are our text for study about the signs that will mark the completion of the dispensation of grace and the end-time apostasy within the worldwide Church of the living God. These characteristics, behaviors, and signs are manifesting now in our culture and in the Church.

II Thessalonians 2:1-12, I Timothy 4:1-5, II Timothy 3:1- 4:18

II Peter 1:3-11, II Peter 2:1-3, II Peter 3:1-18, Jude 1:4-22

After the nation of Israel's religious leaders and ruler's total rejection of the Lord Jesus and their blasphemy of the Holy Spirit recorded in Matthew chapter twelve, that very same day at seaside Jesus began to teach about this mystery we now know as the Church age.

Jesus was clearly instructing us about the corruption and the resulting slow fade away from the Truth that would continue throughout the Church age as seen in the eight prophetic parables recorded in Matthew chapter thirteen, that are all to be taken together and considered as one flowing and congruent message.

(1) The parable of the Sower (Matthew 13:1-9,18-23) teaches that the Gospel of the coming Kingdom will be preached throughout the Church age with varying degrees of success and results depending upon how the individual hearer has prepared his/her own heart and their subsequent chosen level of devotion, obedience, and submission to the Word of Truth. Only twenty-five percent of the hearts are good among those few that find the narrow way (Luke 13:22-30), and even those were at diverse levels of fruitfulness, depending on their level of submission to the Word.

(2) The parable of the Wheat and Tares (Matthew 13:24-30, 36-43) teaches that it will be very difficult to distinguish between the true born-again believers

and those that are unconverted or unsaved with the separation and culling of those not occurring until the conclusion of the age.

(3) The parable of the tiny Mustard Seed (Matthew 13:31-32) teaches that His very small Church will experience incredible growth in numbers and territory, thus spreading throughout the earth; and the birds of the air, symbolic of demons; (Genesis 15:11, Deuteronomy 28:26, Revelation 18:2) will come and strive to infiltrate it and successfully nest within its branches.

(4) The parable of the Yeast (Matthew 13:33) teaches that this leaven/yeast (corruption/sin/apostasy) will be hid and mixed and spread throughout the entire three measures (Genesis 18:6, Judges 6:19) of meal/bread/batch which is symbolic of the Word of God/Bread of Life/Doctrine of Christ. Thus, the whole Church shall experience a constant moral and doctrinal corruption and falling away from the Truth. (study Matthew 16:5-12, Mark 8:14-21, Luke 12:1-3) The yeast of the Pharisees, Sadducees, and Herod is the religious self-righteous spirit and the political spirit. The religious spirit is man's attempt to please and be right with God, and the political spirit is man's self-ambitions and desire to please men more than,

or rather than wanting to please God. (I Corinthians 5:6-8, Galatians 5:7-10) Yeast and leaven are consistently throughout the commands and instructions of God symbolic of sin, evil, iniquity, and insidious perversion. (Genesis 19:3, Exodus 12:8-20, Exodus 34:25, Leviticus 2:11)

These first four parables are all about the corruption and sin within the Church, and the majority of those within the Church would be "broad way" walkers (Matthew 7:13-14) and they would be unfruitful; and were all spoken out in the open with the great crowd assembled around Him at the sea of Galilee. (Matthew 13:2)

And the last four parables were only spoken in the presence of His disciples in the house, (Matthew 13:36) and these are a more encouraging word about those in the Church that are faithful and genuine "narrow gate" entering disciples.

(5) The parable of the Hidden Treasure (Matthew 13:44) teaches that the nation of Israel/field (study Exodus 19:5-6, I Peter 2:9) will remain struggling to believe Jesus is the Messiah until the time of Jacob's trouble (Jeremiah 30:3-9), or the great tribulation, but; they are a treasure to the Lord.

(6) The parable of the Pearl of Great Price (Matthew 13:45-46) teaches that the Gentiles/nations that are earnestly searching for the Savior, will find Him, value Him, and thus place Him above all things in this world and in their lives. These also will inherit the Kingdom. These two: Hidden Treasure/Israel and the Gentiles make up the one Pearl of Great Price, which is the Church.

(7) The parable of the Fishing Net (Matthew 13:47-50) teaches the same basic message as the Wheat and Tares, which is that the Church will have a mixture of true born-again believers and those that are not in genuineness born from above. This will prevail until the conclusion of the age of grace.

(8) The parable of the Old and New Treasure (Matthew 13:51-52) teaches that true disciples of Jesus Christ must diligently study and accordingly receive revelation from the Old and New Covenants/Testaments which is the whole council of God, and when all His precepts are taken together; one can rightly comprehend the value and wisdom of Father God's total redemptive plan and purposes for His faithful saints in the coming Kingdom age.

All eight of these parables are about the Church age, and all must be studied and considered together as one passage and one complete message to thus grasp the whole sweep of what Jesus is teaching about this mystery revelation He now called the Church.

Some in the Church today are preaching a "kingdom now" doctrine, teaching that Christians will take over the seven mountains of our society before the end of the age. These mountains are religion, family, education, government, media, arts, and commerce. According to Jesus, this is not going to happen.

Jesus came preaching the Gospel of the Kingdom and His first followers thought and believed the Messianic Kingdom would be established then too, but; it was not, and the Kingdom age is not coming until the King comes again. So, until then every believer is called to be salt and light in this corrupt and increasingly dark and dying world.

You are the salt of the earth. But if the salt loses its saltiness, how shall it be made salty? It is from then on good for nothing but to be thrown out and to be trampled underfoot by men. You are the light of the world. A city that is set on a hill cannot be hidden. Neither do men light a candle and put it under a basket, but on a candlestick. And it gives light to all who are in the house. Let your light so shine before men that they may see your good works and glorify your Father who is in heaven. Matthew 5:13-16 MEV

Salt is good. But if the salt loses its saltiness, how will you season it? Have salt in yourselves, and have peace with one another. Mark 9:50 MEV

Salt is good [an excellent thing], but if salt has lost its strength and has become saltless (insipid, flat), how shall its saltness be restored? It is fit neither for the land nor the manure heap; men throw it away. He who has ears to hear, let him listen and consider and comprehend by hearing! Luke 14:34-35 AMPC

Again, Jesus spoke to them, saying, I am the light of the world. Whoever follows Me shall not walk in the darkness, but shall have the light of life. John 8:12 MEV

While I am in the world, I am the light of the world. John 9:5 MEV

While you have light, believe in the light that you may become sons of light. John 12:36a MEV

Do all things without grumbling and faultfinding and complaining [against God] and questioning and doubting [among yourselves], that you may show yourselves to be blameless and guileless, innocent and uncontaminated, children of God without blemish (faultless, unrebukable) in the midst of a crooked and wicked generation [spiritually perverted and per-verse], among whom you are seen as bright lights (stars or beacons shining out clearly) in the [dark] world, Philippians 2:14-15 AMPC

For you are all sons of light and sons of the day; we do not belong either to the night or to darkness. Thessalonians 5:5 AMPC

Every believer as overcoming bond-servants of Jesus Christ have all been called and commanded to be *salt* and *light* in our respective world and within our personal sphere of influence wherever our Lord has rooted and grounded and established us, con-sequently; this is not a new concept nor something that is yet to come.

Therefore, the Kingdom age (the seventh day) does not come until after the consummation and the very end of the Church age (the sixth day) ultimately concluded by the awesome and terrible Day of the Lord. That Day will be both great and terrible. For those that survived and did not take the mark of the beast it will be the greatest of all days, however; for the rest that remain, it will be total devastation and utter desolation forever and ever.

Simply stated, we are not living in the seventh day yet, and the seventh Feast of the Lord, more commonly known as the Feast of Tabernacles has not yet begun, and it does not begin until after the Day of Atonement, or Judgement Day, which is the end of the sixth Feast and the sixth day, and we will all gather in Jerusalem (Zechariah 14:16-21) at the forth temple (Ezekiel 40-48) to celebrate the seventh Feast of the Lord, the Feast of Tabernacles throughout the seventh day, which is the one-thousand-year millennial reign of Christ, or the Kingdom age.

We also believe there will be a great outpouring of the Holy Spirit (Joel 2:28-29) on all the people of God, resulting in a great end-time harvest of souls (ingathering of fruit) to wrap-up the age of grace (former and latter rain–James 5:7-9) before the Day of Judgement comes, however; we must and shall continue to witness this great apostasy and falling away resulting in the refinement of the bride which are the overcomer's; just as the Scriptures teach us.

Arise, shine, for your light has come, and the glory of the Lord has risen upon you. For the darkness shall cover the earth and deep darkness the peoples; but the Lord shall rise upon you, and His glory shall be seen upon you. The nations shall come to your light and kings to the brightness of your rising. Isaiah 60:1-3 MEV

Gross darkness and great Light at the same time creating a very clear separation for all to see. No more lukewarm, sleepy, self-confident fence-sitters, spectators, and pew-warmers with one foot in the world and one foot in the Church; and no more shades of gray.

The resulting remnant are those faithful and bold Spirit-filled overcomers who humbly follow Jesus Christ and will not compromise the Word of God.

The true disciples and worshipers of Jesus are beginning to gather in diverse places with no agenda – just Jesus. These are desperately seeking His presence and His manifest glory. This is the remnant Church, and we are living in the last days of the dispensation of grace. Amen.

Will you be found among the remnant worshipping in spirit and in truth?

To become and fulfill your part of the faithful remnant Church is the overcomer's mandate.

CHAPTER THREE

God's Appointed Times.

Foundational Truth: The just shall live by faith. This is an amazing Truth from the Word of God that many Christians profess, but; do we really have revelation of what this teaches us? How do we apply this to our lives? Who are the just? And what exactly does to live by faith mean? And who or what precisely are we to have faith in?

First, we must know whom it was that declared: *The just shall live by faith?*

And the Lord answered me, and said, Write the vision, and make it plain upon tables, that he may run that readeth it. For the vision is yet for an *appointed time*, but at the end it shall speak, and not lie: though it tarry, wait for it; because it will surely come, it will not tarry. Behold, his soul which is lifted up is not upright in him: But *the just shall live by faith*. Habakkuk 2:2-4 KJV

The Hebrew prophet Habakkuk was called by God to warn the leaders of Judah of the coming judgment. The Jewish leaders were wicked, and the common people were suffering a time of oppression, violence, corruption, persecution, and rebellion resulting in an apostasy of the people of God.

The prophet of God was struggling to understand how long God was going to allow this chaos, iniquity, and oppression of the people to continue and allow these corrupted shepherds to seemingly continue to prosper. Habakkuk cried out to the Lord for answers.

Father God answers Habakkuk with a revelation delivered through a vision of what was and is to come in the last days. God commands him to write it down and to make it clear and simple for all to understand. The Lord tells Habakkuk that the events in the vision shall come to pass at the exact appointed time.

God says to take note of those men who are lifted up in pride and that their souls (mind, will, and emotions) are not upright, and because they are corrupted and the judgment of God has been planned for these men, and it would assuredly come upon them at the precise moment in time that God had ordained, but; the righteous shall live because of their patient endurance and faithfulness to God and their complete trust in Him and their unwavering belief in His written Word.

Do we have other witnesses to this bedrock solid Truth?

For I am not ashamed of the Gospel of Christ: for it is the power of God unto salvation to every one that believeth; to the Jew first, and also the Greek. For therein is the righteousness of God revealed from faith to faith: as it is written. The just shall live by faith. Romans 1:16-17 KJV

But that no man is justified by the law in the sight of God, it is evident: for, the just shall live by faith. Galatians 3:11 KJV

For yet a little while, and He that shall come will come, and will not tarry. Now the just shall live by faith: but if any man draw back, My soul shall have no pleasure in him. Hebrews 10:37-38 KJV

What are we to have faith in? The everlasting Word of God. The apostle Paul was quoting an Old Testament Hebrew prophet in his New Testament epistles.

We are to have faith in God. We are to trust in the entire Word of God. We are to believe everything God says shall come to pass in due season – exactly at the right moment. We are righteous and justified by our faith in God's Word. We are saved and have life by our belief in Jesus Christ, who is the Word made flesh and our soon coming King.

God spoke through the prophet that the vision/revelation of the coming judgment was for a very precisely planned and appointed time. We must always remember and never forget that God knows the future better than we know the past.

What does this mean to us? What exactly is an appointed time?

The prophet Daniel had a vision and the Lord sent His angel Gabriel to interpret Daniel's vision. And he said, Behold, I will make thee know what shall be in the last end of indignation: for at the *time appointed* the end shall be. Daniel 8:19 KJV

And Daniel had more visions of the end of the age, just ahead of the beginning of the Kingdom age.

And both these kings' hearts shall be to do mischief, and they shall speak lies at one table; but it shall not prosper: for yet the end shall be at the *time appointed*. Daniel 11:27 KJV

At the *time appointed* he shall return, and come toward the south; but it shall not be as the former, or as the latter. Daniel 11:29 KJV

And some of them of understanding shall fall, to try them, and to purge, and to make them white, even to the time of the end: because it is yet for a *time appointed*. Daniel 11:35 KJV

These visions that Daniel received are of the very last days at end of the age, during the last forty-two months of the tribulation, when the antichrist is in Jerusalem, exalting himself, and claiming to be a god.

God Almighty is telling us that these things must come to pass, but; He has a plan and He has a precise appointed time for all these things to manifest.

Father God had established an appointed time for Jesus the Messiah to come the first time, and Father God has an appointed time for the Alpha and the Omega, the First and the Last, the Beginning and the End to come again at our heavenly Father's **Moed**.

Jesus, the King of Kings and the Lord of Lords shall come to rule and reign at precisely the appointed time that God Almighty has set, just like Jesus came the first time....at precisely the appointed time God established.

The Hebrew word that has been translated appointed time is *Moed.* This word occurs in the Scriptures two hundred twenty-three times in the Hebrew text. Other Scriptures have transliterated

Moed into English as: seasons, feasts, set time, meeting, assembly, and congregation.

Simply stated the word *Moed* means these are God's set appointments that God Almighty has planned and established even before He created time, before all things, and for all eternity.

The first place we find this Hebrew word *Moed* used in the Scriptures is in the report of the creation of the fourth day chronicled in the book of beginnings.

And God said, Let there be lights in the firmament of the heaven to divide the day from the night; and let them be for signs, and for *seasons*, and for days, and years. Genesis 1:14 KJV

The fourth day of creation equals four thousand years. From Adam until Jesus manifested in the flesh as the Son was four thousand years, and we are the moon and stars because the moon and stars thus reflect the light of the Son.

God created the sun, moon, and stars and placed them in the sky to light the earth, to be His message board for us, and to divide time, days, months, and years. God created the heavenly host to establish His special appointed times. God did this before He created man. Here is another witness in our Bible:

He appointed the moon for *seasons*: the sun knoweth his going down. Psalm 104:19 KJV

The Hebrew word *Moed* is translated as seasons in these Scriptures.

The second place we find the word *Moed* used in the Scriptures is in Genesis chapter seventeen and Almighty God is reaffirming His everlasting covenant with Abram. It was at this time that the Lord gave Abram and his wife Sarai their new names and re-established His promise of an heir/son and God said that this son of promise shall be called Isaac.

But My covenant will I establish with Isaac, which Sarah shall bear unto thee at this *set time* in the next year. Genesis 17:21 KJV

Moed is translated set time here.

Was this covenant for all time? He hath remembered His covenant for ever, the Word which He commanded to a thousand generations. Psalm 105:8 KJV

Even if the Lord's covenant is only for one thousand generations of forty-years each generation, that is still forty thousand years! That certainly covers you and me and the grandkids, and great-grandkids. Hallelujah!

So, in Genesis eighteen we see Jesus and two angels come to Abraham for a visit. Abraham ran to meet them, and hastened to Sarah, and told her to quickly make cakes, and Abraham ran unto the herd to get a calf and he hastened to dress it. Abraham sure seems to be in a big hurry? (Could this possibly be a foreshadowing similitude of Exodus 12:11?)

The Lord Jesus reconfirms to Abraham and Sarah the promise of a son named Isaac, who was born exactly one year later to the definite day.

Is any thing too hard for the Lord? At the *time appointed* I will return unto thee, according to the time of life, and Sarah shall have a son. Genesis 18:14 KJV

We see in the Scriptures in Genesis 19:1-3, that this same day the angels went on to Sodom, encountered Lot at the city gate, and went to lodge at Lot's home that evening, and he made them a *feast of unleavened bread*, then the angels led Lot out of the city before the judgment and the wrath of God came upon the cities of the plain and they were completely destroyed. (Could this possibly be a foreshadowing similitude of Exodus 12:8?)

One year later–Precisely one year later:

And the Lord visited Sarah as He had said, and the Lord did unto Sarah as He had spoken. For Sarah conceived, and bare Abraham a son in his old age, at the *set time* of which God had spoken to him. Genesis 21:1-2 KJV

This day–this *Moed*–this set time, the day of Isaac's birth; started the four-hundred-year count-down of the prophetic covenant promise spoken by Father God to Abram regarding his promised heir/ seed Isaac.

And He said unto Abram, Know of a surety that thy seed shall be a stranger in a land that is not theirs, and shall serve them; and they shall afflict them four hundred years; and also that nation, whom they shall serve, will I judge: and afterward shall they come out with great substance. Genesis 15:13-14 KJV

But in the fourth generation they shall come hither again: for the iniquity of the Amorites is not yet full. Genesis 15:16 KJV

The sons of Levi; Gershon, Kohath, and Merari. And the sons of Kohath; Amram, Izhar, and Hebron, and Uzziel. And the children of Amram; Aaron, and Moses, and Miriam. The sons also of Aaron; Nadab, and Abihu, Eleazar, and Ithamar. I Chronicles 6:1-3 KJV

And those four generations were Levi, Kohath, Amram, and Moses.

We know that Moses returns to Egypt, and Egypt suffers the ten plagues, the final plague being the

51

death of all the first-born offspring of every man and beast.

This is when God instructs Moses on the Passover recorded in Exodus chapter twelve, and on that very day, the day of the Passover, the children of Israel walked out of Egypt, after plundering them of their gold and silver and raiment, which was fulfillment of prophecy recorded in Genesis 15:13. God establishes that this day, Father God's *Moed;* shall be kept and remembered every year, in every generation, forevermore.

And this day shall be unto you for a memorial; and ye shall keep it a feast to the Lord throughout your generations; ye shall keep it a feast by an ordinance for ever. Exodus 12:14 KJV

And ye shall observe this thing for an ordinance to thee and to thy sons for ever. Exodus 12:24 KJV

Thou shalt therefore keep this ordinance in his *season* from year to year. Exodus 13:10 KJV

So, we know that after four hundred thirty years— to the very day, that Moses led the nation of Israel out of Egypt. (Exodus 12:40-41) Exactly four hundred thirty years after God spoke to Abram when he was in Ur of the Chaldees to Go!

And God spake on this wise, That his <u>seed</u> should sojourn in a strange land; and that they should bring them into bondage, and entreat them evil four hundred years. Acts 7:6 KJV

We must do some reckoning of the four hundred plus thirty years.

Abram was dwelling with his family and they were all living in the city of Ur of the Chaldees (Babylonia) when God spoke to Abram and charged him to Go!

Now the Lord had said unto Abram, Get thee out of thy country, and from thy kindred, and from thy father's house, unto a land that I will shew thee. Genesis 12:1 KJV

And Terah took Abram his son, and Lot the son of Haran his son's son, and Sarai his daughter in law, his son Abram's wife; and they went forth with them from Ur of the Chaldees, to go into the land of Canaan; and they came to Haran, and dwelt there. And the days of Terah were two hundred and five years: and Terah died in Haran. Genesis 11:31-32 KJV

They all packed up and traveled about six hundred miles and dwelt in Haran (Acts 7:1-4) for some five years (it was five years also per the history book of Jasher) before Abram fully obeyed God. Well he kinda, sorta obeyed.

Abram was not supposed to take his kindred Lot, and Abram was five years behind schedule. Abram was then seventy-five years old when he left Haran to go across the Euphrates river and to sojourn into the promised land of Canaan, that was then occupied by ten heathenistic tribal nations. (Genesis 15:18-21)

Therefore, it was another twenty-five years before the promised seed of Abraham and Sarah was supernaturally conceived, and their son Isaac was born, thus starting the prophesied four-hundred-year countdown clock.

Genesis 12:1,4 Abram left Ur when he was 70 years old.	
Genesis 21:5 Abram was 100 years old at Isaac's birth.	30 years
Genesis 25:26 Isaac was 60 years old at Jacob's birth.	60 years
Genesis 47:8-9 Jacob was 130 years old entering Egypt.	<u>130 years</u>
Total.	220 years

So, we can see that four generations of Israel's children Levi, Kohath, Amram, and Moses dwelt in Egypt two hundred ten years before eighty-year-old Moses and eighty-three-year-old Aaron (Exodus 7:7) led the exodus of God's covenant people out of Egypt. All of this shows us that God spoke to Abram thirty years before–on the very day that Isaac would be born, which was the future day of Passover, which was the very same day that the nation of Israel left Egypt, which was the 14th day of Nisan. Our heavenly Father is amazing. Selah

And the Lord spake unto Moses, saying, Speak unto the children of Israel, and say unto them, concerning the *feasts* of the Lord, which ye shall proclaim to be holy convocations, even these are My *feasts*. Leviticus 23:1-2 KJV

These are the *feasts* of the Lord, even holy convocations, which ye shall proclaim in their *seasons*. Leviticus 23:4 KJV

We believe the Lord God Almighty is trying to impress on us that these *Moedim* (Hebrew for *feasts* plural) are His feasts and they shall be held on the *Moed* time every year. Each feast of the Lord is prophetic of set events in the Master's plan.

The Lord outlines His *Moedim* (seasons, feasts, set times, appointed times) in: Leviticus 23, Numbers 9, Numbers 28, Numbers 29, Deuteronomy 15, Deuteronomy 16, Deuteronomy 31.

(1) The Lord's **Passover**–Nisan 14	*Latter rain*
(2) Feast of **Unleavened Bread**–Nisan 15-21	Season:
(3) Feast of **First Fruits**–Nisan 18 (after Sabbath)	Barley harvest
Genesis 47:8-9 Jacob was 130 years old entering Egypt.	<u>130 years</u>
(4) Feast of Weeks/**Pentecost**–Sivan 6	Wheat harvest
(5) Feast of **Trumpets**–Tishri 1-2	*Former rain*
(6) Day of **Atonement**–Tishri 10	Season:
(7) Feast of **Tabernacles**–Tishri 15-21	Fruit Harvest

We shall take each one of these *Moedim* or appointed times of the Lord and commence to see what our Lord has begun to reveal to His children about His set times and seasons.

The secret things belong unto the Lord our God: but those things which are revealed belong unto us and to our children for ever, that we may do all the words of this law. Deuteronomy 29:29 KJV

Who hath wrought and done it, calling the generations from the beginning? I the Lord, the First, and with the Last; I AM He. Isaiah 41:4 KJV

Remember the former things of old: For I AM God, and there is none else; I AM God, and there is none like Me. Declaring the end from the beginning, and from the ancient times the things that are not yet done, saying, My counsel shall stand, and I will do all My pleasure. Isaiah 46:9-10 KJV

It is the glory of God to conceal a thing: but the honour of kings is to search out a matter. Proverbs 25:2 KJV.

The *Former* and the *Latter rain* is prophetic of the outpouring of the Holy Spirit.

Israel was an agricultural based nation, and their daily lives were centered on seasons and the harvest cycles, thus; the Lord uses all of His creation to communicate to us, including seedtime and harvest, winter and summer, and the *former rain* to germinate the seed, and *latter rain* to bring the fields to maturity leading to the great ingathering of the precious fruit of the earth.

The Lord spoke to us through His prophets Hosea and Joel describing Jesus' first coming as occurring in the season of the latter or spring *rain* and Jesus' second coming as occurring in the season of the *former and latter rain together* to finish the Lord's harvest of fruit/souls in the earth.

Then shall we know, if we follow on to know the Lord: His going forth is prepared as the morning; and

He shall come unto us as the rain, as the latter and the former rain unto the earth. Hosea 6:3 KJV

Be glad then, ye children of Zion, and rejoice in the Lord your God: for He hath given you the former rain moderately, and He will cause to come down for you the rain, the former rain, and the latter rain in the first month. And the floors shall be full of wheat, and the vats shall overflow with wine and oil. Joel 2:23-24 KJV

In the New Testament book of James, we are admonished to have steadfast endurance, or faith; as we wait upon the precious fruit to be ready to harvest during the season of the great harvest rains when Jesus shall return, which will be proceeded by a great outpouring of the Holy Spirit.

Be patient therefore, brethren, unto the coming of the Lord. Behold, the husbandman waiteth for the precious fruit of the earth, and hath long patience for it, until he receive the early and latter rain. Be ye also patient; stablish your hearts: for the coming of the Lord draweth nigh. James 5:7-8 KJV

In the second part of this study, we shall continue to build on the foundation of our comprehension of the Lord's established seasons, of the former and latter rain similitude, harvest cycles, and the Lord's appointed times. We shall look at each season and the individual feasts with their specific appointed time. Everything God does is in cycles, similitudes, and patterns, thus foreshadowing for those who study His Word of the days and events to come.

The thing that hath been, it is that which shall be; and that which is done is that which shall be done: and there is no new thing under the sun. Ecclesiastes 1:9 KJV

That which hath been is now; and that which is to be hath already been; and God requireth that which is past. Ecclesiastes 3:15 KJV

Following in the next chapter we shall look closely at the seven Feasts of the Lord. These are God Almighty's prophetic dress rehearsals that He commanded and ordained to be practiced repeatedly each year, so we would never forget.

The first four of the Lord's Feasts, which are His appointed times; have all been perfectly fulfilled and thus we believe the last three are soon to become manifest at their precisely set time also.

We must be wise and have our lamps trimmed and our flasks of oil ready and prepared to see the Lord, because the just shall live by faith.

This is the overcomer's mandate.

Chapter four

The Feasts of the Lord.

Foundational Truth: The Lord's seven Feasts are a prophetic pattern of God Almighty's total plan of redemption and restoration for man and earth.

In the first part of this teaching, we have studied the word feasts and discovered that the Hebrew word for feasts is *Moed* and we now understand that these feasts outline God's appointed times and seasons for the entirety of His creation.

It is important to get revelation of the Truth that these are the *Lord's Feasts*, and not as some in the body of Christ ignorantly refer to these prophetic landmarks and signs as the Jewish feasts, which clearly, they are not.

The Lord God Almighty has established these very important times and seasons, not man; and we would do well to pay special heed of these events. Each

60

feast is a portion of the puzzle that taken together is a picture of Father God's master plan for the redemption and restoration of all things on this planet.

In Leviticus chapter twenty-three the Lord gave to His people seven *appointed times* for them to keep and observe every year. Woven within these feasts and holy days are types, shadows, and similitudes that are prophetic messages for all believers in each generation to discover these amazing truths and to subsequently teach the next generation.

The first four feasts prophesied the events that came to pass during the first coming of the Lamb of God and the first outpouring of the Holy Spirit and the beginning of the Church age. The final three feasts are prophetic of the events that shall come to pass in the last days of the Church age and the second and greater outpouring of the Holy Spirit, thus leading to the second coming of Christ, then Judgement day, and concluding with the Kingdom age, which is the one-thousand-year millennial reign of King Jesus of this planet from His earthly throne established in Jerusalem.

These are the (*Moed*) feasts of the Lord, even holy convocations, which ye shall proclaim in their (*Moed*) seasons. Leviticus 23:4 KJV

The future *Day of the Lord* shall be the single most important event in the history of this earth and of all mankind. There is simply no forthcoming event that is more important than the soon return of the King of kings and the Lord of lords to rule and reign forever-more! For this reason, we shall devote the time to discover the symbolic form of prophecy (types, shadows, and similitudes) that is embedded within these special times that the Lord has established for His children to discover and thus prepare. Father God doesn't hide things from us, He hides them for His children.

These feasts of the Lord (and many other sacraments) were practiced for centuries and were widely known and understood as sacred holy days and events. These various events and rituals are not required of the body of Christ, or more commonly referred to as "the Church." Again, to observe all or part of these feasts and/or festivals is a blessing for any believer as they sense the leading of the Lord, but; it is not a new covenant requirement. However, we are required to study the whole counsel of God which is all Scripture from Genesis to Revelation.

In addition, the meeting of the church leaders in Jerusalem outlined in Acts chapter fifteen makes it clear that Gentile believers are not required to follow the other Jewish rituals and customs. Also, in the epistle written to the church in Colossae, Paul teaches us not to allow others to condemn us because we don't keep these various Orthodox Jewish rituals, however; he does tell us that these things are in-fact prophetic, and that they all point us to Jesus Christ.

Let no man therefore judge you in meat, or in drink, or in respect of a holy day, or of the new moon, or of the Sabbath days: Which are a shadow of things to come; but the body is of Christ. Colossians 2:16-17 KJV

God commanded that three times of the year that Israel must keep the feasts. Later, there were three times in the year that God required every male over the age of twenty years (every head of household), to show himself in Jerusalem at the temple. Of course, the temple must have been built. The family could come as well, however; the requirement was for each man to come at these *appointed times* to praise, honor and worship the Lord.

Three times thou shalt keep a feast unto Me in the year. Thou shalt keep the feast of Unleavened Bread: (Thou shalt eat unleavened bread seven days, as I commanded thee, in the time appointed of the month Abib; for in it thou camest out of Egypt: and none shall appear before me empty) and the feast of Harvest, the first fruits of thy labours, which thou hast sown in the field: and the feast of Ingathering, which is in the end of the year, when thou hast gathered in thy labours out of the field. Three times in the year all thy males shall appear before the Lord God. Exodus 23:14-17 KJV

These three appointed times or seasons are:

(1) Passover/Unleavened Bread/First Fruits

(2) Pentecost

(3) Trumpets/Atonement/Tabernacles.

We see the commandment repeated in the book of Deuteronomy.

Three times in a year shall all thy males appear before the Lord thy God in the place which He shall choose; in the feast of Unleavened bread, and in the feast of Weeks, and in the feast of Tabernacles: and they shall not appear before the Lord empty. Deuteronomy 16:16 KJV

Three appointed times for the harvest of seven species: (Deuteronomy 8:7-9)

(1) Passover/Unleavened Bread/First Fruits– beginning of the barley harvest.

(2) Pentecost–in concurrence with the wheat harvest.

(3) Trumpets/Atonement/Tabernacles–concluding with the fruit harvest of grapes, figs,
pomegranates, date honey, and olives.

In Numbers chapters twenty-eight and twenty-nine are the instructions concerning all the burnt
offerings, Sabbath offerings, the first day of each
month/moon, and the seven feast-days.

The seven feasts of the Lord are in *two* groups
or seasons:

(1) Passover: (Leviticus 23:5)	(1st) Nisan	March-April
Unleavened Bread: (Leviticus 23:6)	Nisan 15-21	March-April
First Fruits: (Leviticus 23:10)	Nisan 18	March-April
(2) Pentecost: (Leviticus 23:15-16)	Sivan 6	May-June
(3) Trumpets: (Leviticus 23:24)	(7th) Tishri 1-2	Sept-Oct.
Atonement: (Leviticus 23:27)	Tishri 10	Sept-Oct.
Tabernacles: (Leviticus 23:34)	Tishri 15-21	Sept-Oct.

(Nisan is the first month of the sacred calendar) In our vernacular, we would call them *Spring* feasts (latter rain) and *Fall* feasts (former rain). So, shall we look at each one of these feasts to discover the Lord's appointed and prophetic times.

Spring feast: **Passover**

Historically, Passover commemorates the day that God delivered Israel out of bondage in Egypt, and the beginning of their journey to the Promised Land that God promised through a blood covenant with father Abraham. This occurred on the exact day that God had promised and appointed.

The father of the house would go on the 10th of Nisan and select a lamb without blemish or fault and take it home. For the four days leading up to the day of Passover everyone could inspect the lamb to make sure it was without fault. Then at 3:00 pm on the 14th of Nisan, the father would bring the family outside of the house and place the lamb in the doorway to their home and kill the lamb. He would gather the blood in a vessel, command the family back inside the home, and with a hyssop branch dipped in the blood of the lamb, and he would place blood on the lintel and door posts, forming a cross as the blood dripped and ran down the door onto the threshold of the door.

The lamb was then skinned and roasted upright and whole, propped up on a vertical stick, with another horizontal stick across the ribcage to hold it open, with the intestines placed around its head. So, the lamb was roasted on a *cross* with a *crown*. The Lamb must be cooked before sundown, which was the beginning of the 15th of Nisan, when the Passover meal was to begin.

After the temple was built in Jerusalem, and continuing until its destruction in 70 AD, on the 10th of Nisan the High Priest would go to Bethany to choose a lamb without fault and bring it to the temple to be inspected four days. As the lamb was brought to and through the eastern gate to the city, worshippers would line-up along the side of the pathway leading to the gate and wave palm branches and say *"Baruch Ha Shem Adonai"* (blessed is he who comes in the name of the Lord). At 9:00 am on the 14th of Nisan, the lamb would be secured to one of the horns on the altar.

Blessed be he that cometh in the name of the Lord: we have blessed you out of the house of the Lord. God is the Lord, which hath shewed us light:

bind the sacrifice with cords, even unto the horns of the altar. Psalm 118:26-27 KJV

At 3:00 pm, the High Priest would kill the lamb and declare *"it is finished."*

On the **10th of Nisan** (John 12:12) Jesus left **Bethany** to come to Jerusalem. Bethany was to the east of **Jerusalem** on the Mount of Olives, so; Jesus would have come through the **eastern gate** to the city. Many people came along the pathway leading into the city with **palm branches**, crying Hosanna to the son of David: **blessed is he who cometh in the name of the Lord**. (Matthew 21:9) God thundered His approval of the **faultless Lamb** from heaven. (John 12:28). On the **14th of Nisan**, Pilate also declared after his inspection of Jesus **"I find no fault in Him"** (John 19:4). At **9:00 am** Jesus was crucified (Mark 15:25) and at **3:00 pm** (Matthew 27:46) Jesus spoke as the Sacrifice and as Priest when He said, **"it is finished"** and yielded up the ghost (John 19:30).

Twelve prophecies fulfilled by Jesus. Oh, Glory to God.

Summary of events that ALL occurred on the 10th of Nisan:

God commands Abraham to travel three days to sacrifice Isaac.

Select lamb and take home.

High Priest goes to Bethany to select lamb.

Passover lamb placed on display for inspection.

Jesus comes from Bethany.

Jesus comes to Temple.

Jesus is declared faultless by His Father.

Summary of events that ALL took place on the 14th of Nisan:

Abram was told to leave his country, kin, and his father's house.

Isaac was promised to Abraham and Sarah and named by Jesus.

Isaac was born.

Abraham sacrifices ram on Mount Moriah in place of Isaac.

The beginning of the exodus from Egypt.

The faultless lamb was killed at 3pm.

Jesus died at 3 pm on Mount Moriah and placed in tomb.

Spring feast: **Unleavened Bread**

The feast of Unleavened Bread (representing sinless bread) begins on the 15th of Nisan (Sabbath) and goes seven days until the 21st of Nisan. The lamb

is killed and roasted before 6:00 pm on the 14th of
Nisan, and then the ritual meal called the Sedar (set
order) was on the beginning of the 15th of Nisan. Of
course, this Passover Sedar teaches about the exodus
out of Egypt, but; it also points to the Messiah. We
will briefly go over some of the rituals performed
during the Seder.

On the table would be a special cloth container
with three pockets called a Matzah-Tash, with a loaf
of matzah (unleavened bread) in each pocket. This
symbolizes the Holy Trinity. The center loaf of matzah
would be removed and broken in two pieces. One
piece would be placed back inside the middle pocket.
The father would wrap the broken piece of the matzah
in a linen napkin and then he hides it somewhere in
the house.

The Passover meal is eaten along with other rituals, then after the meal the father would send the
children searching for the hidden matzah. Whoever
finds the buried matzah would bring it back to the
father. The child would then receive the promised
gift of the father. All of this is symbolic of the death,
burial, resurrection, and ascension of the Messiah.

Of course, the promised gift of the father (Luke
24:49) is symbolic of receiving the Holy Spirit at

Pentecost. The matzah bread represents Jesus, the sinless sacrifice, made for us all. Jesus said *"this is my body broken for you"* referring to the unleavened bread. The matzah was cooked on a grill that gave its stripes (Isaiah 53:5), and it was pierced with holes (Zechariah 12:10) Jesus also told us He was the Bread of Life (John 6:51). The feast continues for seven days to remind us to not allow sin into our lives, but to remain separated from the world.

Purge out therefore the old leaven, that ye may be a new lump, as ye are unleavened. For even Christ our **Passover** is sacrificed for us: Therefore let us keep the feast, not with old leaven, neither with the leaven of malice and wickedness; but with the unleavened bread of sincerity and truth. I Corinthians 5:7-8 KJV

The Jewish Rabbis teach to leave one chair at the Seder table for Elijah, for his prophesied return (Malachi 4:5). We believe this is a type and shadow of John the Baptists birth. Zachariah was on duty at the temple during Pentecost (mid Sivan) and we know Elisabeth conceived right after Zachariah's service (Luke 1:23-24) and we know she gave birth to John six months before Jesus was born. (Luke 1:36) So, John the Baptist was born on Nisan 15 and Jesus was born on Tishri 15, six months later at Tabernacles.

Jesus said the John the Baptist was Elijah, which was to come (Matthew 11:14)

Summary of events that ALL occurred on the 15th of Nisan.

Exodus from Egypt continues

John the Baptist is born

Jesus is in the garden tomb.

Spring (barley) feast: **First Fruits**

Jesus was crucified and died on Passover (Nisan 14) on Wednesday and buried/placed in the tomb before the (1st) Sabbath of Unleavened Bread (Nisan 15) and rose from the dead on the first day of the week on Sunday, after the end of the weekly (2nd) Sabbath (Nisan 17) on First Fruits (Nisan 18).

For as Jonas was three days and three nights in the whale's belly; so shall the Son of man be three days and three nights in the heart of the earth. Matthew 12:40 KJV

After the end of the **Sabbaths**, the day is beginning to dawn into first day of the week, came Mary Magdalene and the other Mary of the same kind to see the tomb. Matthew 28:1 PureWordBible

After the **Sabbaths**, around dawn on the first day of the week, Mary Magdalene and the other Mary went to take a look at the burial site. Matthew 28:1 ISV

The first ripe fruits of the barley were brought into the Temple, ground into flour, and baked into unleavened cakes that symbolized the death of the grain and its resurrection into a new form. Jesus is the first fruits to receive a glorified body that will never die.

The devout overcomers that are alive at Christ's return for His bride shall receive their incorruptible, glorified bodies when they are *Harpazo* caught up to meet Jesus in the air. (I Thessalonians 4:14-17) For the saints that have gone home before us; at the resurrection at the end of the age. (John 6:39)

But now is Christ risen from the dead, and become the **first fruits** of them that slept. For since by man came death, by man came also the resurrection of the dead. For as in Adam all die, even so in Christ shall all be made alive. But every man in his own order: Christ the **first fruits**; afterward they that are Christ's at His coming. I Corinthians 15:20-23 KJV

And He is the Head of the body, the church: who is the beginning, the First-born from the dead; that in all things He might have the preeminence. Colossians 1:18 KJV

Noah's ark rested on the mountains of Ararat on the 17th of Nisan (Genesis 8:4). The ark was a type and shadow of Jesus Christ, our Ark and Savior from the overwhelming floodwaters.

Which sometime were disobedient, when once the longsuffering of God waited in the days of Noah, while the ark was being prepared, wherein few, that is, eight souls were saved by water. The like figure whereunto even baptism doth also now save us (not the putting away of the filth of the flesh, but the answer of a good conscience toward God) by the resurrection of Jesus Christ. I Peter 3:20-21 KJV

Israel was baptized and raised up into a new life symbolically when they went through the Red sea on the 17th of Nisan. It all began when the Lord told Moses to demand the king of Egypt to let God's people go three days journey into the wilderness (Exodus 3:18) and God said let My people go, that they may hold a feast unto Me in the wilderness (Exodus 5:1)

Moreover, brethren, I would not that ye should be ignorant, how that all our fathers were under the cloud, and all passed through the Red sea; and were all baptized unto Moses in the cloud and the sea. Now all these things happened unto them for ensamples: and they are written for our admonition, upon whom the ends of the world are come. I Corinthians 10:1-2,11 KJV

Summary of events that all occurred on the 17th of Nisan

Noah's ark came to rest on Turkey's Mount Ararat.

Moses leading Israel passed through the Red Sea.

Pharaoh and his army were destroyed in the Red sea.

Haman and his ten sons were hung on the gallows built for Mordecai.

Jesus, our Savior was resurrected from the dead after sunset!

Spring (wheat) feast: **Pentecost**

The word Pentecost is the transliteration of Greek word for fiftieth and we call it that because the Lord commanded Israel to count seven weeks of seven days:

And ye shall count unto you from the morrow after the Sabbath, from the day that ye brought the sheaf of the wave offering; seven Sabbaths shall be complete: even unto the morrow after the seventh Sabbath shall ye number fifty days; and ye shall offer a new meat offering unto the Lord. Leviticus 23:15-16 KJV

The Lord called this the "*Feast of Weeks*" because it was seven weeks beginning the Sabbath after Passover (16th Nisan) and counting fifty days later is Sivan 6.

Sivan 6 is the day that Moses came down from Mount Sinai (Mt. Sinai is the group of mountains in the Sinai desert, Mount Horeb is the specific mountain) and delivered the Ten Commandments to the children of Israel.

The Hebrew children called this day the festival of the "First Trump" and they also called it the festival of the "Giving of the Law." All these names are accurate and correct.

Christians distinguish and celebrate this day as the birth or launch day of the Church age or the beginning of the dispensation of the age of grace because this is also the same day that Jesus instructed all His disciples to wait for the gift promised of the Father (Acts 1:4). This was Pentecost Sunday when at 9:00 am the Holy Spirit came as promised, the gift of the Father:

And when the day of Pentecost was fully come, they were all with one accord in one place. And suddenly there came a sound from heaven as of a rushing mighty wind, and it filled all the house where they were sitting. And there appeared unto them cloven tongues like as of fire, and it sat upon each one of them. And they were all filled with the Holy Ghost, and began to speak with other tongues, as the Spirit gave them utterance. Acts 2:1-4 KJV

God wrote His Words with His finger for the children of Israel on two tablets of (Exodus 24:10, Numbers 15:37-41, Isaiah 54:11, Ezekiel 1:26) sapphire stone, when He spoke to Moses out of the fire. The fire = Giving of the Law.

And the sight of the glory of the Lord was like devouring fire on the top of the Mount in the eyes of the children of Israel. Exodus 24:17 KJV

And the Lord delivered unto me two tables of stone written with the finger of God; and on them was written according to all the words, which the Lord spake with you in the Mount out of the midst of the fire in the day of the assembly. Deuteronomy 9:10 KJV

Father God's presence was manifest in the fire, just like the first time God spoke to Moses was at Mount Horeb, the very same mountain; and God manifest Himself as fire, even out of the bush that burned, but yet; the bush was not burnt.

Now Moses kept the flock of Jethro his father in law, the priest of Midian: and he led the flock to the backside of the desert, and came to the mountain of God, even Mt. Horeb. And the Angel of the Lord appeared unto him in a flame of fire out of the midst of the bush: and he looked, and, behold, the bush burned with fire, and the bush was not consumed. And Moses said, I will now turn aside, and see this great sight, why the bush is not burnt. Exodus 3:1-3 KJV

For the Lord thy God is a consuming fire, even a jealous God. Deuteronomy 4:24 KJV

For our God is a consuming fire. Hebrews 12:29 KJV

And John the Baptist said–I indeed baptize you with water unto repentance: but He that cometh after me is mightier than I, whose shoes I am not worthy to bear: He shall baptize you with the Holy Ghost and with fire. Matthew 3:11 KJV

The fire = the baptism of the Holy Spirit.

Genesis chapter twenty-two documents the final test (of ten tests and trials) that God gave Abraham. God commanded Abraham to take his only son Isaac and sacrifice him on Mount Moriah. As Abraham and Isaac ascended the Mountain, Isaac ask his father about the absence of a sacrificial lamb, and Abraham answers him by saying that God will provide for Himself a lamb for a burnt offering.

Isaac was bound on the altar and at the last moment, the *Angel of the Lord* called to Abraham out of heaven to stop. Abraham lifted his eyes and saw near him a ram caught in the thorn thicket by his two horns. Abraham took the ram and offered him up as a burnt offering in place of his son. This was establishing the law of substitution = a ram for a lamb, and a covenant Son for a covenant son.

Jehovah-Jireh (Lord will provide) provided a ram that was hung-up by his head. The sacrifice was restrained by the thorns around his head.

The ram horn is called a *shofar* and was used by the Hebrews to signal and thus communicate to the people. In the ancient rabbinical teachings, they taught that the ram was a type and shadow of the coming salvation that the Messiah would bring to mankind. The ram's horns are symbolic of the power and authority of the ram and is connected to the redemption of the Messiah.

The Rabbis taught that the first horn – the left horn – represents the start of the nation of Israel and is connected to the Law of God being given on Mount Horeb. This is why the day of Pentecost is also called the festival of the *First Trump*.

The ancient Rabbis taught that the left horn represented the birth of Israel and that the right horn represented Israel's completed restoration, as prophesied; when the Messiah comes. The shofars represent: The

Law given on Mt. Horeb = First Trump, and the res-urrection of the dead = Last Trump

Also take note of the fact that when the covenant was given, and Moses returned to the people that they were out of control and had fallen into sin and broke the covenant, and the tablets; "the covenant" were also broken.

Moses asked who is on God's side and the tribe of Levi gathered with Moses and as commanded by the Lord, they must take up swords and go and slay those involved with this rebellion. Therefore, on the first Pentecost three thousand Hebrews died.

And the children of Levi did according to the word of Moses: and there fell of the people that day about three thousand men. Exodus 32:28 KJV

Then on the second Pentecost the Church was launched, and the Holy Spirit was poured out, thus beginning the dispensation of grace, and that day three thousand Jews that had come to Jerusalem for the feast were saved!

Then they that gladly received his word were bap-tized: and the same day there were added unto them about three thousand souls. Acts 2:41 KJV

Summary of events that ALL occurred on the 6th of Sivan:

The Ten Commandments of the covenant (Torah) given on Mt. Sinai.

Three thousand men died.

The fire came down.

The beginning of the Church.

The launch of the age of grace.

Three thousand men were saved. (II Corinthians 3:6)

The spring feasts: Passover, Unleavened Bread, First Fruits, and Pentecost have all been perfectly fulfilled in and by Jesus Christ's first advent.

Could it be that the three remaining fall feasts of the Lord are the appointed times of the events surrounding Jesus' second coming?

Fall feast: **Trumpets**

Speak into the children of Israel, saying, in the seventh month, in the first day of the month, shall ye have a sabbath, a memorial of blowing of trumpets, an holy convocation. Leviticus 23:24 KJV

And in the seventh month, on the first day of the month, ye shall have an holy convocation; ye shall do no servile work: it is a day of blowing the trumpets unto you. Numbers 29:1 KJV

This feast day has many names because it is symbolic of many things. One of the names is Rosh Hashanah, meaning "Head of the Year" or New Year's Day.

The ancient Rabbi's and sages taught that this is the day of creation. Tishri 1 is the first day of creation, therefore; mankind/Adam's creation day would be Tishri 6. Tishri is the first month of the civil Hebrew calendar, but; the seventh month of the sacred calendar.

Rosh Hashanah is celebrated for *two days* with absolutely no set schedule of sacraments or events. It is considered as one long *48-hour* day, therefore; **no man knows the day or the hour** when the events will occur during this two-day festival of blowing of the trumpets.

But of that day and hour knoweth no man, no, not the angels of heaven, but My Father only. Matthew 24:36 KJV

The New Year of the Hebrew civil year and the new month of Tishri of course occur at the *new moon*. This was the beginning of the agricultural year. It was required that two witnesses would each report the first tiny silver sliver of the waxing new moon before the official New Year could be proclaimed officially at the Temple in Jerusalem. That public announcement was made by a long, waxing louder and louder, blast of the ram's horn shofar.

According to the rabbinical teachings, the blowing of the *shofar* had special meaning. First, the *Last Trump* was a call to the dead to arise and live again, to wake up from sin, to restoration; through repentance. Second, it was a reminder to the Lord that He was in an everlasting covenant relationship with all the faithful established with father Abraham. The ram's horn is used in reverence to Abraham's sacrifice of the ram that the Lord provided as the substitution in place of the life of his only son Isaac.

This *two-day* feast of the Lord is also known as the Festival of the Awakening Blast that comes from the Scripture in where the Hebrew words for "day of blowing the trumpets" is *Yom Teruah*, which means "*day of shouting*" or the day of resurrection of the dead.

Another name for this feast time was the Festival of the *Last Trump*, and was called that from ancient times. As we have covered under Pentecost, the right horn of Abraham's ram is called the *last trump* and will be blown to herald the coming of the Messiah.

As Christians we can see this truth, and we can see that the *first trump* was the beginning of the Church age and the *last trump* as the harpazo "catching away" of the Church, or the close of the dispensation of grace.

The apostle Paul taught that the (*Harpazo*) rapture or the "*catching away*" of the Church would occur at the "*last trump*" and with a "*shout*" of the archangel.

Behold, I shew you a mystery; we shall not all sleep, but we shall all be changed, In a moment, in the twinkling of an eye, at the last trump: for the trumpet shall sound, and the dead shall be raised incorruptible, and we all shall be changed. I Corinthians 15:51-52 KJV

For the Lord Himself shall descend from heaven with a shout, with the voice of the Archangel, and with the trump of God: and the dead in Christ shall rise first: Then we which are alive and remain shall be *caught up* together with them in the clouds to meet the Lord in the air: and so shall we ever be with the Lord. I Thessalonians 4:16-17 KJV

In Psalm 81 we see the *shofar* being blown during the first of Tishri (new moon) and again at the beginning of the Feast of Tabernacles (full moon) on the 15th of Tishri. This was a call for all of Israel to repent and praise God.

Blow up the trumpet in the new moon, in the time appointed, on our solemn feast day. Psalm 81:3 KJV

The word "*trumpet*" in each of these Scriptures is the Hebrew word *shofar*, or ram's horn. This is important because there are different trumpets spoken of in Scripture. Those trumpets are composed of silver and are called for at different times and for different reasons.

Another word of caution about teachings on trumpets. Many Christians are ignorant of the seven Feasts of the Lord, and His appointed times, and assume that the "*last trump*" Paul wrote about in I Corinthians 15:52 is in reference to the seventh trumpet in Revelation 11:15. This seventh trumpet (of judgment) is sounded during the last forty-two months of the tribulation.

The significant issue here to notice is that Paul wrote the letter to the church at Corinth around 55 AD, and apostle Paul was killed by Nero in Rome in the spring of 68 AD. The beloved apostle John wrote the book of Revelation while on the Isle of Patmos at approximately 95 AD. We know, therefore; that Paul was not referencing the book of Revelation that was written 40 years after Paul wrote the first letter to the Corinthians, and approximately 28 years after Paul's death.

As we stated earlier that the Feast of Trumpets is a *two-day* festival with no set agenda of specific times. Therefore, we *do not* and *can not* predict which day or hour the new moon will be, hence; we *do not* know the day or hour of the sounding of the *Last Trump*, proclaiming the beginning of the New Year.

In the gospels, Jesus taught that we should *watch* and pay close attention to the signs of the times, and that we should know the *season* of His return. He also taught that it would be as it was in the days of Noah (Matthew 24:37-42) when He returns. Jesus said that they were eating and drinking, marrying and giving in marriage...until *the day* that Noah entered into the Ark (Genesis 7:1-10) and that they knew not until the flood came, and took them away, so shall the coming of the Son of man be.

The people of the world will be going about their normal day to day business, ignoring the preaching of the righteous until *the day*.... the day Noah entered the Ark, which was *seven days* before the flood. Then judgment rain started falling and the saints were safe inside the Ark. This is a picture of the God protecting the nation of Israel during of the days of awe or the Tribulation. (Matthew 24:32-44)

A few years ago, at Passover 2013 and again at Passover 2014, groups of Jewish worshippers were arrested during their attempts to sacrifice lambs on the Temple Mount (Mount Moriah) in Jerusalem, but; they continue within the walls of the old city to this day.

The Sanhedrin (council of seventy) has been re-established and has appointed the new High Priest in anticipation of the completion of the third temple. All the architectural plans for the third temple have been completed and all the furnishings, fixtures, and equipment have been created and are in storage. The priest's garments have been made and the Temple Institute have identified and have been training descendants from the tribe of Levi in the procedures of proper Temple sacrificial worship. They even have a red heifer breeding program in place. The third temple will be built soon.

After the destruction of the temple and seventy years of captivity in Persia, the Lord stirred-up king Cyrus and he released faithful Ezra (Ezra 1:1) to lead a company of nearly fifty thousand Hebrews back to Jerusalem to rebuild the Temple. The first thing they did was to rebuild the altar and offer sacrifices unto the Lord. They did this even before they started on the foundations to the Temple.

This re-dedication of the altar and re-establishing the sacrifices to the Lord was done at the *appointed time*. It was conducted on Rosh Hashanah for *two days* and stated that these days were holy.

They then continued to keep the set feasts of the Lord. (Ezra 3:1-6) We can watch and see what unfolds, but; we would speculate that we will see the Jewish folks sacrificing on the Temple site before the new foundations are laid for the third Temple. This is yet another *sign of the end-times*.

Permission must be granted by the controlling authorities before the construction of the third Temple can begin on-site, however; everything else is ready for the Temple to be fully functional just as it did in 70 AD before its destruction. We can accurately predict that with modern methods and equipment, the third temple could be constructed in less than one calendar year.

Currently at this writing, Jewish prayer on the Temple Mount is absolutely forbidden. It is illegal for Jewish believers and Christians to go to the Temple Mount to pray, sing, or worship overtly.

There has been a proposed law submitted to Israel's Knesset (Parliament) to allow prayer on-site, but; it is not law yet. We do not believe that the Jews will have any rights to pray, worship, sacrifice, and certainly not build on the Temple Mount until a peace agreement is in place with (Ishmael/Esau) the Arabs/Palestinians.

We also believe there will need to be some very significant event (perhaps the Psalm 83 war) to occur before this will manifest. This "covenant" confirmed by many could very well be brokered by the antichrist. We believe this will be the seven year *"covenant with many for one week"* prophesied in Daniel 9:27.

Summary of events that occurred on the 1st of Tishri:

First day of Creation of the earth.

Ezra's re-dedication of the altar and the people.

Sacrifices re-established before second temple.

The first ten days of Tishri: Day 1 2 **3 4 5 6 7 8 9** 10

Days 1+2 are *Rosh Hashanah*, or Trumpets.

Days 3+4+5+6+7+8+9 are *Yamin Noraim*, or the **7** Days of Awe.

Day 10 is *Yom Kippur,* or the Day of Atonement.

We will now look at the 7 Days of Awe, the *seven days* between Trumpets and Atonement. The rabbinical teachings call these the *Yamin Noraim* which means the *terrible days*, or the *days of awe*. They took this name from the prophet Joel.

And the Lord shall utter His voice before His army: for His camp is very great: for He is strong that executeth His word: for the day of the Lord is great and very terrible: who can abide it? Joel 2:11 KJV

Alas! For that day is great, so that none is like it: it is even the time of *Jacob's trouble*; but he shall be saved out of it. Jeremiah 30:7 KJV

Blow ye the trumpet in Zion, and sound an alarm in My Holy mountain: let all the inhabitants of the land tremble: for the day of the Lord cometh, for it is nigh at hand. Joel 2:1 KJV This is Rosh Hashanah– the *Last Trump.*

Could it be the *Harpazo* the catching away of the Church described in I Thessalonians 4:17?

And the Lord shall utter His voice before His army: for His camp is very great: for He is strong that executeth His word: for the day of the Lord is great and very terrible: who can abide it? Joel 2:11 KJV

This is Yamin Noraim–the *Days of Awe* the seven-year Tribulation.

Blow the trumpet in Zion, sanctify a fast, call a solemn assembly: Gather the people, sanctify the congregation, assemble the elders, gather the children, and those that suck the breasts: let the bridegroom go forth of His chamber, and the bride out of her closet. Joel 2:15-16 KJV

This is the 10th day Yom Kippur – the *Great Trump* this is Judgment day when King Jesus returns with the faithful overcomers to stand on the Mount of Olives and enter the eastern gate of the Temple.

The days of awe, the terrible days, the time of Jacob's trouble–All of these names are symbolic for the seven-year Tribulation when the antichrist brings hell on earth and God Almighty is pouring out His wrath until King Jesus returns to destroy the beast, false prophet, and the armies of His enemies.

We believe that the Feast of Trumpets is when Jesus could return for His bride (the overcomers) and they shall be *caught up to meet the Lord in the air*. They will be at the marriage supper of the Lamb (Jewish wedding is seven days) with the Bridegroom for the seven years of Tribulation until judgment day, the *Day of the Lord*, the day that Jesus returns to stand on the Mount of Olives, and His bride will then return with Him.

The Tribulation–First 42 months: *These must be fulfilled before the Day of the Lord begins.

*Apostasy – the falling away of believers from Truth.

*Restrainer taken away – the gathering together of the faithful Bride.

Antichrist revealed. (2 Thessalonians 2:1-10)

Covenant signed in Israel. (Daniel 9:27)

Midpoint of the tribulation: The antichrist sits in the Temple, proclaims himself to be god, and stops the Jewish sacrifices, and breaks the seven-year peace covenant with many, and then the *Great Tribulation* begins.

The seven-year Tribulation–Second 42 months:

The two witnesses shall prophesy in Jerusalem (Revelation 11:3-12)

The King of kings returns on the Mount of Olives (Zechariah 14:4)

Armageddon (Revelation 19:16)

The beast and the false prophet are cast into the lake of fire. (Revelation 19:20)

There is much to be said regarding the *End of the Age*. We have just touched upon some of the various eschatological prophecies that teach us about these days, but; there is still a great deal of information to be gleaned from Scripture.

This teaching is focused on the Feasts of the Lord, and what they reveal to us, so; we shall move on to the next very important appointed time.

Fall feast: **Day of Atonement**

Also on the tenth day of this seventh month there shall be a day of atonement: it shall be an holy convocation unto you; and ye shall *afflict* your souls, and offer an offering made by fire unto the Lord. And ye shall do no work in that day: for it is a day of atonement for you before the Lord your God. Leviticus 23:27-28 KJV

This appointed time teaches us about the second coming of Jesus Christ, the Son of the living God. The Feast of Trumpets is called the *Last Trump* and this Day of Atonement is called the festival of the *Great Trump*. This trump is blown on the fast. This is the only *fast* day of all the *Feasts of the Lord*. This is *the day* that the Lord (Bridegroom) comes out of His bridal chamber, where He has been with His bride for seven years:

Blow the trumpet in Zion, sanctify a *fast*, call a solemn assembly: Gather the people, sanctify the congregation, assemble the elders, gather the children, and those that suck the breasts: let the bridegroom go forth of His chamber, and the bride out of her closet. Let the priests, the ministers of the Lord, weep between the porch and the altar, and let them say, spare thy people, O Lord, and give not thine heritage to reproach, that the heathen should rule over them: wherefore should they say among the people, where is their God? Joel 2:15-17 KJV

Immediately after the Tribulation of those days shall the sun be darkened, and the moon shall not give her light, and the stars shall fall from heaven, and the powers of the heavens shall be shaken: And then shall appear the sign of the Son of man in heaven: and then shall all the tribes of the earth mourn, and they shall see the Son of man coming in the clouds of heaven with power and great glory. And He shall send His angels with a *great* sound of a *trumpet,* and they shall gather together His elect from the four winds, from one end of heaven to the other. Matthew 24:29-31 KJV

This is the Day of Atonement–The prophesied judgment day for the world, this is the very end of the *Day of the Lord*. The Lord will send His angels at the *Great Trump* to gather the elect, those believers that survived the Tribulation; to Jerusalem to be with

Jesus as He takes His throne as King of kings and Lord of lords. The kings and lords are the overcomers.

This day was the day that the ritual of the two goats was performed. (Leviticus 16) One goat was "for the Lord" and the other the "scapegoat". They cast lots to determine which was which. The Lord's goat was sacrificed for the sins of the people, and the other was released to die in the wilderness. This is a picture of Jesus, the Son of the Father and Barabbas (which means *son of the father*) and a picture of Jesus and the antichrist. One goat dedicated to God, and one goat dedicated to satan.

There were many rituals and ceremonial proceedings involved with this one day that we will summarize: The Day of Atonement was the one day of the year that the High Priest put on special garments after the ceremonial purification in the mikveh and entered the Holy of Holies behind the veil, to place blood on the mercy seat that rests on top of the Ark of the Covenant.

When the Glory of the Lord would come down between the two golden Cherub on the top of the mercy seat, God would *see the blood*, not the sins of the people. The blood atoned for, or "covered" the iniquities of the people for another year. If the High

Priest was not properly consecrated and prepared, he would drop dead in the Holy of Holies.

Therefore they would attach a small bell to the hem of the High Priest's garment, so others could listen for the bell tinkling. It is told in historical writings that they would also tie a rope around the High Priests ankle, so if he dropped dead behind the veil, other priests could pull his corpse out of the Holy of Holies.

If they didn't take such precautions, they too could perish in their attempt to remove the dead body of the High Priest from behind the veil.

Summary of events that occurred on the 10th of Tishri:

Day of release, every seventh *Shemitah* year. (Deuteronomy 15:1-3)

Day of the year of *Jubilee* (7 x7 years) the 50th year. (Leviticus 25:8-10)

The Day of Freedom and the final Jubilee.

The Day of the Lord.

Fall feast: **Tabernacles**

Speak unto the children of Israel, saying, the fifteenth day of this seventh month shall be the Feast of Tabernacles for seven days unto the Lord. On the first day shall be an holy convocation: ye shall do no servile work therein. Seven days ye shall offer an offering made by fire unto the Lord: on the eighth day shall be an holy convocation unto you; and ye shall offer an offering made by fire unto the Lord: it is a solemn assembly; and ye shall do no servile work therein. Leviticus 23:34-36 KJV

This appointed time of the Lord teaches us about the seventh day–the millennial reign of Christ, or the Kingdom age. Our day of rest from sin and Satan. (Revelation 20:4)

The eighth day will be the new heaven and earth and the New Jerusalem, or the end of the Kingdom age on earth and the new beginning of our eternity with the Lord. (Revelation 21-22)

Also in the fifteenth day of the seventh month, when ye have *gathered in* the fruit of the land, ye shall keep a feast unto the Lord seven days: on the first day shall be a Sabbath, and on the eighth day shall be a Sabbath. Leviticus 23:39 KJV

This appointed time of the Lord is also called the Feast of Ingathering.

Ye shall dwell in booths seven days; all that are Israelites born shall dwell in booths: That your generations may know that I made the children of Israel to dwell in booths, when I brought them out of the land of Egypt: I AM the Lord your God. Leviticus 23:42-43 KJV

This was a time that Israel was to remember that God Almighty brought them out of bondage in the land of Egypt into the Promised Land. They were to *remember* that the Lord led them, watered them, fed them, clothed them, healed them, and protected them in the wilderness for forty years. God Almighty *tabernacled* (dwelt) among the people!

And Moses declared unto the children of Israel the feasts of the Lord. Leviticus 23:44 KJV

This was the most important feast of the year for the children of Israel. This was the greatest celebration and the most joyful of all the appointed times. It was a time to remember and celebrate Almighty God's provisional care in the wilderness, and it marked the final *ingathering* of the harvest of the precious fruit of the earth. This is why each day the burnt offerings began with the sacrifice of bulls (Numbers 29:12-40) for seven days, thus equaling a seven-day total of seventy bulls offered as a sacrifice representing all the nations of the world.

We believe that Jesus was born on the first day of the Feast of Tabernacles, and this is why we will gather each year during the millennial reign for this feast – to celebrate the coronation of our awesome King!

And the Word was made flesh, and *dwelt* among us, (and we beheld His glory, the glory as of the only begotten of the Father) full of grace and truth. John 1:14 KJV

The Greek word *skenoo* that is translated *dwelt* in this verse means *tabernacled.* John wrote "the Word was made flesh, and *tabernacled* among us."

Also, the shepherds did not stay in the field with the sheep in December and January in and around Bethlehem because it was too cold at night. We also see where Jacob built booths or *tabernacles* for his livestock and rested in Genesis 33:17 at *Succoth* which means tabernacle.

The feast of Tabernacles is foreshadowing the one-thousand-year millennial reign, the seventh day; the day of rest, when once again the Word shall come to *tabernacle* with His people, and we shall rule and reign with Him until the new beginning on the eighth day, which is the beginning of eternity.

The eighth day is the last day, that great day (John 7:37) of the feast. (Leviticus 23:34-36,39, Numbers 29:35) which is the new beginning: The new heaven and the new earth and the New Jerusalem. (Revelation 21:1-3) Oh, praise the Lord!

Of all the appointed times that the Lord established the feast of Tabernacles is the only one that the Bible tells us shall continue in the millennium:

And it shall come to pass, that every one that is left of all the nations which came against Jerusalem shall go up from year to year to worship the King, the Lord of Hosts, and to keep the feast of tabernacles. Zechariah 14:16 KJV

Summary of the events that occur, beginning on the 15th of Tishri:

Great time of rest and celebration.

The most precious Fruit of the earth harvested.

We believe Jesus was born and tabernacled with us and shall again very soon.

We pray that this introduction to the Feasts of the Lord and God Almighty's appointed times will cause your faith to grow to new levels and shall add strength to your good foundation as you continue your study of the Word of God and walk in victory as you keep watch and pray because the time is near. Amen.

But of that day and that hour knoweth no man, no, not the angels which are in heaven, neither the Son, but the Father. Take ye heed, watch and pray: for ye know not when the time is. For the Son of man is as a man taking a far journey, who left his house, and gave authority to his servants, and to every man his work, and commanded the porter to watch. Watch ye therefore: for ye know not when the master of the house cometh, at even, or at midnight, or at the cockcrowing, or the morning: Lest coming suddenly he find you sleeping. And what I say unto you I say unto all, Watch. Mark 13:32-37 KJV

Jesus has commanded us to: Take heed, watch and pray. Watch ye therefore.

Watch–This is the overcomer's mandate.

CHAPTER FIVE

God's Prophetic Time Clock.

Foundational Truth: God loves Israel and the city of Jerusalem, and those that bless Israel are blessed and those that come against Israel will perish.

It is also foolish to think, as some do; that God is finished with Israel. No, in-fact Israel is God's time piece and if we want to know where we are in the end-time scenario of events we must look at and carefully consider Israel and Jerusalem.

It is very clear in the Scriptures how God loves and cares for land and people of Israel. First, a quick review: We see (Genesis 12:1-3) how God calls Abram, the first Hebrew; (Genesis 14:13) out of his country to a place God Almighty promises him land and makes an everlasting covenant with Abram, to give him and his seed forevermore as an inheritance, (Genesis 12:7, 13:15, 15:18, 17:7, 22:18,

26:4) which was confirmed many times by Father God in the Word.

And he dreamed that there was a ladder set up on the earth, and the top of it reached to heaven; and the angels of God were ascending and descending on it! And behold, the Lord stood over and beside him and said, I am the Lord, the God of Abraham your father [forefather] and the God of Isaac; I will give to you and to your descendants the land on which you are lying. And your offspring shall be as [countless as] the dust or sand of the ground, and you shall spread abroad to the west and the east and the north and the south; and by you and your Offspring shall all the families of the earth be blessed and bless themselves. Genesis 28:12-14 AMPC

He has remembered His covenant forever, the word which He commanded to a thousand generations, the covenant which He made with Abraham, and His oath to Isaac. Then He confirmed it to Jacob for a statute, to Israel as an everlasting covenant, saying, To you I will give the land of Canaan as the portion of your inheritance, when they were only a few men in number, very few, and strangers in it. And they wandered about from nation to nation, from one kingdom to another people. He permitted no man to oppress them, and He reproved kings for their sakes: Do not touch My anointed one, and do My prophets no harm. Psalm 105:8-15 NSAB

God says that He will bless those that bless Israel and He shall curse those that curse Israel, and that all families of the earth shall be blessed through Israel. (Genesis 12:3,18:18) Of course we know this eternal blessing to all people and every family on earth is speaking of Jesus, the Lion from the tribe of Judah and the Root of David. (Genesis 49:8-12, Revelation 5:5)

We find it interesting that there seems to be so much debate about who has rightful claim to the Holy Land and especially the city of Jerusalem. El Shaddai – God Almighty – The great I AM – The Master and Creator of the universe said this land of promise is *My land,* and we believe Him!

The land, moreover, shall not be sold permanently, for *the land is Mine*; for you are but aliens and sojourners with Me. Leviticus 25:23 NASB

Behold, to the Lord your God belong heaven and the highest heavens, the earth and all that is in it. Deuteronomy 10:4 NASB

A land which the Lord thy God careth for: the eyes of the Lord thy God are always upon it, from the beginning of the year even unto the end of the year. Deuteronomy 11:12 KJV

For behold, in those days and at that time, when I restore the fortunes of Judah and Jerusalem, I will gather all the nations and bring them down to the valley of Jehoshaphat. Then I will enter into judgement with them there on behalf of My people and My inheritance, Israel, whom they have scattered among the nations; and they have divided up *My land*. Joel 3:1-2 NASB

Additionally, and very explicitly the Lord God Almighty said that He has chosen Jerusalem as the place that He would put His eye and His name and His heart forever. (I Kings 8:29, I Kings 11:13, II Kings 21:7, Zechariah1:17, Zechariah 2:12, Zechariah 3:2, Zechariah 8:1-8)

The Lord said to him, I have heard your prayer and your supplication, which you have made before Me; I have consecrated this house which you have built by putting My name there forever, and My eyes and My heart will be there perpetually. I Kings 9:3 NSAB

For the Lord has chosen Zion; He has desired it for His habitation. This is My resting place forever; here I will dwell, for I have desired it. Psalm 132:13-14 NASB

Therefore thus says the Lord, I will return to Jerusalem with compassion; My house will be built in it, declares the Lord of hosts, and a measuring line will be stretched over Jerusalem. Again, proclaim, saying, Thus says the Lord of hosts, My cities will again overflow with prosperity, and the Lord will again comfort Zion and again choose Jerusalem. Zechariah 1:16-17 NASB

We are commanded by God to bless Israel.

God also says what He will do to those that come against Israel and try to divide His land. (Joel 3:1-21). The nation of Israel is very special to our Lord and He will defend her, and He commands us to pray for prosperity and peace within Israel.

For thus says the Lord of hosts; After glory He has sent me against the nations which plunder you, for he who touches you, touches the apple of His eye. Zechariah 2:8 NASB

In that day will the Lord guard and defend the inhabitants of Jerusalem, and he who is [spiritually] feeble and stumbles among them in that day [of persecution] shall become [strong and noble] like David; and the house of David [shall maintain its supremacy] like God, like the Angel of the Lord Who is before them. And it shall be in that day that I will make it My aim to destroy all the nations that come against Jerusalem. Zechariah 12:8-9 AMPC

Pray for the peace of Jerusalem! May they prosper who love you [the Holy City]! May peace be within your walls and prosperity within your palaces! For my brethren and companion's sake, I will now say, Peace be within you! For the sake of the house of the Lord our God, I will seek, inquire for, and require your good. Psalm 122:6-9 AMPC

We could go on-and-on about how much Almighty God loves Israel. The bottom line is you must be totally ignorant of the Holy Bible or just simply dishonest not to see and believe that we as Christians are commanded by God's Word to love, pray for, and support Israel. Whosoever is *not* a friend of Israel, is on the wrong side of the will of God. This is not a good place to be.

But you, Israel, My servant, Jacob, whom I have chosen, the offspring of Abraham My friend, you whom I [the Lord] have taken from the ends of the earth and have called from the corners of it, and said to you, You are My servant – I have chosen you and not cast you off [even though you are exiled]. Fear not [there is nothing to fear], for I am with you; do not look around you in terror and be dismayed, for

I am your God. I will strengthen and harden you to difficulties, yes, I will help you; yes, I will hold you up and retain you with My [victorious] right hand of rightness and justice. Isaiah 41:8-10 AMPC

For the nation and kingdom that will not serve you in that day [Jerusalem] shall perish; yes, those nations shall be utterly laid to waste. Isaiah 60:12 AMPC

Therefore [earnestly] wait for Me, says the Lord, [waiting] for the day when I rise up to the attack [as a witness, accuser, or judge, and a testimony]. For My decision and determination and right it is to gather the nations together, to assemble the king-doms, to pour upon them My indignation, even all [the heat of] My fierce anger; for [in that day] all the earth shall be consumed with the fire of My zeal and jealousy. Zephaniah 3:8 AMPC

Behold, all these promises and proclamations made by the Lord apply to all of Father God's chil-dren because we are all the spiritual seed of Abraham.

There is [now no distinction] neither Jew nor Greek, there is neither slave nor free, there is not male and female; for you are all one in Christ Jesus. And if you belong to Christ [are in Him Who is Abraham's Seed], then you are Abraham's offspring and [spiritual] heirs according to promise. Galatians 3:28-29 AMPC

Now, we shall have a good look at God's prophetic time clock and see where we are.

One of the most momentous events of history and fulfillment of Bible prophecy is the nation of Israel being established as a sovereign State on May 14,1948 AD exactly as it was prophesied by the prophet-priest Ezekiel in the Word of God.

Ezekiel's time-line prophecy and Daniel's seventy weeks are the two most outstanding signs that we are living in the last days, or the very end of the Church age, before the return of our Lord and King, Jesus Christ to rule and reign for one thousand years (Revelation 20:6) here on earth from His earthly throne in Jerusalem (Zechariah 14:16-17) which is the Kingdom age to come, that Jesus taught us all to pray to the Father about. (Matthew 6:9-13)

God also said He would (1) *resuscitate the off-spring* and the (2) *land* of Israel. And God prophesied that He would then (3) *re-gather* the sons and daughters of Israel back to their promised land and establish them as a sovereign (4) *nation in one day*. They would be no longer divided nation but restored as (5) *one people*. And the Lord said He would watch over them as their (6) *Shepherd*, and that their (7) *defense forces* would be victorious despite facing overwhelming enemies, and that God would restore their (8) *wealth and prosperity*. And God prophesied that He would restore the (9) *Hebrew language* to the people. God showed the prophet the holocaust, where two-thirds of the Jewish population in Europe would be murdered, and then God told us exactly (10) *when* the children of Israel would become a sovereign State again, despite the whole world trying to exterminate them from the face of the earth. Our heavenly Father loves Israel.

(1) So I prophesied as I was commanded; and as I prophesied, there was a noise, and behold, a rattling; and the bones came together, bone to bone. And I looked, and behold, sinews were on them, and flesh grew and skin covered them; but there was no breath in them. Then He said to me, Prophesy to the breath, prophesy, son of man, and say to the breath, Thus says the Lord God, Come from the four winds, O breath, and breathe on these slain, that they come to life. So I prophesied as He commanded me, and the breath came into them, and they came to life and stood on their feet, an exceedingly great army.

(2) Also I will restore the captivity of My people Israel, and they will rebuild the ruined cities and live in them; they will also plant vineyards and drink their

wine, and make gardens and eat their fruit. I will also plant them on their land, and they will not again be rooted out from their land which I have given them, says the Lord your God. Amos 9:14-15 NASB

(3) Then He said to me, Son of man, these bones are the whole house of Israel; behold, they say, Our bones are dried up and our hope has perished. We are completely cut off. Therefore prophesy and say to them, Thus says the Lord God, Behold, I will open your graves and cause you to come up out of your graves, My people; and I will bring you into the land of Israel. Then you will know that I am the Lord, when I have opened your graves and caused you to come up out of your graves, My People. I will put My Spirit within you and you will come to life, and I will place you on your own land. Then you will know that I, the Lord, have spoken and done it, declares the Lord. Ezekiel 37:7-14 NASB

(4) Before she travailed, she brought forth; Before her pain came, she gave birth to a boy. Who has heard such a thing? Who has seen such a thing? Can a land be born in one day? Can a nation be brought forth all at once? As soon as Zion travailed, she also brought forth her sons. Shall I bring to the point of birth and not give delivery? Says the Lord. Or shall

I who gives delivery shut the womb? Says your God. Isaiah 66:7-9 NASB

(5) Then say to them, Thus says the Lord God: Behold, I will take the children of Israel from among the nations to which they have gone, and will gather them from every side and bring them into their own land. And I will make them one nation in the land, upon the mountains of Israel, and one King shall be King over them all; and they shall be no longer divided into two kingdoms any more. Ezekiel 37:21-22 AMPC

(6) Hear the word of the Lord, O nations, and declare in the coastlands afar off, and say, He who scattered Israel will gather him and keep him as a shepherd keeps his flock. Jeremiah 31:10 NASB

(7) If you walk in My statues and keep My commandments and do them, And you shall chase your enemies, and they shall fall before you by the sword. Five of you shall chase a hundred, and a hundred of you shall put ten thousand to flight, your enemies shall fall before you by the sword. Leviticus 26:3,7-8 AMPC

(8) then the Lord your God will restore you from captivity, and have compassion on you, and will gather you again from all the peoples where the Lord your God has scattered you. If your outcasts are at

the ends of the earth, from there the Lord your God will gather you, and from there He will bring you back. The Lord your God will bring you into the land which your fathers possessed, and you shall possess it; and He will prosper you and multiply you more than your fathers. Deuteronomy 30:3-5 NASB

(9) For then [changing their impure language] I will give to the people a clear and pure speech from pure lips, that they may all call upon the name of the Lord, to serve Him with one unanimous consent and one united shoulder [bearing the yoke of the Lord]. Zephaniah 3:9 AMPC

All of these things that Father God prophesied about the nation of Israel have all come to pass and are easily verified, and there are many more in the Word that also have been fulfilled, but; we just took a sampling to establish that whatever God says is gonna happen shall become manifest.

(10) Father God told us precisely when the nation of Israel would be re-born.

Ezekiel's time-line prophecy.

Over two thousand five hundred years ago, the prophet Ezekiel was part of the skilled working-class exiles from Judah carried away into bondage during the seventy-year Babylonian captivity (606-536 BC). The Lord gave him revelation through a vision the year that the Hebrew children would be restored permanently to the Promised Land.

The Scriptures hold many prophecies about the return of the descendants of Israel to the Holy Land in the very *last days*. Ezekiel was aware of Jeremiah's prophecy about the people of the southern kingdom of Judah being carried away captive by the king of Babylon for seventy years (Jeremiah 25:11) because they were not honoring (Leviticus 25:4) every seventh Sabbatical year or the Shemitah years. (II Chronicles 36:21) And, of course; Ezekiel knew that the people of the ten northern tribes, known as Israel; were carried away captive by the Assyrians (II Kings 15:29) approximately one hundred thirty years earlier because of their gross sin and rebellion of worshiping idols and even the sacrificing of their children to their idols. Today we call this sin of child sacrifice to our idols *pro-choice.*

The prophet Ezekiel was given another revelation about the Hebrew people and God's judgment and discipline upon them for their sin and disobedience and how long the children of Israel people would be exiled from the Promised Land.

Lie upon thy left side, and lay the iniquity of the house of Israel upon it: According to the number of days that thou shalt lie upon it thou shalt bear their iniquity. For I have laid upon thee the years of their iniquity, according to the number of the days, three hundred and ninety days: So shalt thou bear the iniquity of the house of Israel. And when thou hast accomplished them, lie again on thy right side, and thou shalt bear the iniquity of the house of Judah forty days: I have appointed thee each day for a year. Ezekiel 4:4-6 KJV

Jerusalem is the center of the world and East is always first or before. (Numbers 3:38, Ezekiel 43:1-7, Matthew 24:27) Imagine as if one were standing in the land of Israel facing east, then north would be to your left hand and south would be to your right hand, hence your left side represents the northern kingdom–the house of Israel, and your right side represents the southern kingdom–the house of Judah.

God declared that all of Israel would be disciplined for a total of four hundred thirty years of total exile from the Promised Land. (390 + 40 = 430)

However, let us not forget that Jeremiah's prophecy established the Babylonian captivity at seventy years, which ended in 536 BC, in the month of Nisan, but only a remnant of exiles (42,360) returned to Jerusalem with Ezra, under the decree of Cyrus. (Ezra 1:1-3, Ezra 2:64) Most chose to remain in Babylon, but; we must deduct the seventy years of the Babylonian captivity from the total number of four hundred thirty years. (430–70 = 360) So, now we have an additional three hundred sixty years of exile remaining after the Babylonian captivity ended in 536 BC.

Any student of the Scriptures knows that when you study the history of Israel you will not find any event that would correspond with this three hundred sixty-year period. The fact is, the majority of the God's people never returned to Israel when they had the opportunity to do so and even the ones that did failed to truly repent for their past sin, iniquity, and rebellion against God. The vast majority of the Jewish people chose to remain in Babylon, a pagan nation of idol worshippers. (study the book of Esther)

The answer to our three hundred sixty-year mystery is found in the Torah given to Moses and recorded in Leviticus chapter twenty-six. God has established the principle of judgment that says that after Father

God disciplined His children for their sin and iniquity, and they did not repent and turn from their
prideful and rebellious ways and return to the Lord,
then God would multiply the original judgment by
seven (7x) times.

And if ye will not yet for all this hearken unto Me,
then I will punish you seven times more for your sins.
And I will break the pride of your power; and I will
make your heaven as iron, and your earth as brass.
Leviticus 26:18-19 KJV

Israel did not genuinely repent after the first
seventy years of Babylonian captivity, therefore;
God multiplied the remaining three hundred sixty
years by seven.

360 x 7 equals 2,520 Biblical years of additional
exile from their inheritance, or the promised land; for
the Jewish people.

Now, just as we calculate a Biblical year when we
study the time-line prophecy in the book of Daniel,
the same shall apply here. The prophetic or Father
God's calendar year is three hundred sixty days,
based on the Hebrew lunar calendar year. (not on
our 365.25-day pagan solar calendar year).

We know from other studies that this twelve
month–thirty days per month–three hundred sixty

days per year reckoning is established in Scripture in Noah's day (Genesis 7:11, Genesis 8:3-4) five thirty-day months equaled one hundred fifty days, (Revelation 12:6) and also one thousand two hundred sixty days are forty-two months or three and one-half years.

To fully understand the prophecy, we must convert from three hundred sixty-day Hebrew lunar calendar to our current way of reckoning days, months, and years.

Therefore, Ezekiel's prophecy reveals to us that the Jewish people would be allowed to return to their Promised Land in the springtime of 1948 AD.

2,520 prophetic years x 360 days = 907,200 days. The end of the Babylonian captivity was in the spring of 536 BC. (per Jewish the sages' historical writings)

So, we divide our 907,200 prophetic days by our 365.25-day year and we get 2,483.8 solar calendar years. Also remember there is no zero-year AD between one BC and one AD, so we subtract one year from our total calculations accordingly.

The seventy-year Babylonian captivity ended in the spring of 536.4 BC, so we subtract 536.4 from our 2,483.8 and we have the sum of 1,947.4 minus

1 year between the years of 1 AD and 1 BC, and you arrive at springtime 1,948.4 AD

The sovereign State of Israel was proclaimed on: **Friday May 14th, 1948** on the Gregorian calendar (366-day leap year), which was before sundown on the 6th day of the week, of the eighth month of Lyar on the 5th day, 5708

The fulfillment of Moses, Isaiah, Jeremiah, Ezekiel, Amos, and Zephaniah's prophecies in our generation is truly awesome. Of course, they are all inspired by the Holy Spirit. This is how we prove to unbelievers and doubters that the Word of God is Truth.

This event of the formation of the sovereign nation of Israel after 2,500 years, and to the month and year that was prophesied is simply awe inspiring. There are many, many more prophetic events and patterns throughout the Scriptures that have been fulfilled to build our faith and thus help others believe in our Lord and His Holy written Word.

This prophecy is of the utmost importance because it started the final countdown to the second coming of the King of kings and the Lord of lords: Jesus Christ our Lord and soon coming King. However, we need to study one more very important prophetic time clock prophecy that will tell what season of time we are in now.

Daniel's seventy weeks' time-line prophecy.

Daniel was a very intrepid and faithful man that was devoted to serving his Lord. Throughout the more than seventy years in Babylonian captivity, and even when facing certain death; Daniel never once compromised his faith as he endeavored to do all he could to honor and follow all the precepts of his Lord.

Here in chapter nine of the book of Daniel, we find Daniel attempting to honor God's **moed** or His *appointed times*, that we know as the Feasts of the Lord, and specifically the Day of Atonement. (see Leviticus 23:26-32, Numbers 29:7-11)

We see Daniel humbling himself by fasting and praying to the Lord, confessing his guilt and inter-ceding on behalf of the sin-guilt of his kinsmen. This is what was done on *Yom Kippur*, (sixth feast) the Day of Atonement, at the Temple in Jerusalem.

Obviously, Daniel could not be physically present in Jerusalem as commanded by God, and the Temple had been destroyed by Nebuchadnezzar, conse-quently; faithful Daniel did the very best he could within the limitations and circumstances he had to cope with in this pagan nation. Our heavenly Father God knows our heart, and the Lord surely knew the condition and motivation of Daniel's heart that day in Shushan, Persia as he was in servitude to king Darius.

As Daniel was praying, the angel Gabriel came from heaven with a message at three pm, at the very time that the two goat (the Lord's goat and the scapegoat) sacramental offering would be performed at the Temple. (see Leviticus 16:2-34)

Gabriel came to teach Daniel about the first coming of the promised Messiah, His death, and the end of the age. Can you imagine how overwhelming it would be for Gabriel to appear and join you during your prayer time and to deliver a message for all of mankind directly from the throne room of Almighty God, and to inform you that you are known in heaven and that you are greatly beloved! Wow, how incredible would that be?

Seventy weeks are determined upon thy people and upon thy holy city, to finish the transgression, and to make an end of sins, and to make reconciliation for iniquity, and to bring in everlasting righteousness, and to seal up the vision and prophecy, and to anoint the most Holy. Daniel 9:24 KJV

Seventy weeks of years is four hundred ninety years. The English word weeks was transliterated from the Hebrew word *shabua* which means *a period of seven*, thus; the Scripture could literally read *seventy sevens are determined* and be accurate. And we know Daniel had studied the Scriptures and the prophecies (Jeremiah 25:11-12, Jeremiah 29:10) as recorded in Daniel 9:2, and he understood that the seventy years of captivity was the judgment of God on the nation of Israel (Leviticus 26) for the seventy Sabbatical or Shemitah years that was utterly ignored by the kingdom of Judah. (II Chronicles 36:9-21)

Seventy Sabbath-years would span four hundred ninety years, and Daniel was literally living-out the fulfillment of this timeline prophecy.

And this whole land shall be a desolation, and an astonishment; and these nations shall serve the king of Babylon seventy years. And it shall come to pass, when seventy years are accomplished, that I will punish the king of Babylon, and that nation, saith the Lord, for their iniquity, and the land of the Chaldeans, and will make it perpetual desolations. Jeremiah 25:11-12 KJV

The angel Gabriel explained to Daniel that there would be seventy weeks of years from the decree to rebuild the city of Jerusalem until the Messiah the "Most Holy" would be anointed King of the earth.

We know from the study of Genesis 1:14 that God created the sun, moon, and stars for us as signs and for us to keep seasons, or God's *moed* appointed times; and for counting days and years. Then we see in Genesis chapter seven that God's prophetic year is three hundred sixty days, or twelve moons/months of thirty days each. The Lord specifically told us that five moons/months was one hundred fifty days (Genesis 7:24). We must comprehend these things to be able to calculate and reckon the timeline prophecies that the Lord gives us. The "one day equals a year" principle we will find in Scripture in Numbers 14:34 and Ezekiel 4:6.

Know therefore and understand that from the going forth of the commandment to restore and to build Jerusalem unto the Messiah the Prince shall be seven weeks, and threescore and two weeks: the street shall be built again, and the wall, even in troublous times. Daniel 9:25 KJV

Gabriel explained to Daniel that from the *decree* to rebuild Jerusalem it would be seven weeks or forty-nine years until the walls and streets of the city would be rebuilt plus another sixty-two weeks until the Messiah, for a total of sixty-nine weeks until the Messiah would be cut off. Therefore, it would be four hundred eighty-three years until the Messiah would be killed.

In the book of Nehemiah 2:1-8, we see that in the month of Nisan in the twentieth year of Artaxerxes reigning as the Persian king, that the King's *decree* releasing Nehemiah (the cupbearer of the king) to go and rebuild Jerusalem's walls and gates was given. Artaxerxes took the throne mid-year of 465 BC, thus; his twentieth year would have been summer of 445 BC. The following month of Nisan would have been in spring 444 BC, before the conclusion of his twentieth year as King. (Historical documentation per Wikipedia)

And after threescore and two weeks shall Messiah be cut off, but not for Himself: and the people of the prince that shall come shall destroy the city and the sanctuary; and the end thereof shall be with a flood, and unto the end of the war desolations are determined. Daniel 9:26 KJV

Again, the messenger angel Gabriel told Daniel starting at the decree given to rebuild Jerusalem to the Messiah being *cut-off* was a total of sixty-nine weeks, or four hundred eighty-three years.

The prophecy states that Messiah would be cut off (killed) not for anything He had done, but; for a sacrifice. After the Messiah is cut off, a prince would come and destroy Jerusalem and the sanctuary (Temple) and then the land would be totally desolate after the war.

Next, let's do some reckoning and calculations of years.

In 1894 in Great Brittan, a devout Christian by the name of *Sir Robert Anderson* wrote an excellent book called *The Coming Prince* about Bible prophecy, and Anderson was the first we know to convert the Hebrew prophetic calendar to the Gregorian modern calendar like thus:

69 x 7 = 483 years x 360 days (Hebrew lunar calendar) equals a total of 173,880 days. 173,880 days applied on the modern sun calendar becomes 476 years and 21 days. 476 years x 365.25 days per the modern sun calendar equals 173,859 days and 173,880 days less <173,859 days> leaves 21 days.

March 14, 444 BC (the day of the *Decree*) plus 476 years would be March 14, 31 AD. March 14 + 21 days is April 6. Add one year because there is no "0" year between BC and AD and the final date we arrive at is April 6, 32 AD.

We have researched various sources for the conversion dates for The Feast of Passover in 32 AD, and there is conflicting data, however; they all agree that Passover that year was in April, so; we are satisfied with a margin of error in the human calculations being within (plus or minus) a few days. We also know that according to the Gospel of Luke, John the Baptist's ministry began in 28 AD.

Now in the fifteenth year of the reign of Tiberius Caesar, Pontius Pilate being governor of Judaea, and Herod being tetrarch of Galilee, and his brother Philip tetrarch of Ituraea and of the region of Trachonitis, and Lysanias the tetrarch of Abilene, Luke 3:1 KJV

The Romans kept good records and we know Caesar Augustus, the first Roman Emperor reigned until his death August 19, 14 AD. Rome's second Caesar, Tiberius began his *co-reign* the last year of Augustus's life and reigned until 37 AD at his death. (13 AD plus 15 years equals 28 AD plus the three and on-half years of Jesus' ministry and you have 32 AD) It is also documented that Pontius Pilate was the Roman Governor of Judaea from 26 AD till 36 AD.

After Jesus was *cut off* in 32 AD, Titus marshalled ten Legions of Roman soldiers in Antioch, Syria (now in Turkey) before they marched to lay siege at Jerusalem in 67 AD and ultimately destroyed the Temple in 70 AD. Titus and his father Vespasian were the field Generals who led the Roman siege on Jerusalem and the Temple Mount. Neither of these men were a king or a prince.

During the siege, Caesar Vitellius died (assassinated in a military coup) and the Roman senate voted General Vespasian in as the new Caesar and recalled him back to Rome. Unknown to Titus, at the very time his soldiers broke through the walls and were destroying the Temple complex, he had literally become a prince of Rome! Just another amazing truth that only God Almighty could make happen. The Temple was destroyed on the 9th day of AV in 70 AD. (The exact same day as the first temple) The Jewish historian from the tribe of Levi *Flavius Josephus*, was an eye witness to the Jewish-Roman war and he claims one million one hundred thousand non-combatants, of which the vast majority were Jews; perished during this more than three-year siege from violence, starvation, and disease.

In summary, angel Gabriel said that it would be sixty-nine weeks equaling four hundred eighty-three years until Messiah would be cut off in 32 AD. That leaves a *Gap* of time until Daniel's seventieth week.

In 71 AD, the Romans fulfilled prophet Micah's more than seven hundred fifty-year-old prophecy about plowing under the city of Jerusalem, (Micah 3:12) and Jesus prophesied that not one stone (Matthew 24:2) would be left on top of another. In 132 AD the final Jewish insurgency of war was totally crushed by the Roman army that left the country of Israel "no more." The nation of Israel ceased to exist for one thousand eight hundred sixteen years until its miraculous supernatural rebirth May 14, 1948. (In Daniel chapter eleven, the messenger angel prophesied a comprehensive list of events from 536 BC up to 1948 AD)

And *he* shall confirm the covenant with many for one week: and in the midst of the week *he* shall cause the sacrifice and the oblation to cease, and for the overspreading of abominations *he* shall make it desolate, even until the consummation, and that determined shall be poured upon the desolate. Daniel 9:27 KJV

We believe Daniel's seventieth week shall begin at the catching away (*Harpazo*) or the rapture of the Church. The seventieth and final week begins when *the beast* system and the antichrist comes on the geo-political world scene and forces a seven-year peace treaty/covenant with Israel and the surrounding nations, thus we have the *Gap* time:

Week sixty-nine was concluded at the crucifixion of Jesus Christ at Passover in the spring of 32 AD.

The Temple in Jerusalem was destroyed in 70 AD on the 9th of AV.

Roman war against the last Jewish revolt in 130 AD.

Israel completely and utterly desolated in132 AD.

Israel restored as a sovereign nation May 14,1948 AD

The Harpazo/rapture of the Church in [unknown] AD will mark the beginning of the 70th week.

The *Gap* time between the 69th and the 70th week is the age of grace, or the Church age. We are living at the very end of the *Gap* time right now.

The **he** mentioned in Daniel 9:27 that shall confirm the peace treaty is the antichrist. Paul called him the *man of sin* and the *son of perdition*.

Let no man deceive you by any means: for that day shall not come, except there come a falling away first, and that man of sin be revealed, the son of perdition. II Thessalonians 2:3 KJV

Daniel wrote that the seventieth week *beginning* is marked by the antichrist confirming the covenant (peace treaty) with Israel and many others. In the *middle* of the week, (Matthew 24:15) the antichrist would enforce the stop of the sacrifices at the Temple, and at the end of the week the antichrist would be made desolate or destroyed.

This is Daniel's seventieth week, which is the seven-year Tribulation, and that its beginning shall be marked by the seven-year covenant/agreement with Israel and many. We must keep watching the Middle East and especially Israel because the nation of Israel is the apple of God's eye (Zechariah 2:8) and Jerusalem is God Almighty's prophetic time clock.

We believe that the Middle East war prophesied in Psalm 83 and the Gog/Magog war prophesied in Ezekiel chapters thirty-eight and thirty-nine must occur before the beginning of the seven-year Tribulation because we believe these incredible defeats suffered by the sons of Ishmael surrounding Israel will prompt the disposition of the Arab nations and other nations and people to desire and seek a treaty or compact with Israel and allow the third temple to be built it its proper place.

These middle eastern wars are what necessitates the seven-year *covenant with many* that will be *confirmed* by this dynamic leader of the world–the antichrist, which he breaks after forty-two months. God has sent His two witnesses (Revelation 11:3) to preach for the first forty-two months and the antichrist kills them and their bodies are in the street for the world to see for three and one-half days before God resurrects them.

This is the beginning of the last forty-two months of the Tribulation when antichrist breaks the seven-year covenant with many, stops the sacrifices at the Temple, and declares that he is "god" and the real savior of humanity and the ecosystem. (Climate change/global warming nonsense is satanic)

We believe the antichrist's plan must include convincing the people of the world that the two witnesses of God were the antichrist and the false prophet that he has killed. This is when all those living must declare and worship him as their *god* and take the *mark* (Revelation 13:15-18) or be killed.

This will be a time of such mass confusion, chaos, and utter destruction that many will believe anyone telling them that they are the "savior" and will be deceived into taking the "mark" or the name of the beast. These individuals that receive this mark of the beast shall be irrevocably doomed to the eternal lake of fire. (Revelation 14:9-12)

There is much more to be said about this time-line Bible prophecy and all the details of this period in history. This cursory review is not an exhaustive work on the topic, but rather it should be viewed as just a good primer for your further study. Amen.

General comments and closing notes regarding Bible Prophecy:

The study of the prophetic messages within the Holy Bible is simply just "Bible study" because approximately one third of all the Scriptures are prophetic; meaning that it is literally predicting a specific future event or is a type, shadow, similitude, or pattern pointing to future people, places, things, and events.

Eschatology is the specific and focused study of the "last things" or End-Time Bible Prophecy.

There are many individuals, ministers, pastors, teachers, theologians, and scholars that study the prophetic Scriptures with many different opinions and conclusions. We consider ourselves as mere students of Bible prophecy. The more we study the Scriptures, the more we realize how much more we must learn. We believe every serious student should be as the Bereans, and therefore (Acts 17:11) searching the Scriptures daily to find out if these things being taught were so. There is no one individual that knows it all or ever will. There are some that "know" more than others, but; we have not encountered too many absolute *experts* in Bible prophecy.

For our knowledge is fragmentary (incomplete and imperfect). And our prophecy (our teaching) is fragmentary (incomplete and imperfect). I Corinthians 13:9 AMPC

God intended it that way. When the Holy Spirit calls us "the body of Christ" (I Corinthians 12:27) we know Holy Spirit is referring to the Church and He teaches that the "body" has many parts, and so too the Church has many parts. Therefore, we all need each other. We need all the parts to make-up a whole fully functioning body. We need your part and you need our part. Amen.

There are many good men and women of God that stand in the office of Teacher, placed there by our Lord Jesus; for the perfecting (maturing) of the saints (Ephesians 4:1-16). Not all Teachers are called to focus their teaching on the same topics or sub-jects, therefore; there are some Teachers that focus their teaching ministry on Bible Prophecy. Certainly, not everyone in the following list stands in the min-istry office of Teacher, however; we believe the Lord has anointed them and led them to write for Him specifically for the building-up and equipping the saints for the work of the ministry.

We have included a short list of Bible teachers that help clarify the prophetic Scriptures, and that we believe do a good job. We might suggest that if you wish to study Bible Prophecy at a deeper level that you consider some of these individuals work to aid your personal study and growth in your understanding of God's Word.

*Sir Robert Anderson, John Ankerberg, Kay Arthur, Mark Biltz, Richard Booker, Billye Brim, Jonathan Cahn, Morris Cerullo, *J.R. Church, Bobby Conner, Paul Keith Davis, Jimmy DeYoung, Lou Engle, *Les Feldick, John Hagee, Ed Hindson, Mark Hitchcock, Thomas Horn, *Noah Hutchings, Thomas Ice, *John Paul Jackson, *Grant Jeffrey, Robert Jeffress, David Jeremiah, Ken Johnson, Rick Joyner, *Tim LaHaye, *Zola Levitt, Hal Lindsey, L.A. Marzulli, *Chuck Missler, Ron Phillips, David Reagan, Joel Richardson, Joel Rosenberg, Bill Salus, Gary Stearman, Perry Stone, Jack Van Impe, *David Wilkerson

Other good general Bible teachers that don't necessarily focus on Prophecy:

Adrian Beale, John Bevere, Mel Bond, Reinhard Bonnke, *F.F. Bosworth, *E. M. Bounds, Michael L.

Brown, Rodney Howard-Browne, *Charles Capps, *Howard Carter, Mahesh Chavda, Randy Clark, Bill Cloud, Kenneth Copeland, Jesse Duplantis, Jimmy Evans, *Charles Finney, *Kenneth E. Hagin, Bill Hamon, Mark Hankins, Norvel Hayes, Leif Hetland, Marilyn Hickey, *Steve Hill, Bill Johnson, Jeremiah Johnson, Beth Jones, Flavius Josephus, R.T. Kendall, *E.W. Kenyon, *John G. Lake, Roberts Liardon, Joyce Meyer, *Dwight L. Moody, Robert Morris, *Andrew Murray, *T.L. Osborn, Frederick K.C. Price, *Derek Prince, *Chris Putnam, *Leonard Ravenhill, Rick Renner,*Oral Roberts, *R.W. Schambach, *David A. Seamands, Dutch Sheets, *Charles H. Spurgeon, *Lester Sumrall, Charles Swindoll, Adam F. Thompson, *A.W. Tozer, *James Ussher *Smith Wigglesworth, Andrew Woods, Andrew Wommack,*Lilian B. Yeomans.

(*Signifies those promoted to heaven.)

We have yet to find anyone that we would absolutely agree with everything that comes out of their mouth or pen, so; please understand that we are unequivocally *not* providing any sort of blanket endorsement of any of these individuals and/or their teachings or opinions.

We have and could find points of disagreement with each of these individuals as we are quite sure they could find points of disagreement with our views also. Please accept this as simply our attempt at providing a reference list of various authors/expounders/preachers/teachers that we are familiar with and are introduced to their works. Some represented here we have read dozens of their books and others only one, but; found it beneficial.

As simply as we know how to express this, we respect and honor the gift (past or present) in these men and women of God and believe we all could possibly glean and prosper from their revelation and exposition of the Scriptures.

Folks, we are living in the very last of the last days and we need to be helping others to see and know the Truth and help them to prepare for the incredible things that are about to come upon this planet earth and those who choose to live as the lord of their life.

Time is short friend and Jesus is coming sooner than we think.

This is the overcomer's mandate.

CHAPTER SIX

The Harpazo of the Faithful.

Foundational Truth: The righteous bond-servants of Jesus Christ will be caught-up to meet their King Jesus in the air before the great and terrible Day of the Lord begins.

Of all the topics that seem to stir believers up is a discussion about the rapture of the Church. For beginners, there are those that want to argue that the word rapture is not found in the Holy Bible and to that we must agree. The word rapture is not in the original Holy Bible and either is the word Bible, or the word Trinity, or the word Godhead, or the word Easter. None of these words are in the original Hebrew, Aramaic, or Greek manuscripts. Yes, we are fully aware that the 1611 Authorized Version, or the immensely popular King James Version English translation has the word Easter once and the word

Godhead three times, however; these are not correct transliterations from the original language.

The word rapture originated from the Latin Vulgate, or the Latin translation of the Holy Bible and the Latin word for the Greek word harpazo is rapturo, thus; we transliterate this word into English as rapture. We do not wish to enter this spurious dispute, so we have used the proper word from the original Greek text to title this portion of our dissertation, and from the passage where we find this word harpazo, will mark the beginning of our search of the Scriptures.

For the Lord Himself will descend from heaven with a shout, with the voice of the archangel and with the *trumpet* of God, and the dead in Christ will rise first. Then we who are alive and remain will be *caught up* together with them in the clouds to meet the Lord in the air, and so we shall always be with the Lord. Therefore comfort one another with these words. I Thessalonians 4:16-18 NASB

Trumpet (Greek noun 11x) *Salpigx*: war trumpet. This is the Greek transliteration for the Hebrew word Shofar which was used to call God's people to war and to announce victory wrought by Him. (Other Scripture examples where these words are used: Matthew 24:31, I Corinthians 14:8, I Corinthians

15:52, Exodus 19:16,19, Exodus 20:18, Joshua 6:20, Joel 2:1,15)

Caught up (Greek verb 14x) *Harpazo*: to seize, catch up, snatch away, take by force. (Other Scripture examples where this word is used: John 6:15, John 10:28,29, Acts 8:39, II Corinthians 12:2,4, Hebrews 12:19, Jude 1:23)

The apostle Paul is writing to the church at Thessalonica and is describing the moment that King Jesus returns in the clouds for His bride that has made herself ready and all the faithful saints will be *harpazo* or caught up to meet the Lord in the clouds and to be with Him forevermore. What a glorious day that will be.

As we have said and have repeatedly confirmed that God Almighty teaches and prepares us about the things to come by and through types, shadows, similitudes, and patterns and this prophetic event is no exception. Therefore, we shall begin with the prophetic patterns in the Hebrew Scriptures and end with the Greek Scriptures.

Has anyone living ever been harpazo or raptured or caught up before? Yes, there are seven events in the Holy Book of Scriptures we must look at carefully.

Faithful Enoch was the first.

Enoch lived sixty-five years, and became the father of Methuselah. Then Enoch walked with God three hundred years after he became the father if Methuselah, and he had other sons and daughters. So all the days of Enoch were three hundred and sixty-five years. Enoch walked with God; and he was not, for God took him. Genesis 5:21-24 NASB

Enoch (which means *Teacher*) was the seventh from Adam and he could possibly be the second most righteous and faithful man that has ever walked the earth (First place is Jesus). We do know this fact, he is the record holder for the oldest living man because Enoch is more than five thousand four hundred years old now because he has yet to taste death. Enoch lived in a day that was overwhelmingly violent, reprobate, and wretched and yet he still walked with his God. Enoch is a faithful overcomer and he is the prophetic similitude of the Church.

By faith Enoch was taken up so that he would not see death; And he was not found because God took him up; for he obtained the witness that before his being taken up he was pleasing to God. And without faith it is impossible to please Him, for he who comes to God must believe that He is and that He is a rewarder of those who seek Him. Hebrews 11:5-6 NASB

The Lord showed Enoch the coming judgement and destruction of all the wickedness through the deluge. This is why Enoch named his firstborn son Methuselah, which means *When he is dead it shall be sent*, and that which would be sent was the flood. Methuselah lived to be nine hundred sixty-nine years, and the day of his death Noah entered the ark, seven days before the flood event began. Enoch was also shown the judgement at the end of days also. Here Jude, the half-brother of Jesus; was quoting from the Ancient Book of Enoch 1:9

It was also about these men that Enoch, in the seventh generation from Adam, prophesied, saying, Behold, the Lord came with many thousands of His holy ones, to execute judgement upon all, and to convict all the ungodly of all their ungodly deeds which they have done in an ungodly way, and of all the harsh things which ungodly sinners have spoken against Him. Jude 1:14-15 NASB

God Almighty took His righteous servant Enoch out of the world before the Judgement began to fall on the earth in his day because Enoch's devoted and faithful lifestyle pleased Father God very much, just as Jesus will come to harpazo His faithful and righteous overcoming bond-servants before the Day of the Lord and judgement falls on this earth thus marking the end of the age of grace.

The humble leader Moses was the second.

Some very astute Bible scholars would say that the second Harpazo event would have been Moses because Moses on his one hundred and twentieth birthday climbed Mount Nebo (approximately 2,500 ft. above sea level) and that his natural life force was not abated nor was his eyesight dim and from on top of the mountain God Almighty showed Moses the promised land. We believe this is the results of Moses spending so much time under or within the glorious Presence of the Lord that his body just didn't wear-out much like the peoples clothing and their shoes (Deuteronomy 8:4, 29:5) didn't wear-out during their forty-year sojourn in the wilderness (Exodus 13:21-22, Nehemiah 9:19) of which they were continuously under the glory cloud by day and the pillar of fire by night.

So Moses the servant of the Lord died there in the land of Moab, according to the word of the Lord. And He buried him in the valley in the land of Moab, opposite Beth-peor; but no man knows his burial place to this day. Although Moses was one hundred and twenty years old when he died, his eye was not dim, nor his vigor abated. Deuteronomy 34:5-7 NASB

However, the Scripture plainly stated that Moses died that day and God took his body, nevertheless; to complicate this a bit we also know that the archangel Michael got in a scrap with the devil over Moses' body.

But Michael the archangel, when he disputed with the devil and argued about the body of Moses, did not dare pronounce against him a railing judgement, but said, The Lord rebuke you! Jude 1:9 NASB

We believe it is very clear and we can safely say that Moses' death and the final disposition of his body was not typical. We can also say that there are undeniably extraordinary circumstances recorded here to say the least. Thus, we are not dogmatic about this episode and we accept that there are things in the Scriptures that we do not fully understand. So, we simply believe it should be considered a harpazo event when we add to the contemplation the following event that definitely includes Moses and our next raptured man who was a participant in this incredible supernatural occurrence on the Mount of Transfiguration with our Lord.

Some eight days after these sayings, He took along Peter and John and James, and went up on the mountain to pray. And while He was praying, the appearance of His face became different, and His clothing became white and gleaming. And behold, two men were talking with Him; and they were Moses and Elijah, who, appearing in glory, were speaking of His departure which He was about to accomplish at Jerusalem. Luke 9:28-31 NASB

If you can accept Moses as the second "God modified" rapture occurrence, then the prophet Elijah is our third harpazo happening to consider.

The power prophet Elijah was the third.

Now Elijah the Tishbite, who was of the settlers of Gilead, said to Ahab, As the Lord, the God of Israel lives, before whom I stand, surely there shall be neither dew nor rain these years, except by my word. I Kings 17:1 NASB

Elijah is from the Tishbite tribe which no one knows who they are, and he is from an unknown location in Gilead. So, this unknown prophet named (my God is Jehovah) Elijah just shows up one day ordained by God Almighty to confront the evil king Ahab. Of course, the exploits of Elijah are well known to any Bible student including his exit from this world when Elijah was taken to heaven after crossing the river Jordan with his protégé Elisha.

And it came about when the Lord was about to take up Elijah by a whirlwind to heaven, that Elijah went with Elisha from Gilgal. II Kings 2:1 NASB

As they were going along and talking, behold, there appeared a chariot of fire and horses of fire which separated the two of them. And Elijah went up by a whirlwind to heaven. II Kings 2:11 NASB

The Old Testament righteous saints were the fourth.

All the righteous and faithful and the wicked and unfaithful people of the Old Testament that passed away have all gone to a place called *Sheol* in Hebrew, which means place of the dead; and is referred to as *Hades* and Abraham's bosom in the New Testament. Hades was the holding place for the unfaithful dead souls and Abraham's bosom was the place for the faithful and righteous ones.

Now the poor man died and was carried away by the angels to Abraham's bosom; and the rich man also died and was buried. In Hades he lifted up his eyes, being in torment, and saw Abraham far away and Lazarus in his bosom. Luke 16:22-23 NASB

When our Lord Jesus died His tortured death on the Roman cross for our sins and iniquities, He went to Hades to confront our adversary and He took back the keys and the authority over death, hades, and the grave. Oh, glory to God!

But He answered and said to them, An evil and adulterous generation craves for a sign; and yet no sign will be given to it but the sign of Jonah the prophet; for just as Jonah was three days and nights in the belly of the sea monster, so will the Son of Man be three days and three nights in the heart of the earth. Matthew 12:39-40 NASB

When I saw Him, I fell at His feet like a dead man. And He placed His right hand on me, saying, Do not be afraid; I am the first and the last, and the living One; and I was dead, and behold, I am alive forevermore, and I have the keys of death and of Hades. Revelation 1:17-18 NASB

When resurrection power was manifest, and Jesus rose from the grave some absolutely incredible events were displayed on the earth and specifically witnessed at Jerusalem.

And behold, the veil of the temple was torn in two from top to bottom; and the earth shook and the rocks were split. The tombs were opened, and many bodies of the saints who had fallen asleep were raised; and coming out of the tombs after His resurrection they entered the holy city and appeared to many. Matthew 27:51-53 NASB

Now on the first day of the week Mary Magdalene came early to the tomb, while it was still dark, and saw the stone already taken away from the tomb. John 20:1 NASB

Jesus said to her, Woman, why are you weeping? Whom are you seeking? Supposing Him to be the gardener, she said to Him, Sir, if you have carried Him away, tell me where you have laid Him, and I will take Him away. Jesus said to her, Mary! She turned and said to Him in Hebrew, Rabbioni! (which means, Teacher). Jesus said to her, Stop clinging to Me, *for I have not yet ascended to the Father*; but go to My brethren and say to them, I ascend to My Father and your Father, and My God and your God.

Jesus is our great High Priest (Hebrews 4:14) and He had *not yet ascended* back to heaven where the real ark of the covenant is in the heavenly tabernacle (Hebrews 9:24) and He had to go there and apply His own precious blood (Hebrews 9:11-12) on the mercy seat in heaven. As our High Priest, He could not be touched by anyone lest He be defiled (Leviticus 16) before He entered the real Holy of Holies and applied His powerful and perfect blood on the mercy seat for our everlasting atonement.

Jesus Christ was the fifth.

Our fifth harpazo occurrence is by far the most important of all because it is centered on the life, death, and resurrection of our Lord Jesus Christ the Son of the living God. Jesus Christ came to this earth born under the Law, born of a virgin, lived a sinless life as the Son of Man and as the Son of God. The death of Jesus Christ ended the dispensation of the Law and His resurrection from the grave and His subsequent rapture marked the beginning of the dispensation of grace, or the Church age.

When you were dead in your transgressions and the uncircumcision of your flesh, He made you alive together with Him, having forgiven us all our transgressions, having canceled out the certificate of debt consisting of decrees against us, which was hostile to us; and He has taken it out of the way, having nailed it to the cross. When He had disarmed the rulers and authorities, He made a public display of them, having triumphed over them through Him. Colossians 2:13-15 NASB

As we saw above, when Jesus came back into the tomb to possess and resurrect His body and come forth out of the garden tomb, He was leading the captive saints out of Abraham's bosom and leading them into heaven when He paused to minister to little Mary there at the empty tomb. Mary of Magdala could have been the very first person to be born-again.

But to each one of us grace was given according to the measure of Christ's gift. Therefore it says, When He ascended on high, He led captive a host of captives, and He gave gifts to men. (Now this expression, He ascended, what does it mean except that He also had descended into the lower parts of the earth? He who descended is Himself also He who ascended far above all the heavens, so that He might fill all things.) Ephesians 4:7-10 NASB

And after He had said these things, He was lifted up while they were looking on, and a *cloud* received Him out of their sight. And as they were gazing intently into the sky while He was going, behold, two men in white clothing stood beside them. They also said, why do you stand looking into the sky? This Jesus, who has been taken up from you into heaven, will come in just the same way as you have watched Him go into heaven. Acts 1:9-11 NASB

The overcoming Church will be the sixth.

When King Jesus returns to harpazo His faithful bond-servants, this will mark the closing of the dispensation of grace and the consummation of the Church age. Just as His rapture marked the beginning of the Church age, Jesus' return to rapture His Church will be the close of the Church age, and the beginning of the seven-year Tribulation, or Daniel's seventieth week, thus followed by the Kingdom age.

Do not let your heart be troubled; believe in God, believe also in Me. In My Father's house are many dwelling places; if it were not so, I would have told you; for I go to prepare a place for you. If I go and prepare a place for you, I will come again and receive you to Myself, that where I am, there you may be also. John 14:1-3 NASB

The coming Tribulation is a time of judgement being wrought upon the inhabitants of the earth for wickedness, rebellion, idolatry, sexual perversion, and the shedding of innocent blood. It is also a time that God Almighty will be dealing with the nation of unbelieving Israel.

For the wrath of God is revealed from heaven against all ungodliness and unrighteousness of men who suppress the truth in unrighteousness, Romans 1:18 NASB

Let no one deceive you with empty words, for because of these things the wrath of God comes upon the sons of disobedience. Ephesians 5:6 NASB

However, we can see from the prophetic patterns that the Lord always has mercy on His faithful and righteous remnant and removes them before His wrath is poured out on the unfaithful, incredulous backsliders, and the evil reprobates.

Take heed, keep on the alert; for you do not know when the appointed time will come. Mark 13:33 NASB

But we should always give thanks to God for you, brethren beloved by the Lord, because God has chosen you from the beginning for salvation through sanctification by the Spirit and faith in the truth. II Thessalonians 2:13 NASB

Because you have kept the word of My perseverance. I also will keep you from the hour of testing, that hour which is about to come upon the whole world, to test those who dwell on the earth. I am coming quickly; hold fast what you have, so that no one will take your crown. Revelation 3:10-11 NASB

The Two Witnesses in Jerusalem will be the seventh.

During the time of Jacobs trouble (Jeremiah 30:1-3,7-9) or more commonly known as the Tribulation, God Almighty is pouring out His wrath on the unrepentant earth dwellers and dealing with the now reunified nation of unbelieving Israel. Besides the one hundred forty-four thousand Israeli evangelists (Revelation 7:1-4) that God has sealed and sent out, there will be manifest two witnesses that will preach repentance in Jerusalem for forty-two months and instigating great signs and wonders in the earth.

These are the two olive trees and the two lampstands that stand before the Lord of the earth. And if anyone wants to harm them, fire flows out of their mouth and devours their enemies; so if anyone wants to harm them, he must be killed in this way. These have the power to shut up the sky, so rain will not fall during the days of their prophesying; and they have power over the waters to turn them into blood, and strike the earth with every plague, as often as they desire. Revelation 11:4-6 NASB

After their work is accomplished by the midpoint of the Tribulation, these two witnesses are killed by the Antichrist and the rebellious world throws a party in delight over their deaths.

When they have finished their testimony, the beast that comes up out of the abyss will make war with them, and overcome them and kill them. And their dead bodies will lie in the street of the great city which mystically is called Sodom and Egypt, where also their Lord was crucified. Those from the peoples and tribes and tongues and nations will look at their dead bodies for three and a half days, and will not permit their dead bodies to be laid in a tomb. And those who dwell on the earth will rejoice over them and celebrate; and they will send gifts to one another, because these two prophets tormented those who dwell on the earth. Revelation 11:7-10 NASB

Then after they lay in the streets of Jerusalem for three and one-half days, the Lord raises these two men from the dead and raptures them back to heaven before the eyes of the entire world as yet another sign and wonder, and then God Almighty gives them a good shaking. The arrogance and stubbornness of some folks is simply amazing.

But after the three and a half days, the breath of life from God came into them, and they stood on their feet; and great fear fell upon those who were watching them. And they heard a loud voice from heaven saying to them, Come up here. Then they went up into heaven in the cloud, and their enemies watched them. And in that hour there was a great earthquake, and a tenth of the city fell; seven thousand people were killed in the earthquake, and the rest were terrified and gave glory to the God of heaven. Revelation 11:11-13 NASB

The identity of these two witnesses is a bit of a mystery. Some prophecy experts believe that these two men are Moses and Elijah primarily because these two prophets are doing the same sort of miracles that Moses and Elijah did during their respective ministries. Some additionally believe that because Moses and Elijah both were in attendance with Jesus on the Mount of Transfiguration, therefore; that event was foreshadowing these men as the two witnesses.

These are all valid Scripturally based views, yet there are still some astute Bible scholars that believe these two witnesses are Elijah and Enoch because we know without dispute neither of these men ever tasted death, and that would solve the issues surrounding Moses' departure from the land of the living.

And inasmuch as it is appointed for men to die once and after this comes judgement, Hebrews 9:27 NASB

And Enoch and Elijah are both prophets and because righteous Enoch would represent the witness to the Gentiles and Elijah would then represent the witness to the Israelites thus God would be providing a witness to the whole world, then they would then both die as it is appointed for every man, and then the judgment.

We believe that the time of Jacob's trouble is Daniel's seventieth week. We also believe that the Day of the Lord is the whole Tribulation and that all these names describe the very same seven-year period. The faithful overcomers, or the Church if you prefer; have now been removed and the dispensation of grace is now concluded. Enoch represents the faithful overcomers that walk in love and obedience to Jesus Christ now and have been removed from the earth.

However, those that have chosen to live as the lord of their own life and unbelieving Israel is now left on the earth. Father God will now deal with His enemies, and He will be fulfilling His Word to the nation of Israel.

Therefore, we believe the two witnesses are Moses and Elijah representing the Law and the Prophets testifying to the nation of Israel and because of their witnessing along with the one hundred forty-four thousand evangelists that the Lord has commissioned by sealing them with the mark of the covenant and released, there will be many Jews and Gentiles that come to faith in the Word of God during this incredibly difficult time. The age of grace is over, and the Old Testament Law is now reinstituted with the temple sacrifices. This period of chaos will be such as the world has never seen before.

That concludes our survey of the specific caught up/harpazo/rapture events in the Scriptures where one or more individuals were caught up into the clouds. These are provided for us to carefully study and thus glean yet greater insight into Father God's Word and His ways.

Now we will continue to survey other types, shadows, similitudes and other events found recorded in the Scriptures that are prophetic patterns pointing to the forthcoming end-time events that will indeed follow the rapture of the Church and the close of the age of God's amazing grace.

Noah and his family in the Ark.

Then the Lord said to Noah, Enter the ark, you and all your household, for you alone I have seen to be righteous before Me in this time. Genesis 7:1 NASB

For after seven more days, I will send rain on the earth forty days and forty nights; and I will blot out from the face of the land every living thing that I have made. Noah did according to all that the Lord had commanded him. Genesis 7:4-5 NASB

It came about after the seven days, that the water of the flood came upon the earth. Genesis 7:10 NASB

Those that entered, male and female of all flesh, entered as God had commanded him; and the Lord closed it behind him. Genesis 7:16 NASB

God found Noah and his household to be righteous and commanded Noah to enter the safety of the earthbound ark seven days before the deluge came upon the earth, and God Himself closed the door. This is a type and shadow of Israel during the Tribulation and the believers and the animals on earth being super-naturally protected during the seven-year Tribulation and ultimately ends with King Jesus returning with the overcomers at the end of the seven years as the ark covers and protects these people and the animals to thus be ushered into the Kingdom age to come, and these will then begin to repopulation the earth during the one-thousand-year millennium.

For the coming of the Son of Man will be just like the days of Noah. For as in those days before the flood they were eating and drinking, marrying and giving in marriage, until the day that Noah entered the ark, and they did not understand until the flood came and took them all away; so will the coming of the Son of Man be. Matthew 24:37-39 NASB

For if God did not spare angels when they sinned, but cast them into hell and committed them to pits of darkness, reserved for judgement; and did not spare the ancient world, but preserved Noah, a preacher of righteousness, with seven others, when He brought a flood upon the world of the ungodly; II Peter 2:4-5 NASB

Noah and his family and the animals are a type and shadow if unbelieving Israel that believe in God but did not believe or accept Jesus. God will supernaturally protect these, so they will survive during the Day of the Lord which means the seven years of war, pestilence, plagues, famine, economic lack, natural disasters, violence, and doom.

Lot the backslidden kindred of Abraham.

Lot and his family dwelling in Sodom are a type and shadow of backslidden believers that have been living their own way and are left behind after the faithful overcomers are raptured before the Day of the Lord begins. But, because of the prayers and intercession of devoted believers, God shows these His great mercies and provides a means of escape, so these can survive the Tribulation and enter the Kingdom age.

And the Lord said, The outcry of Sodom and Gomorrah is indeed great, and their sin is exceedingly grave. Genesis 18:20 NASB

Now the two angels came to Sodom in the evening as Lot was sitting in the gate of Sodom. When Lot saw them, he rose to meet them and bowed down with his face to the ground. Genesis 19:1 NASB

Lot the self-ambitious nephew of faithful Abraham deliberately became increasingly involved in the activities of the cities of the plain and selfishly chose to live within the comforts and worldliness that the cosmopolitan city of Sodom could offer. Lot chose a Canaanite wife and had sons and daughters and even became involved with the political system there and served as a participant and a leader within the governmental structure and activities.

Lot was a backslidden believer in God, and he lived in a city overflowing with violence, wickedness, carnality, decadence, and sexual perversion. The Lord sent messenger angels to warn and thus lead Lot and his household outside to safety in the mountain before God's wrath and final judgement fell upon these abhorrent settlements of the reprobate Canaanite tribes.

Then the two men said to Lot, Whom else have you here? A son-in-law, and your sons, and your daughters, and whomever you have in the city, bring them out of the place; for we are about to destroy this place, because their outcry has become so great before the Lord that the Lord has sent us to destroy it. Genesis 19:12-13 NASB

When morning dawned, the angels urged Lot, saying, Up, take your wife and your two daughters who are here, or you will be swept away in the punishment of the city. *But he hesitated.* So the men seized his hand and the hand of his wife and the hands of his two daughters, for the compassion of the Lord was upon him; and they brought him out, and put him outside the city. When they had brought them outside, one said, Escape for your life! Do not look behind you, and do not stay anywhere in the valley; escape to the mountains, or you will be swept away. Genesis 19:15-17 NASB

Lot and his two young daughters and his wife were the only ones of his family in the city that believed the warning that utter destruction was literally about to fall upon them. Even then, as they were escaping the judgement, Lot's wife looked back at this carnal world of ungodly filth that she just could not separate from and she was swept away in the falling wrath and judgement being poured out on the satanic world system.

It was the same as happened in the days of Lot: they were eating, they were drinking, they were buying, they were selling, they were planting, they were building; but on the day that Lot went out from Sodom it rained fire and brimstone from heaven and destroyed them all. It will be just the same on the day that the Son of Man is revealed. Luke 17:28-30 NASB

And if He condemned the cities of Sodom and Gomorrah to destruction by reducing them to ashes, having made them an example to those who would live ungodly lives thereafter; and if He rescued righteous Lot, oppressed by the sensual conduct of un principled men (for by what he saw and heard that righteous man, while living among them, felt his righteous soul tormented day after day by their lawless deeds), then the Lord knows how to rescue the godly from temptation, and to keep the unrighteous under punishment for the day of judgement, and especially those who indulge the flesh in its corrupt desires and despise authority. II Peter 2:6-10 NASB

Do you see the pattern: (1) God Almighty clearly instructs the people how to live righteously, (2) and after a very long time of patiently waiting for them to humble themselves and repent, (3) God prepares to bring judgement upon the exceedingly wicked, rebellious, and unrepentant people, (4) and then Father God warns those that know He is God of the coming wrath and doom, (5) and finally our gracious and merciful Lord provides a way of escape for those that believe, (6) and ultimately in dramatic conclusion judgement day comes.

As incredible as it seems, there will be people that believe in God and miraculously survive the Day of the Lord and thus live to *enter* the Kingdom age that follows the great Tribulation.

To be included as part of the harpazo before the Day of the Lord is one of the rewards for the faithful that live as true bond-servants of the Lord Jesus Christ and thus fulfilling the overcomer's mandate.

CHAPTER SEVEN

In Training for Reigning.

Foundational Truth: Our heavenly Father has a divinely designed sanctifying process that He initiates through the ministry of the Holy Spirit to transform all willing and submissive believers into faithful overcomers.

Therefore, the genuine bond-servants of Jesus Christ are actively in training for reigning.

[You should] be exceedingly glad on this account, though now for a little while you may be distressed by <u>trials</u> and suffering temptations, so that [the genuineness] of your faith may be <u>tested</u>, [your faith] which is infinitely more precious than the perishable gold which is <u>tested</u> and purified by fire. [This proving of your faith is intended] to redound to [your] praise and glory and honor when Jesus Christ (the Messiah, the Anointed One) is revealed. I Peter 1:6-7 AMPC

Beloved, do not be amazed and bewildered at the fiery <u>ordeal</u> which is taking place to test your quality, as though something strange (unusual and alien to you and your position) were befalling you. I Peter 4:12 AMPC

*Ordeal, *Trials (Greek noun 21x) *Peirasmos:* a temptation and/or test depending on the context. An experiment, a trial, probation, or testing.

Consider it wholly joyful, my brethren, whenever you are enveloped in or encounter <u>trials</u> of any sort or fall into various temptations. Be assured and understand that the trial and <u>proving</u> of your faith bring out endurance and steadfastness and patience. But let endurance and steadfastness and patience have <u>full play</u> and do a thorough work, so that you may be [people] <u>perfectly</u> and fully developed [with no defects], lacking in nothing. James 1:2-4 AMPC

*Proving, *Tested (Greek noun 2x) *Dokimion:* test, trial, what is genuine. What is found acceptable and approved after testing. Put to the test, examine; proof.

*Full play, *Perfect: (Greek adjective 19x) *Teleios:* Mature, having reached its end, perfect, complete, and full-grown. Wholeness of all its parts and of full age, specially of the completeness of Christian character.

You, therefore, must be <u>perfect</u> [growing into complete maturity of godliness in mind and character, having reached the proper height of virtue and integrity], as your heavenly Father is <u>perfect</u>. Matthew 5:48 AMPC

The Lord God Almighty desires and commands every one of His children to be continually growing up and maturing in our faith, and to progressively become transformed into the image of His Son Jesus Christ. This process is designed and ordained by our heavenly Father, and it will be completely and repeatedly executed in the life of every born-again believer that confesses Jesus as their Lord, and truly walks in submission to His living Word.

The good news is that if you don't pass the test that you are currently experiencing, you get to take it again and again; until you do successfully pass the test. This is Father God's way for the faithful believers to prepare themselves as the future bride of Christ and make themselves ready for the marriage supper of the Lamb.

Let us rejoice and be glad and give the glory to Him, for the marriage of the Lamb has come and *His bride has made herself ready*. I was given to her to clothe herself in fine linen, bright and clean;

for the fine linen is the righteous acts of the saints. Then he said to me, Write, Blessed are those who are invited to the marriage supper of the Lamb. And he said to me, These are true words of God. Then I fell at his feet to worship him. But he said to me, Do not do that; I am a fellow servant of yours and your brethren who hold the testimony of Jesus; worship God. For the testimony of Jesus is the spirit of prophecy. Revelation 19:7-10 NASB

The overcoming believers invited to the marriage supper are those spiritually mature and obedient, or stated another way; the bride who has made herself ready: these are the faithful overcomers.

We can see this clearly illustrated in the teaching of Jesus in The Parable of the Ten Virgins which were all bridesmaids waiting on the Groom as recorded in Matthew's gospel.

Then the kingdom of heaven shall be likened to ten virgins who took their lamps and went to meet the bridegroom. Five of them were foolish (thoughtless, without forethought) and five were wise (sensible, intelligent, and prudent). For when the foolish took their lamps, they did not take any [extra] oil with them; But the wise took flasks of oil along with them [also] with their lamps. While the bridegroom lingered and was slow in coming, they all began nodding their heads, and they fell asleep. But at midnight there was a shout, Behold, the bridegroom! Go out to meet him! Then all those virgins got up and put their own lamps in order. And the foolish said to the wise, Give us some of your oil, for our lamps are going out. But the wise replied, There will not be enough for us and for you; go instead to the dealers and buy for yourselves. But while they were going away to buy, the bridegroom came, and those who were <u>prepared</u> went in with him to the marriage feast; and the door was shut. Later the other virgins also came and said, Lord, Lord, open [the door] to us! But He replied, I solemnly declare to you, I do not know you [I am not acquainted with you]. Watch therefore [give strict attention and be cautious and active], for you know neither the day nor the hour when the Son of Man will come. Matthew 25:1-13 AMPC

*Prepared (Greek adjective 17x) *Hetoimos:* fitness, standing by, to be in readiness. ready to meet the opportunity at hand; ready because the necessary preparations are done. To make ready, the act of getting prepared, making all the necessary preparations and arrangements.

All ten of these young people were virgins (Christians), and all ten were aware and waiting on the bridegroom. Five were foolish and did not prepare themselves and were not ready when the bridegroom came suddenly with a shout (rapture) at a day and hour they did not know. However, five were wise and had made themselves ready and were then taken into the marriage supper with their Lord. These five wise and prepared virgins were overcomers.

I have fought the good (worthy, honorable, and noble) fight, I have finished the race, I have kept (firmly held) the faith. [As to what remains] henceforth there is laid up for me the [victor's] crown of righteousness [for being right with God and doing right], which the Lord, the righteous Judge, will award to me and recompense me on that [great] day – and not to me only, but also to all those who have loved and yearned for and welcomed His appearing (His return). II Timothy 4:7-8 AMPC

The apostle Paul had certainly denied himself (crucified his flesh) and taken up his cross (surrendered his plans) and followed Jesus (led by the Holy Spirit). Paul knew there were rewards for those who are faithful in serving the Lord Jesus to the very end of his natural life here on earth. Those divine eternal rewards are for all the faithful overcomers. This Scripture passage bears repeating.

Let us rejoice and shout for joy [exulting and triumphant]! Let us celebrate and ascribe to Him glory and honor, for the marriage of the Lamb [at last] has come, and His bride has <u>prepared</u> herself. She has been permitted to dress in fine (radiant) linen, dazzling and white – for the linen is (signifies, represents) the righteousness (the upright, just, and godly living, deeds, and conduct, and right standing with God) of the saints (God's holy people). Then [the angel] said to me, Write this down: Blessed (happy, to be envied) are those who are summoned (invited, called) to the marriage supper of the Lamb. And he said to me [further], These are the true words (the genuine and exact declarations) of God. Revelation 19:7-9 AMPC

*Prepared (Greek verb 40x) *Hetomazo:* To make ready, the act of getting prepared, making all the necessary preparations and arrangements.

Now, we shall take a closer look at this foundational Truth: The perfecting and maturing process designed by our heavenly Father for us to become genuine faithful overcomers.

Our awesome heavenly Father gives us a promise in His Word, which is directly connected to a principle rule or condition that must be obeyed; and this will be followed by a problem, test, or trial in our own personal wilderness, and when we have stood in faith on God's Word; then we shall see the manifestation of the Lord's provisional promise flow in our lives. Promise + Principle + Problem = Provision. If the test is aborted by us and thus unsuccessful, we must then proceed back to step one and start over again.

This is the Lord God Almighty's way. This is how the bride of Christ will prepare herself for her Bridegroom. This is the life of the overcomer. (John 17:17, I Thessalonians 5:23-24, Ephesians 5:26-27, I Corinthians 10:6,11, II Timothy 2:15, II Timothy 3:16-17)

The nation of Israel was tested in the wilderness for 40 years. Why? Because they responded to the problem presented in the wilderness with fear, doubt, grumbling, murmuring, whining, and unbelief. (Numbers 13-14)

It was only a three-day journey from Egypt, across the Red sea to Mount Horeb; and then it was an eleven-day journey from there on to Kadesh-barnea, which is the southern boundary of the promised land.

(Deuteronomy 1:2-3) All of those that were fear-filled, unbelieving, whining, rebellious, and grumbling adults of that generation died in the wilderness except two men of the (Exodus 12:37) six hundred thousand men: Caleb and Joshua. What was the difference? Faith in God.

Jesus was tested in the wilderness <u>40 days</u>. Why? Because He responded to the tests and temptations in faith, hope, and love; which He demonstrated by quoting the written Word of God. (Matthew 4:1-11, Mark 1:12-13, Luke 4:1-14)

How you and I see and perceive the problem, is the problem. The Lord will allow trials and tests to prove our faith in His Word and our belief in His unfailing love for us. Do you really believe that God Almighty is good at all times and will always keep His promise regardless of the circumstances? This is genuine faith.

After these things God tested Abraham and said to him, "Abraham!" And he said, "Here I am." Genesis 22:1 MEV

By faith Abraham, when he was tested, offered up Isaac, and he who had received the promises offered up his only begotten son. Hebrews 11:17 MEV

But the envoys came from the officials of Babylon who were sent to him to inquire about the sign that had been given in the land. God left him alone in order to test Hezekiah, to know what was in his heart. II Chronicles 32:31 MEV

I, the Lord, search the heart, I test the mind, even to give to every man according to his ways, and according to the fruit of his deeds. Jeremiah 17:10 MEV

You must remember that the Lord your God led you all the way these forty years in the wilderness, to humble you, and to prove you, to know what was in your heart, whether you would keep His command-ments or not. Deuteronomy 8:2 MEV

Blessed (happy, to be envied) is the man who is patient under trial and stands up under temptation, for when he has stood the test and been approved. He will receive [the victor's] crown of life which God has promised to those who love Him. James 1:12 AMPC

The Lord will allow trials to come into our lives to test and to prove the genuine quality of our faith. Why? To reveal to us **if** we are really trusting Him and sincerely believing His Word is His will. Remember our omniscient God sees and knows everything, but; we don't.

If you will listen diligently to the voice of the Lord your God, being watchful to do all His command-ments which I command you this day, the Lord your

God will set you high above all the nations of the earth. And all these blessings shall come upon you and overtake you **if** you heed the voice of the Lord your God. Deuteronomy 28:1-2 AMPC

But **if** you will not obey the voice of the Lord your God, being watchful to do all His commandments and His statutes which I command you this day, then all these curses shall come upon you and overtake you. Deuteronomy 28:15 AMPC

If you are willing and obedient, you shall eat the good of the land; but **if** you refuse and rebel, you will be devoured by the sword. For the mouth of the Lord has spoken it. Isaiah 1:19-20 AMPC

And Jesus said, [You say to Me], **If** you can do anything? [Why,] all things can be (are possible) to him who believes! Mark 9:23 AMPC

So Jesus said to those Jews who had believed in Him, **If** you abide in My word [hold fast to My teachings and live in accordance with them], you are truly My disciples. And you will know the Truth, and the Truth will set you free. John 8:31-32 AMPC

Jesus said to her, Did I not tell you and promise you that **if** you would believe and rely on Me, you would see the glory of God? John 11:40 AMPC

If you live in Me [abide vitally united to Me] and My words remain in you and continue to live in your hearts, ask whatever you will and it shall be done for you. John 15:7 AMPC

If you keep My commandments [if you continue to obey My instructions], you will abide in My love and live on in it, just as I have obeyed My Father's commandments and live on in His love. John 15:10 AMPC

You are My friends **if** you keep on doing the things which I command you to do. John 15:14 AMPC

Many of the promises in God's Word are conditional and therefore based on our level of submission to His Word and His ways. This is how we truly love Him: **If** we choose to faithfully obey Him.

I have been young, and now I am old; yet I have not seen the righteous forsaken, nor their offspring begging bread. Psalm 37:25 MEV

But seek first the kingdom of God and His righteousness, and all these things shall be given to you. Matthew 6:33 MEV

We know that all things work together for good to those who love God, to those who are called according to His purpose. Romans 8:28 MEV

We all desire these awesome promises to be manifest in and through our lives, however; the Word is clear. Father God promises to take care of our business **if** we take care of His business first. The blessings of God follow the obedience to His Word and His ways.

How do we love the Lord? By trusting Him. How is our faith in His Word proven to be genuine? Through quick and absolute obedience to His Word and His way of doing things.

Should we expect God Almighty to meet all our needs **if** we do not put Him first in every facet our lives? Do you think Father God should bless us **if** we don't care about His righteousness; which is simply His Word and His way of doing things?

Can you honestly say that you love Jesus **if** you do not obey His teachings, and you are not making a sincere effort every day to study His Word and build your relationship with Him?

God promises us that everything that happens or doesn't happen in our lives will all ultimately work for our good **if** we love Him and continue to walk in His ways. This promise is not for those living in rebellion.

So, how do we truly love Him? Jesus answers this question very clearly and succinctly.

By total submission to His Word and His ways, which equals obedience to His plan and His purposes, and explicitly not your plans and purposes; because that would make you lord of your life and there is only room for one on the throne ruling your life.

Please remember that we cannot change the Truth, the Truth changes us; and God's Word is Truth. We do not get to define or have an opinion about what loving Jesus looks like.

Jesus Christ our Savior and Lord has made some incredible promises to those called, chosen, and faithful believers who overcome to the very end.

Little children, you are of God [you belong to Him] and have [already] defeated and overcome them [the agents of the antichrist], because He who lives in you is greater (mightier) than he who is in the world. I John 4:4 AMPC

For the [true] love of God is this: that we do His commands [keep His ordinances and are mindful of His precepts and teaching]. And these orders of His are not irksome (burdensome, oppressive, or grievous). For whatever is born of God is victorious over the world; and this is the victory that conquers the world, even our faith. I John 5:3-4 AMPC

He who is able to hear, let him listen to and give heed to what the Spirit says to the assemblies (churches). To him who overcomes (is victorious), I will grant to eat [of the fruit] of the tree of life, which is in the paradise of God. Revelation 2:7 AMPC

He who is able to hear, let him listen to and heed what the Spirit says to the assemblies (churches). He who overcomes (is victorious) shall in no way be injured by the second death. Revelation 2:11 AMPC

He who is able to hear, let him listen to and heed what the Spirit says to the assemblies (churches), To him who overcomes (conquers), I will give to eat of the manna that is hidden, and I will give him a white stone with a new name engraved on the stone, which no one knows or understands except he who receives it. Revelation 2:17 AMPC

And he who overcomes (is victorious) and who obeys My commands to the [very] end [doing the works that please Me], I will give him authority and power over the nations; and he shall rule them with a scepter (rod) of iron, as when earthen pots are broken in pieces, and [his power over them shall be] like that which I Myself have received from My Father; and I will give him the Morning star. He who is able to her, let him listen to and heed what the [Holy] Spirit says to the assemblies (churches). Revelation 2:26-29 AMPC

Yet you still have a few [persons'] names in Sardis who have not soiled their clothes, and they shall walk with Me in white, because they are worthy and deserving. Thus shall he who conquers (is victorious) be clad in white garments, and I will not erase or blot out his name from the Book of Life; I will acknowledge him [as Mine] and I will confess his name openly before My Father and before His angels. He who is able to hear, let him listen to and heed what the [Holy] Spirit says to the assemblies (churches). Revelation 3:4-6 AMPC

He who overcomes (is victorious), I will make him a pillar in the sanctuary of My God; he shall never be put out of it or go out of it, and I will write on him the name of My God and the name of the city of My God, the new Jerusalem, which descends from My God out of heaven, and My own new name. He who can hear, let him listen to and heed what the Spirit says to the assemblies (churches). Revelation 3:12-13 AMPC

He who overcomes (is victorious), I will grant him to sit beside Me on My throne, as I Myself overcame (was victorious) and sat down beside My Father on His throne. He who is able to hear, let him listen to and heed what the [Holy] Spirit says to the assemblies (churches). Revelation 3:21-22 AMPC

And they have overcome (conquered) him by means of the blood of the Lamb and by the utterance of their testimony, for they did not love and cling to life even when faced with death [holding their lives cheap till they had to die for their witnessing]. Revelation 12:11 AMPC

He who is victorious shall inherit all these things, and I will be God to him and he shall be My son. Revelation 21:7 AMPC

Wow, King Jesus has promised those who choose to believe Him and follow Him an incredible and adventurous life of faith here and now along with establishing an awesome hope for our eternal future and our inheritance and rewards in the Kingdom age.

Each believer is called to deny themselves, take up their cross and follow Jesus. We are not called to live for Christ; we are called to crucify our carnal desires and lay down our self-ambitions, so Jesus can live through us. This is real life!

This is what it means to truly know Him, and to see Him manifest Himself to you, and through you. This is how we can accurately and powerfully proclaim Jesus Christ to this lost and dying world. (Colossians 1:24-29) This is the great mystery, Christ in us, the hope of glory!

The person who has My commands and keeps them is the one who [really] loves Me; and whoever [really] loves Me will be loved by My Father, and I [too] will love him and will show (reveal, manifest) Myself to him. [I will let Myself be clearly seen by him and make Myself real to him.] John 14:21 AMPC

Jesus answered, **If** a person [really] loves Me, he will keep My word [obey My teaching]; and My Father will love him, and We will come to him and make Our home (abode, special dwelling place) with him. John 14:23 AMPC

Quick, total, and absolute obedience–this is what it means to say Jesus is the Lord of my life!

And as we are faithful to follow Him, we shall be transformed to become more than conquers and overcomers now in these last days of the age of grace, and then we shall be kings and lords ruling and reigning with the King of kings and Lord of lords in the forthcoming Kingdom age that is rapidly approaching. Oh, hallelujah, Amen.

To live a sanctified and separated life faithfully walking in obedience to the Word, and thus becoming one of the honored saints as a lord or a king ruling and reigning with King Jesus in His domain is the overcomer's mandate.

CHAPTER EIGHT

Christic is our Plumb Line.

Foundational Truth: The Word is the Way, the Truth, and the Life; and those that overcome must measure everything by the Word daily and adjust their love walk accordingly as they are led by Holy Spirit.

In the beginning was the Word, and the Word was with God, and the Word was God. He was in the beginning with God. All things came into being through Him, and apart from Him nothing came into being that has come into being. John 1:1-3 NASB

What is a plumb line, or plummet? A plumb line is a cord with a pointed weight on one end of the cord which is used by builders as a vertical reference line to establish and maintain vertical accuracy and uprightness as one begins to build upon the established footing, pier or foundation of a structure.

For a significant portion of my adult life, I was involved in the construction and development business, therefore; because of those life experiences, many of my analogies have a construction related theme. As an example of this, I can testify to the fact that establishing the foundation correctly of any structure is the first and most important phase of the entire construction sequence and it must be done right.

Simply stated, if you do not get the foundation correct, absolutely nothing else will be correct either, and you will find yourself constantly struggling all the way through to completion of your structure and the reality is that building will never be plumb, square, or true. Therefore, we begin building each of our chapters with a Foundational Truth stone.

As you know, our heavenly Father is the great Master Builder and He sent His Son to this earth to be our example and the Cornerstone of our life foundation.

Where were you when I laid the foundations of the earth? Declare, if you have understanding. Who has determined its measurements, if you know? Or who has stretched the line upon it? To what are its foundations fastened? Or who laid its cornerstone when the morning stars sang together, and all the sons of God shouted for joy? Job 38:4-7 MEV

The stone that the builders rejected has become the cornerstone. This is what the Lord has done; it is marvelous in our eyes. Psalm 118:22-23 MEV

Therefore thus says the Lord God, Behold, I am laying in Zion for a foundation a Stone, a tested Stone, a precious Cornerstone of sure foundation; he who believes (trusts in, relies on, and adheres to that Stone) will not be ashamed or give way or hasten away [in sudden panic]. I will make justice the measuring line and righteousness the plummet; and hail will sweep away the refuge of lies, and waters will overwhelm the hiding place (the shelter). Isaiah 28:16-17 AMPC

You are built upon the foundation of the apostles and prophets with Christ Jesus Himself the chief Cornerstone. In Him the whole structure is joined (bound, welded) together harmoniously, and it continues to rise (grow, increase) into a holy temple in the Lord [a sanctuary dedicated, consecrated, and sacred to the presence of the Lord]. In Him [and in fellowship with one another] you yourselves also are being built up [into this structure] with the rest, to form a fixed abode (dwelling place) of God in (by, through) the Spirit. Ephesians 2:20-22 AMPC

According to the grace of God which has been given to me, as a wise master builder, I have laid the foundation, but another builds on it. Now let each one take heed how he builds on it. For no one can lay another foundation than that which was laid, which is Jesus Christ. I Corinthians 3:10-11 MEV

Since you have [already] tasted the goodness and kindness of the Lord. Come to Him [then, to that] Living Stone which men tried and threw away, but which is chosen [and] precious in God's sight. [Come] and, like living stones, be yourselves built [into] a spiritual house, for a holy (dedicated, consecrated) priesthood, to offer up [those] spiritual sacrifices [that are] acceptable and pleasing to God through Jesus Christ. For thus it stands in Scripture: Behold, I am laying in Zion a chosen (honored), precious chief Cornerstone, and he who believes in Him [who adheres to, trusts in, and relies on Him] shall never be disappointed or put to shame. To you then who believe (who adhere to, trust in, and rely on Him) is the preciousness; but for those who disbelieve [it is true], The [very] Stone which the builders rejected has become the main Cornerstone, and, A Stone that will cause stumbling and a Rock that will give [men] offence; they stumble because they disobey and disbelieve [God's] Word, as those [who rejected Him] were destined (appointed) to do. I Peter 2:3-8 AMPC

Jesus Christ is our true foundation and in Him and on His Word we all are to build-up our spiritual house. This building, growing, and expanding of our spirit-man is the process of sanctification, however; every wise builder knows he or she must take heed to build straight, plumb, and true. This means that we also must soberly inspect, judge, measure, and train ourselves, and we must have an infallible tool by which to measure, and the only tool that never needs recalibration is the incorruptible and eternal and living Word of God.

I consider my ways, and I turn my feet to Your testimonies. I made haste, and I did not delay to keep Your commandments. Psalm 119:59-60 MEV

Let us examine and probe our ways, And let us return to the Lord! Lamentations 3:40 NASB

Examine and test and evaluate your own selves to see whether you are holding to your faith and showing the proper fruits of it. Test and prove yourselves [not Christ]. Do you not yourselves realize and know [thoroughly by an ever-increasing experience] that Jesus

Christ is in you – unless you are [counterfeits] disapproved on trial and rejected. II Corinthians 13:5 AMPC

But let every person carefully scrutinize and examine and test his own conduct and his own work. He can then have the personal satisfaction and joy of doing something commendable [in itself alone] without comparison with his neighbor. Galatians 6:4 AMPC

Little children, let us not love [merely] in theory or in speech but in deed and in truth (in practice and in sincerity). By this we shall come to know (perceive, recognize, and understand) that we are of the Truth, and can reassure (quiet, conciliate, and pacify) our hearts in His presence, whenever our hearts in [tormenting] self-accusation make us feel guilty and condemn us. [For we are in God's hands.] For He is above and greater than our consciences (our hearts), and He knows (perceives and understands) everything [nothing is hidden from Him]. And, beloved, if our consciences (our hearts) do not accuse us [if they do not make us feel guilty and condemn us], we have confidence (complete assurance and boldness) before God, And we receive from Him whatever we ask, because we [watchfully] obey His orders [observe His suggestions and injunctions, follow His plan for us] and [habitually] practice what is pleasing to Him. I John 3:18-22 AMPC

Therefore, to properly evaluate, measure, and judge our progress, we must have established an ideal model or standard. And to accurately assess and guide our growth, we must have something to compare to and measure from; such as the builder's plumb line. The ideal pattern or standard that we all must look at to do any such comparisons is the Lord Jesus Christ, and we measure and guide our growth with and by His Word and His Word alone.

Blessed is the man who walks not in the counsel of the ungodly, nor stands in the path of sinners, nor sits in the seat of scoffers; but his delight is in the law of the Lord, and in His law he meditates day and night. He will be like a tree planted by the rivers of water, that brings forth its fruit in its season; its leaf will not wither, and whatever he does will prosper. Psalm 1:1-3 MEV

How shall a young man keep his way pure? By keeping it according to Your word. With my whole heart I seek You; do not allow me to wander from Your commandments. Your word I have hidden in my heart, that I might not sin against You. Psalm 119:9-11 MEV

Let's summarize what we have established thus far in this foundational truth. We know that we are to become increasingly Christlike in word and deed, and we must judge and evaluate ourselves to determine our progress. And to do these deliberate measurements accurately we must take every thought, belief, deed, and action plan back to the plumb line, which is the whole counsel of God's Word – Genesis to Revelation. We will next look at some simple examples of "plumb lines" for everyone to seek and aspire to attain within the Scriptures.

Jesus gave us a summation of nine clear measurements in His longest recorded teaching discourse at the foot of the unspecified mountain, probably near the sea of Galilee. These nine precepts have become commonly known as the beatitudes.

Blessed are the poor in spirit, for theirs is the kingdom of heaven. Blessed are those who mourn, for they shall be comforted. Blessed are the meek, for they shall inherit the earth. Blessed are those who hunger and thirst for righteousness, for they shall be filled. Blessed are the merciful, for they shall obtain mercy. Blessed are the pure in heart, for they shall see God. Blessed are the peacemakers, for they shall be called the sons of God. Blessed are those who are persecuted for righteousness' sake, for theirs is the kingdom of heaven. Blessed are you when men revile you and persecute you, and say all kinds of evil against you falsely for My sake. Rejoice and be very glad, because great is your reward in heaven, for in this manner they persecuted the prophets who were before you. Matthew 5:3-12 MEV

The gospel of Luke chapter six has a succinct and similar portion of Scripture recording clear and specific measures for overcomers to use as a "plumb line" for their daily walk with the Lord.

He lifted up His eyes on His disciples, and said: Blessed are you poor, for yours is the kingdom of God. Blessed are you who hunger now, for you shall be filled. Blessed are you who weep now, for you shall laugh. Blessed are you when men hate you, and when they separate you from their company and insult you, and cast out your name as evil, on account of the Son of Man. Rejoice in that day, and leap for joy, for indeed, your reward is great in heaven. For in like manner their fathers treated the prophets. But woe to you who are rich, for you have received your consolation. Woe to you who are filled, for you shall hunger. Woe to you who laugh now, for you shall mourn and weep. Woe to you, when all men speak well of you, for so their fathers spoke of the false prophets. Luke 6:20-26 MEV

The apostle Paul, bond-servant of Christ; also gave us comprehensive and very clear "plumb line" for us to utilize in measuring and evaluating our success in denying ourselves and taking up our cross and thus being led by the Holy Spirit as overcomers.

For the whole Law [concerning human relationships] is complied with in the one precept, You shall love your neighbor as [you do] yourself. But if you bite and devour one another [in partisan strife], be careful that you [and your whole fellowship] are not consumed by one another. Galatians 5:14-15 AMPC

But I say, walk and live [habitually] in the [Holy] Spirit [responsive to and controlled and guided by the Spirit]; then you will certainly not gratify the cravings and desires of the flesh (of human nature without God). For the desires of the flesh are opposed to the [Holy] Spirit, and the [desires of the] Spirit are opposed to the flesh (godless human nature); for these are antagonistic to each other [continually withstanding and in conflict with each other], so that you are not free but are prevented from doing what you desire to do. But if you are guided (led) by the [Holy] Spirit, you are not subject to the Law. Now the doings (practices) of the flesh are clear (obvious): they are immorality, impurity, indecency, idolatry, sorcery, enmity, strife, jealousy, anger (ill temper), selfishness, divisions (dissensions), party spirit (factions, sects with peculiar opinions, heresies), envy, drunkenness, carousing, and the like. I warn you beforehand, just as I did previously, that those who do such things shall not *inherit* the kingdom of God. Galatians 5:16-21 AMPC

But the fruit of the [Holy] Spirit [the work which His presence within accomplishes] is **love**, **joy** (gladness), **peace**, **patience** (an even temper, forbearance), **kindness**, **goodness** (benevolence), **faithfulness**, **gentleness** (meekness, humility), **self-control** (self-restraint, continence). Against such things there is no law [that can bring a charge]. And those who belong to Christ Jesus (the Messiah) have crucified the flesh (the godless human nature) with its passions and appetites and desires. If we live by the [Holy] Spirit, let us also walk by the Spirit. [If by the Holy Spirit we have our life in God, let us go forward walking in line, our conduct controlled by the Spirit]. Let us not become vainglorious and self-conceited, competitive and challenging and provoking and irritating to one another, envying and being jealous of one another. Galatians 5:22-26 AMPC

Please note that we broke-up this passage of Scripture in Galatians 5:14-26 for ease of study and reference, however; it must be considered together as one congruent and flowing thought. Also, take special notice of the portion of Scripture which is in italics in verse twenty-one because we shall discuss the very important difference between *entering* the Kingdom of God and *possessing* and *inheriting* the Kingdom within the thirteenth chapter in this volume.

Peter, the bond-servant of Christ; also gave us all a clear "plumb line" and a nine step-by-step outline by which we can use to measure, evaluate, and track our spiritual growth and maturity.

Simon Peter, a servant and apostle (special messenger) of Jesus Christ, to those who have received (obtained an equal privilege of) like precious faith with ourselves in and through the righteousness of our God and Savior Jesus Christ: May grace (God's favor) and peace (which is perfect well-being, all necessary good, all spiritual prosperity, and freedom from fears and agitating passions and moral conflicts) be multiplied to you in [the full, personal, precise, and correct] knowledge of God and of Jesus our

Lord. For His divine power has bestowed upon us all things that [are requisite and suited] to life and godliness, through the [full, personal] knowledge of Him Who called us by and to His own glory and excellence (virtue). By means of these He has bestowed on us His precious and exceedingly great promises, so that through them you may escape [by flight] from moral decay (rottenness and corruption) that is in the world because of covetousness (lust and greed), and become sharers (partakers) of *the divine nature.* II Peter 1:1-4 AMPC

For this very reason, adding your **diligence** [to the divine promises], employ every effort in exercising your **faith** to develop **virtue** (excellence, resolution, Christian energy), and in [exercising] virtue [develop] **knowledge** (intelligence), and in [exercising] knowledge [develop] **self-control**, and in [exercising] self-control [develop] **steadfastness** (patience, endurance), and in [exercising] steadfastness [develop[**godliness** (piety), and in [exercising] godliness [develop] **brotherly affection**, and in [exercising] brotherly affection [develop] **Christian love**. For as these qualities are yours and increasingly abound in you, they will keep [you] from being idle or unfruitful unto the [full personal] knowledge of our Lord Jesus Christ (the Messiah, the Anointed One). II Peter 1:5-8 AMPC

The synopsis of this teaching thus far can be condensed into one concept, one instruction, one precept, one action, and one Word: *Agape* (Love). Which is *the divine nature* of God.

Love does no wrong to one's neighbor [it never hurts anybody]. Therefore love meets all the requirements and is the fulfilling of the Law. Romans 13:10 AMPC

But clothe yourself with the Lord Jesus Christ (the Messiah), and make no provision for [indulging] the flesh [put a stop to thinking about evil cravings of your physical nature] to [gratify its] desires (lusts). Romans 13:14 AMPC

To become an overcomer is to become like our Lord and Savior Jesus Christ in every way, and to become like our Lord Jesus is to deliberately choose to order our daily walk and lives consistently in accordance with the unconditional and sacrificial *agape* love of God.

A new commandment I give to you, that you love one another, even as I have loved you, that you also love one another. By this all men will know that you are My disciples, if you have love for one another. John 13:34-35 MEV

This is My commandment: that you love one another, as I have loved you. Greater love has no man than this: that a man lay down his life for his friends. You are My friends if you do whatever I command you. John 15:12-14 MEV

This I command you: that you love one another. John 15:17 MEV

Do you hear the clarion call of our Lord and Master? We are to walk like Him, talk like Him, act like Him, be like Him, and follow Him in all our ways.

Therefore be imitators of God as beloved children. Walk in love, as Christ loved us and gave Himself for us as a fragrant offering and a sacrifice to God. Ephesians 5:1-2 MEV

By this it is made clear who take their nature from God and are His children and who take their nature from the devil and are his children: no one who does not practice righteousness [who does not conform to God's will in purpose, thought, and action] is of God; neither is anyone who does not love his brother (his fellow believer in Christ). I John 3:10 AMPC

He who does not love has not become acquainted with God [does not and never did know Him], for <u>God is love</u>. I John 4:8 AMPC

And we know (understand, recognize, and are conscious of, by observation and by experience) and believe (adhere to and put faith in and rely on) the love God cherishes for us. <u>God is love</u>, and he who dwells and continues in God, and God dwells and continues in him. In this [union and communion with Him] love is brought to completion and attains perfection with us, that we may have confidence for the day of judgement [with assurance and boldness to face Him], because as He is, so are we in this world. I John 4:16-17 AMPC

The youngest and last living apostle of the Lamb was John, born 6 AD, who went home to be with his Lord in 100 AD. We believe that no person on earth knew Jesus Christ better than John. No one knows with absolute confidence when John scribed these oracles, but; many Bible scholars believe that it was during the last decade of John's life when he composed the five books of which authorship is credited to him and included in the canon of Scripture comprising the New Testament books and epistles.

The English word canon is derived from the Greek word *Kanon,* which is defined as: a rule or regulation, a rule of conduct or doctrine; or a cane, or reed used as a standard of measure or ruler. (*Kanon* is used four times in the New Testament in II Corinthians 10:13,15,16 and Galatians 6:16) Therefore, one could proclaim very precisely and astutely that the canon of inspired Scripture, widely known as the Holy Bible; is our measuring standard or our plumb line, by which we measure and guide the building and conduct of our lives in Christ Jesus.

We do not desire to enter the deliberation over the exact dates that these epistles were composed, but rather; we want to inform and help us all gain understanding of the significantly less than ideal conditions of which the elderly apostle John was subjected to when he at great personal suffering and sacrifice, wrote these inspired books for our benefit.

The first Roman persecution of the Church occurred under the diabolical and depraved Emperor Nero, in which thousands of Christians were tortured and killed in the most horrendous ways imaginable. The apostle Paul was beheaded, and apostle Peter was crucified during this time. Reliable history as chronicled that Peter was crucified upside-down at

his request because he was unworthy of being crucified in the same fashion as his Master and Lord.
There is no doubt that both Peter and Paul were genuine bond-servants of our Lord and true examples of
faithful overcomers.

The widespread persecution of Christians subsided
after the homosexual and cross-dressing Nero killed
himself in June of 68 AD, but; the Roman military was
busy putting down the Jewish rebellion of Roman rule
and taxation in Judaea which mostly ended with the
total destruction of the Temple in Jerusalem on the 9th
day of Av in 70 AD. Rome was in political turmoil and
had a leadership crisis for about a decade while going
through five different Emperors during that season,
which gave the Church a much-needed break and the
opportunity for the faith to spread.

The Christian Church was experiencing a second
period of extreme and fierce persecution from the
Roman government under the rule of the cruel
Emperor Domitian, who reigned from 81 AD until his
assassination in 96 AD. The elder John was considered the esteemed leader of the church in the city of
Ephesus, and therefore he was indeed a prime target
for maltreatment.

Thus, a nearly ninety-year-old John was arrested and taken to Rome, severely and cruelly mistreated and banished to the prison colony on the Isle of Patmos. John certainly had many great opportunities to begin to doubt or at the very least develop a bad attitude, however; he obviously maintained his faith in his Master because it was in this harsh environment of a penal work camp that John, now a cave dweller; received the Revelation of our Lord. Wow, what a blessing his faithful obedience has been to the world.

The Revelation of Jesus Christ, which God gave Him to show to His bond-servants, the things which must soon take place; and He sent and communicated it by His angel to His bond-servant John, who testified to the word of God and to the testimony of Jesus Christ, even to all that he saw. Blessed is he who reads and those who hear the words of the prophecy, and heed the things which are written in it; for the time is near. Revelation 1:1-3 NASB

I, John, your brother and fellow partaker in the tribulation and kingdom and perseverance which are in Jesus, was on the Island called Patmos because of the word of God and the testimony of Jesus. I was in the Spirit on the Lord's day, and I heard behind me a loud voice like the sound of a trumpet, Revelation 1:9-10 NASB

It inspires, confronts, and humbles me to think about the loyalty and faithfulness of our brother John the Revelator. He was the only disciple of Christ with enough gumption to be present at the foot of the cross when our Lord Jesus was crucified, and he witnessed His last breath.

John was entrusted and charged by Jesus to care for His mother Mary until she died in 54 AD. He was the first disciple to enter and thus witness the empty garden tomb. He saw the utter destruction of the Temple in 70 AD and the fall of the city of Jerusalem in 71 AD. The beloved brother John no doubt witnessed and experienced the heart-break of the cruel and seemingly meaningless tortured deaths of innumerable friends and loved-ones – all devout and sincere disciples of Jesus our Lord.

I indeed wonder how my faith would have held-up as I ponder all that the aged and abused bond-servant John must have patiently endured for the Word and his testimony of Jesus over the decades, and yet, he was still loving and worshiping his Lord in spirit and in truth on the Lord's day, irrespective of his own personal sufferings, aches, pains, and lack of comforts there on that harsh prison isle. How do you think you would have done in this place? Selah.

We have included the entire second epistle of John here because we all need to be reminded of what message was of such great importance to John that he would literally risk being tortured to death for communicating the Truth with the true followers of Jesus Christ. We believe it is safe to say that brother John, the beloved bond-servant of Jesus Christ; was unquestionably an overcomer.

This second letter from apostle John is addressed in code to *Cyria,* a Greek word which means "a lady" and that lady is the Church and was probably sent to a specific leader of one of the house churches for copying and distribution. John knew he could be issuing a death warrant to anyone specifically named in any such letter known to be from him because Domitian was hunting down and arresting these Christians and especially any known family or friends of apostle John. Domitian was having them tortured and killed in his attempts to stop the spread of this prohibited religion called Christianity that did not acknowledge and worship him as a demigod.

The elderly elder [of the church addresses this letter] to the elect (chosen) lady (Cyria) and her children, whom I truly love – and not only I but also all who are [progressively] learning to recognize and know and understand the Truth – Because of the Truth which lives and stays on in our hearts and will be with us forever: Grace (spiritual blessing), mercy, and [soul] peace will be with us, from God the Father and from Jesus Christ (the Messiah), the Father's Son, in all sincerity (truth) and love.

I was greatly delighted to find some of your children walking (living) in [the] Truth, just as we have been commanded by the Father [Himself]. And now I beg you, lady (Cyria) not as if I were issuing a new charge (injunction or command), but [simply recalling to your mind] the one we have had from the beginning, that we love one another. And what this love consists in is this: that we live and walk in accordance with and guided by His commandments (His orders, ordinances, precepts, teachings). This is the commandment, as you have heard from the beginning, that you continue to *walk in love* [guided by it and following it].

For many imposters (seducers, deceivers, and false leaders) have gone out into the world, men who will not acknowledge (confess, admit) the coming of Jesus Christ (the Messiah) in bodily form. Such a one is the imposter (the seducer, the deceiver, the false leader, the antagonist of Christ) and the antichrist. Look to yourselves (take care) that you may not lose (throw away or destroy) all that we and you have labored for, but that you may [persevere until you] win and receive back a perfect reward [in full]. Anyone who runs on ahead [of God] and does not abide in the doctrine of Christ [who is not content with what He taught] does not have God; but he who continues to live in the doctrine (teaching) of Christ [does have God], he has both the Father and the Son. If anyone comes to you and does not bring this doctrine [is disloyal to what Jesus Christ taught], do not receive him [do not accept him, do not welcome or admit him] into [your] house or bid him Godspeed or give him any encouragement. For he who wishes him success [who encourages him, wishing him Godspeed] is a partaker in his evil doings.

I have many things to write to you, but I prefer not to do so with paper and ink; I hope to come to see you and talk with you face to face, so that our joy may be complete. The children of your elect (chosen) sister wish to be remembered to you. Amen (so be it). II John 1:1-13 AMPC

John, the disciple whom Jesus loved according to Scripture; (John 13:23, 19:26, 20:2, 21:7, 21:20) repeatedly risked his life to encourage others to patiently endure whatever they must as they walk, live, teach, preach, follow, and love the Truth to the very end. Therefore, you and I are thus commanded and must do the same.

Jesus is the Truth – Jesus said to him, I am the way, the truth, and the life. No one comes to the Father except through Me. John 14:6 MEV

The Word is Truth – Sanctify them by Your truth. Your word is truth. John 17:17 MEV

The Holy Spirit is Truth – But when the Spirit of truth comes, He will guide you into all truth. For He will not speak on His own authority. But He will speak whatever He hears, and He will tell you things that are to come. John 16:13 MEV

Father God is Truth – And we know that the Son of God has come and has given us understanding, so that we may know Him who is true, and we are in Him who is true – His Son Jesus Christ. He is the true God and eternal life. I John 5:20 MEV

Beloved overcomer, this is exactly what our King Jesus meant when He said:

And whoever does not bear his cross and follow Me cannot be My disciple. Luke 14:27 MEV

And he who does not take his cross and follow after Me is not worthy of Me. Matthew 10:38 MEV

We all must learn to humbly walk in the Way of Agape, because this is loving the Truth and that is the overcomer's mandate. Amen.

CHAPTER NINE

Prophetic Patterns of Overcomers: Abraham

Foundational Truth: The Lord of Hosts is faithful to fulfill His Word, just as we must as overcomers be faithful to obey and be doers of what He asks of us.

In the first book the Holy Spirit gave to us to write called *The Believer's Mandate,* we covered the Foundational Truth of how God teaches us through prophetic types, shadows, similitudes, and patterns within several chapters. Therefore, we would recommend that you study this book also, but; we won't go over that plowed ground again here because we will continue to build on that established Truth and illuminate some additional prophetic patterns within the Scriptures.

For our first prophetic pattern we will go to the book of beginnings, Genesis; and the father of the faithful: Abraham. The days of Abraham and Sarah are charted beginning in Genesis chapter eleven and continuing through chapter twenty-five. Their lives were so incredibly rich with nuggets of revelatory light and incredible lessons for us all, that it is difficult sometimes to focus on just one of those lessons embodied within their lives. Nevertheless, we will attempt to be disciplined and not wander-off our subject matter and run down any rabbit trails here while in Genesis.

Go! Go forth! (Hebrew: *Lekh-Lekha*) The clarion call of Abram –

Now the Lord said to Abram, Go forth from your country, And from your relatives And from your father's house, To the land which I will show you; And I will make you a great nation, And I will bless you, And make your name great; And so you shall be a blessing; And I will bless those who bless you, And the one who curses you I will curse. And in you all the families of the earth will be blessed. Genesis 12:1-3 NASB

The Lord said, Shall I hide from Abraham what I am about to do, since Abraham will surely become a great and mighty nation, and in him all the nations of the earth will be blessed? Genesis 18:17-18 NASB

In your seed all the nations of the earth shall be blessed, because you have obeyed My voice. Genesis 22:18 NASB

The Lord God Almighty emphatically called Abram (*Exalted father*) to Go and Go now! Father God was calling Abram unto separation: To leave his father Terah's house and dominion, to leave the other family members and relatives, to leave his city, and to leave this land and kingdom of idolaters behind and journey unto a new land and a new way of life.

It is important to understand and take notice of other historical records, such as the Book of Jasher, Midrashim, and the Rabbinical commentaries; indicating that Terah was an officer of the government and held a high position within king Nimrod's court. Consequently, Terah would have been a man of great affluence and distinction within the society and culture of those days.

Special acknowledgement here: Please note that we do not support or advocate the building of doctrine with any extra-biblical or non-canonical works, writings, or records. However, we do recognize the value of the study of other chronicles of historical documents available to help us gain insights to the customs and the cultural values of these important civilizations. The Book of Jasher is distinctive and of specific interest to us because the Holy Spirit references it within the Scriptures specifically in Joshua 10:13, II Samuel 1:18, and II Timothy 3:8.

Abram was called by God unto total separation from this corrupt worldly system, the land, and its customs and culture. Abram was called to cross over the Euphrates (*to bear fruit*) river and to sojourn in this new land that the Lord would lead Abram into and through.

The Lord God Almighty called Abram to come out from Ur of the Chaldeans, which means *Light* of the *Astrologers*. This ancient city was in the southern part of the kingdom of Babylonia (*Confusion*) ruled by Nimrod (*To be rebellious*) and it is characteristic and symbolic of the world system then and now. This city and nation of idolaters and moon-god worshippers were under the control of the god of this world and its entirely carnal, immoral, and corrupt structure.

Definition of *Astrologers*: Clairvoyants, soothsayers, fortune-tellers, diviners, psychics, spiritualists, and mediums. (All of which are under the influence of familiar, unclean, and demonic spirits)

We study the life of Abraham (*Father of many nations*) because we are thus commanded in the Scriptures (Romans 15:4, I Corinthians 10:1-11, II Timothy 2:15, II Timothy 3:16-17) to study these chronicled examples, and because Abraham is the Gentile that fathered the Jewish people, and he is the father of all the faithful in the worldwide family of God. Therefore, if you are a born-again follower of Jesus Christ, you too are born of the promised Seed of Abraham and are truly the spiritual son or daughter of faithful Abraham.

Jesus said to him, Today salvation has come to this house, because he also is a son of Abraham. For the Son of Man has come to seek and to save that which was lost. Luke 19:9-10 MEV

Therefore the promise comes through faith, so that it might be by grace, that the promise would be certain to all the descendants, not only to those who are of the law, but also to those who are of the faith of Abraham, who is the father of us all (as it is written, I have made you a father of many nations) before God whom he believed, and who raises the dead, and calls those things that do not exist as though they did. Romans 4:16-17 MEV

Even Abraham believed God, and it was credited to him as righteousness. Therefore know that those who are of faith are the sons of Abraham. And the Scripture, foreseeing that God would justify the Gentiles by faith, preached the gospel in advance to Abraham, saying, In you shall all the nations be blessed. So then those who are of faith are blessed with faithful Abraham. Galatians 3:6-9 MEV

Christ has redeemed us from the curse of the law by being made a curse for us – as it is written, Cursed is everyone who hangs on a tree–so that the blessing of Abraham might come on the Gentiles through Jesus Christ, that we might receive the promise of the Spirit through faith. Galatians 3:13-14 MEV

What does it mean to be a son or daughter of Abraham? It means that we are still under the original unconditional and everlasting blood covenant (Genesis 12,15,17) that God made with Abram and that everything Father God promised Abraham is yours and mine too.

Every promise, all the protection, all the provision, and the blessing are yours because we receive by faith all of this through the same promise that Father God made to Abraham – the Son of promise: Jesus Christ. Amen.

When Abram was ninety-nine years old, the Lord appeared to him and said, I am Almighty God. Walk before Me and be blameless. And I will make My covenant between you and Me and will exceedingly multiply you. Abram fell on his face and God said to him, As for Me, My covenant is with you, and you shall be the father of a multitude of nations. No longer will your name be called Abram, but your name will be Abraham, for I have made you the father of a multitude of nations. I will make you exceedingly fruitful; and I will make nations of you, and kings will come from you. I will establish My covenant between Me and you and your descendants after you throughout their generations for an everlasting covenant, to be God to you and your descendants after you. All the land of Canaan, where you now live as strangers, I will give to you and to your descendants for an everlasting possession, and I will be their God. Genesis 17:1-8 MEV

Wow, the Lord God Almighty said "I will" ten times in this passage of Scripture. Faith comes when the *will* of God is known, therefore; we believe and declare by faith that we know the *will* of God concerning His blood covenant with His people.

However, we need to identify and emphasize a specific portion of the everlasting blood covenant that *El Shaddai*–Almighty God–made with Abraham. We will now focus on the real estate that was part of this unconditional and everlasting covenant known as the promised land. The land that Almighty God said, *I have given* (past tense) to the descendants of Abraham, which God said *I have made* (past tense) the father of a multitude of nations.

Our heavenly Father is a faith God that speaks and operates in faith, therefore; He expects His children to walk and live by faith in Him too. This land of the covenant was identified specifically by the Lord as the territory extending from the Nile river in Egypt to the Euphrates river. Consequently, this encompassed the territories of the ten tribal people groups that occupied the land during Abraham's sojourn in the land.

On the same day the Lord made a covenant with Abram, saying, To your descendants I have given this land, from the river of Egypt to the great Euphrates River – the land of the Kenites, the Kenizzites, the Kadmonites, the Hittites, the Perizzites, the Rephaites, the Amorites, the Canaanites, the Girgashites, and the Jebusites. Genesis 15:18-21 MEV

Behold, this complete list of <u>ten</u> tribes is never again named in the Bible, and specifically; the first three tribes named here are never mentioned by name again in any listing of the Canaanite tribes. Thus, we surmise by this fact of omission that these first three clans and tribal groups had become very weak or perhaps even extinct in the roughly four hundred years between Abraham sojourning in the land until the time of Moses (1400 BC) receiving the Torah and Joshua's crossing over the Jordon river to begin the conquest of the remaining tribal people occupying the coveted promised land.

Therefore, each one of these ten natural tribal clans of people represent the characteristics of spiritual entities and are symbolic of iniquities and oppressive influences that are in the land and must be overcome.

This is where we will begin detailing the two prophetic patterns of many within the Scriptures, that we have chosen to study. The following two are illustrative of the overcomers in the land promised by Almighty God first to Abraham and then to his descendants, which ultimately are you and me.

As you probably know, the Bible is a progressive revelation of God's Truth to His creation and we will begin with Abram and his journey as the first similitude and then progress to Joshua as the second example pattern of the overcomer's life.

Walking with Abraham.

As we know God called Abram to completely separate from this place of evil polytheism to a new life of monotheism. God called Abram to separate from his father and his relatives, his home and his inheritance, his city and the kingdom. Abram was called to go out from his family, and he was promised a family.

Abraham was called to go. Go where? To the place God would show him and God promised Abram that he would receive a family, home, land, and an eternal inheritance for his future descendants, even though Sarai his wife was barren.

Terah and his family's life is chronicled in other ancient books of historical writings and it is recorded that Abram was around seventy years old when God called to Abram to Go forth! God called Abram to go out for his sake.

After Terah had lived 70 years, he became the father of [at different times], Abram and Nahor and Haran, [his firstborn]. Now this is the history of the descendants of Terah. Terah was the father of Abram,

Nahor, and Haran; and Haran was the father of Lot. Haran died before his father Terah [died] in the land of his birth, in Ur of the Chaldees. And Abram and Nahor took wives. The name of Abram's wife was Sarai, and the name of Nahor's wife was Milcah, the daughter of Haran the father of Milcah and Iscah. But Sarai was barren; she had no child. And Terah took Abram his son, Lot the son of Haran, his grandson, and Sarai his daughter-in-law, his son's Abram's wife. And they went forth together to go from Ur of the Chaldees into the land of Canaan; but when they came to Haran, they settled there. And Terah lived 205 years; and Terah died in Haran. Genesis 11:26-32 AMPC

And he answered, Brethren and fathers, listen to me! The God of glory appeared to our forefather Abraham when he was still in Mesopotamia, before he [went to] live in Haran, and He said to him, Leave your own country and your relatives and come into the land (region) that I will point out to you. So then he went forth from the land of the Chaldeans and settled in Haran. And from there, after his father died, [God] transferred him to this country in which you are now dwelling. Yet He gave him no inheritable property in it, [no] not even enough ground to set his foot on; but He promised that He would give it to him for a permanent possession and to his descendants after him, even though [as yet] he had no child. Acts 7:2-5 AMPC

Abram was tentative, selfish, and bound by traditions; thus, he was only partially obedient. Abram was still with his father Terah and his nephew Lot even after they had left the Persian Gulf coast city of Ur that was about fifty miles south of Babylon and relocated six hundred miles to the northwest to the city of Haran until Terah died approximately five years later. Abram was still dwelling in his father's house and he still had his nephew Lot with him.

Although they did leave Ur of the Chaldees, but he did not leave behind the kingdom of Babylonia; not until Abram's father had died in Haran.

So Abram departed, as the Lord had directed him; and Lot [his nephew] went with him. Abram was seventy-five years old when he left Haran. Genesis 12:4 AMPC

Abram was now ready to heed the call of God and cross over the great river Euphrates into the land of Canaan. Crossing over such a body of water is symbolic of dying to our old life and coming out of the water birthed into our new life. Therefore, Abram leaving his old life behind and crossing over the Euphrates river was symbolic and foreshadowing of our born-again experience, and now as one who *crossed over* Abram the Hebrew, chose to heed and did cross over in obedience.

The four altars of Abraham – The altars of sacrifice are the place of altering us.

<u>The first altar</u> Abram built at Shechem – Choosing to be obedience to the call and receiving new life by faith. (being born-again and becoming good soil)

Abram took Sarai his wife, and Lot his brother's son, and all their possessions that they had gathered, and the persons [servants] that they had acquired in Haran, and they went forth to go to the land of Canaan. When they came to the land of Canaan, Abram passed through the land to the locality of Shechem, to the oak or terebinth tree of Moreh. And the Canaanite was then in the land. Then the Lord appeared to Abram and said, I will give this land to your posterity. So Abram built an altar there to the Lord, Who had appeared to him. Genesis 12:5-7 AMPC

Shechem means *early rising* and the oak tree (Judges 6:11, I Kings 13:14, Isaiah 61:3) is always symbolic of *righteousness* and Moreh means *Teacher,* so Abram obeyed God and become the early rising or the first righteousness teacher in the land of Canaan.

[Urged on] by faith Abraham, when he was called, obeyed and went forth to a place which he was destined to receive as an inheritance; and he went, although he did not know or trouble his mind about where he was to go. Hebrews 11:8 AMPC

The second altar Abram built between Bethel and Ai – Our choice to deny our flesh and walk in His ways. (denying our physical desires and fleshly lusts to become 30-fold fruitful soil)

From there he pulled up [his tent pegs] and departed to the mountain on the east of Bethel and pitched his tent, with Bethel on the west and Ai on the east; and there he built an altar to the Lord and called upon the name of the Lord. Genesis 12:8 AMPC

Abram deliberately selected to dwell on the mountain, or *the high ground* in front of, or *before*, or east of, Bethel which means the *House of God* and beyond Ai which means *a heap of ruins*, or *to act perversely*. Thus, Abram has chosen to dwell on the high ground before the House of God and beyond the ruinous heaps of those acting perversely.

[Prompted] by faith he dwelt as a temporary resident in the land which was designated in the promise [of God, though he was like a stranger] in a strange country, living in tents with Isaac and

Jacob, fellow heirs with him of the same promise. Hebrews 11:9 AMPC

The third altar Abram built at Hebron – Our choice to separate from our dreams, plans, and all our self-ambitions. (lay down all our soulish desires and yield our mind/will/emotions to become 60-fold fruitful soil)

So Abram said to Lot, Let there be no strife, I beg of you, between you and me, or between your herdsmen and my herdsmen, for we are relatives. Is not the whole land before you? Separate yourself, I beg of you, from me. If you take the left hand, then I will go to the right; or if you choose the right hand, then I will go to the left. Genesis 13:8-9 AMPC

The Lord said to Abram after Lot had left him, Lift up now your eyes and look from the place where you are, northward and southward and eastward and westward; for all the land which you see I will give to you and to your posterity forever. And I will make your descendants like the dust of the earth, so that if a man could count the dust of the earth, then could your descendants be counted. Arise, walk through the land, the length of it and the breadth of it, for I will give it to you. Then Abram moved his tent and came and dwelt among the oaks or terebinths of Mamre, which are at Hebron, and built there an altar to the Lord. Genesis 14-18 AMPC

Abram finally separated from his insubordinate and backslidden relative Lot, who should have never been there to begin with; and allowed him to claim and take whatever land he might choose. God promptly rewarded Abram for his act of faith and obedience with confirming with Abram His promise to give him a huge family, and to lift his eyes and walk and look in every direction because God was going to give it all to his great multitude of descendants, even the land that knot head Lot just claimed and left to occupy which begins Lot's slow-fade away from walking in the ways of God.

Abram then moved his tent and dwelt among the oaks at Mamre which means *from the vision,* at Hebron which means *Confederation.* Thus, Abram dwelt in peace and righteousness that he now had revelation of that comes from his faith confederation with the Lord and not others.

For he was [waiting expectantly and confidently] looking forward to the city which has fixed and firm foundations, whose Architect and Builder is God. Now those people who talk as they did show plainly that they are in search of a fatherland (their own country) If they had been thinking with [homesick] remembrance of that country from which they were emigrants, they would have found constant opportunity to return to it. But the truth is that they were yearning for and aspiring to a better and more desirable country, that is, a heavenly [one]. For that reason God is not ashamed to be called their God [even to be surnamed their God – the God of Abraham, Isaac, and Jacob], for He has prepared a city for them. Hebrews 11:10,14-16 AMPC

The fourth altar that Abraham built at Moriah – Our choice to utterly lay down our life and future for others, in absolute submission to the Lord. (yielding our spiritual life in complete faith to become 100-fold fruitful soil)

After these events, God tested and proved Abraham and said to him, Abraham! And he said, Here I am. [God] said, Take now your son, your only son Isaac, whom you love, and go to the region of Moriah; and offer him there as a burnt offering upon one of the mountains of which I will tell you. Genesis 22:1-2 AMPC

This event recorded in Genesis chapter twenty-two is one of the most prophetic passages in the Bible, and is so incredibly rich with revelatory Truth, it is difficult to not expound just a bit here. First, Moriah means *chosen of the Lord*, and this place is where one thousand years later king David is instructed (II Samuel 24) to build an altar and offer sacrifices unto God and thus David purchased this site. Of course, following David's lead, the anointed son Solomon (II Chronicles 3:1) would take the plans and build the Temple of God here at this God chosen site.

When they came to the place of which God had told him, Abraham built an altar there; then he laid the wood in order and bound Isaac his son and laid him on the altar on the wood. Genesis 22:9 AMPC

By faith Abraham, when he was put to the test [while the testing of his faith was still in progress], had already brought Isaac for an offering; he who had gladly received and welcomed [God's] promises was ready to sacrifice his only son, of whom it was said, Through Isaac shall your descendants be reckoned. For he reasoned that God was able to raise [him] up even from the dead. Indeed in the sense that Isaac was figuratively dead [potentially sacrificed], he did [actually] receive him back from the dead. Hebrews 11:17-19 AMPC

This account is usually the one that comes to mind when someone speaks of the faith of Abraham, and it has confronted and provoked many through the years as they consider what they might have done that day upon Mount Moriah.

The journey of Abraham and his sanctifying altars and spiritual maturing process is a type and shadow and similitude of the overcomers mandate, just as is the parable of the Sower that Jesus taught us is a pattern of the overcomer.

Jesus Christ began His parable teaching (Mark 4:20) with the born-again good soil, followed by the self-denying 30-fold soil, leading to the soul yielding cross-bearing 60-fold soil, thus followed by the fully mature Spirit-led 100-fold soil as also a prophetic picture of the believer's maturing process as we submit to the sanctifying power of the Holy Spirit and deliberately choose to become overcomers in this present world.

Abram submitted to God and journeyed into the land of Canaan. It the process of God's testing and trials, Abram was altered, and he discovered his destiny and became Abraham, thus fulfilling Father God's master plan and purpose for his life.

By trusting Almighty God Abram learned to overcome his timidity, selfish ambitions, folk customs, and fears. Through faith, he overcame his self-seeking and deceitful nature, and by faith he overcame the patriarchal family dictates, traditions, and cultural mindset.

Abraham sojourned in the land by faith and over time, in full obedience to Almighty God, and therefore became an excellent example of a genuine overcomer for us all to emulate.

Every aspect of Abraham's life is a faith-filled adventure and prophetic pattern of the overcomer's mandate.

CHAPTER TEN

Prophetic Patterns of Overcomers: Joshua.

Foundational Truth: The Lord of Hosts is faithful to fulfill His Word, just as we must as over-comers be faithful to obey and be doers of what the Lord specifically asks of us, not what He asked of our ancestors.

<u>Walking with Joshua.</u>

Now we will advance to our next example found in Joshua, the servant of Moses.

Remember, each one of these natural tribal groups of people dwelling in the land characterize a spiritual truth and a spiritual entity, and by studying their heritage and the tribal names we can gain great insight to what sort of familiar, unclean, and oppressive spirits they manifest.

When the Lord your God brings you into the land which you are entering to possess and has driven out many nations before you, the Hittites and the Girgashites and the Amorites and the Canaanites and the Perizzites and the Hivites and the Jebusites, seven nations greater and mightier than you, and when the Lord your God delivers them before you and you strike them down, then you must utterly destroy them. You shall make no covenant with them nor show mercy to them. Deuteronomy 7:1-2 MEV

You must not be frightened of them, for the Lord your God is among you, a great and awesome God. The Lord your God will drive out those nations before you, little by little. You will not be able to destroy them all at once, lest the beasts of the field become too numerous for you. But the Lord your God will deliver them to you and will throw them into a great confusion until they are destroyed. Deuteronomy 7:21-23 MEV

Behold, why would our loving heavenly Father full of mercy and grace instruct Joshua to lead all God's people across the Jordan river to literally invade and conquer the land of Canaan with extreme prejudice, utterly wiping-out all those people dwelling in the land?

For us to properly comprehend this very important command of God, we must return to the post-flood days of Noah in the Scriptures. We must take an in-depth look into Noah and his family's dysfunction, and the resulting consequences of the treasonous actions and the resulting immoral behavior. To reveal the answer to this incredibly significant and most critical question, we shall study the following inspired passage of Scripture recorded in Genesis chapter nine:

The sons of Noah who went forth from the ark were Shem, Ham, and Japheth. Ham was the father of Canaan. These were the three sons of Noah, and from them the whole earth was populated.

Noah began to be a man of the soil, and he planted a vineyard. Then he drank some wine and become drunk, and lay uncovered in his tent. And Ham, the father of Canaan, saw the nakedness of his father and told his two brothers outside. So Shem and Japheth took a garment, and laid it upon both their shoulders, and went backward, and covered the nakedness of their father. Their faces were turned away, and they did not see their father's nakedness.

When Noah awoke from his wine and knew what his younger son had done to him, he said, *Canaan be cursed! He will be a servant of servants to his brothers.*

He also said, *Blessed be the Lord God of Shem, and let Canaan be his servant. May God enlarge Japheth, and may he dwell in the tents of Shem, and may Canaan be his servant.*

Noah lived after the flood three hundred and fifty years. All the days of Noah were nine hundred and fifty years, and then he died. Genesis 9:18-29 MEV

We would like to begin by pointing out that the Bible is written in abridged cliff-notes, or a condensed summary of the history of God's creation and God's people. It is important to keep this in mind when we study because we all have the tendency to read over a selected passage and not consider the total elapsed time and the chronology of the recorded events.

As a prime example of this, we know Noah lived a total of nine hundred fifty years and was five hundred years old (Genesis 5:32) before he became a father, and we know Noah was six hundred years old (Genesis 7:6) when the floodwaters came upon the earth, and the flood lasted one hundred fifty days (Genesis 8:3) and then Noah lived for another three hundred fifty years after the flood receded. The twelve verses of Scripture recorded in Genesis 9:18-29 that we are studying now cover the last three hundred fifty years of Noah's life, and it is important to keep this truth in mind as we continue our study here.

To put these things in proper perspective, consider the fact that the forefathers of the great nation of the United States of America signed the United States Declaration of Independence on July 4th, 1776. Therefore, the United States of America has not yet celebrated her two hundred fiftieth anniversary of being a sovereign nation, and will not until July 4th, 2026, and only if Jesus tarries. Now, just pause and take a moment to contemplate all the things that have come to pass and all the radical changes that have occurred in the culture and in lives of the people living in the U.S. of A. since the Revolutionary War. Now, begin to imagine the events and changes that will come to pass in the next one hundred years, should the Lord Jesus not come for his bride before.

Now, shall we return to Genesis chapter nine – Why did the Holy Spirit tell us that Ham was the father of Canaan in verse eighteen and again in verse twenty-two when Canaan was Ham's fourth born son according to Genesis 10:6? Could it be that as the Holy Spirit is citing the begotten sons of Noah and Noah's wife, the Lord wants to reveal to us all that this other male child, specifically Canaan; that came from Noah's wife's womb was not sired by Noah, as it might appear?

In verse twenty it states that Noah began to be a man of the soil, or in the Hebrew text: *Adamah* which means earth, ground, land. We know someone else that was notoriously known as man of the earth in Genesis 4:2-3 by the name of Cain, who overly esteemed the works of his hands and his own efforts.

We also have learned that Noah planted a vineyard. Consider other vineyards within the Scriptures (Numbers 6:1-4, Judges 13:4-5, I Kings 21:1-16, Ecclesiastes 2:4) The vineyard and the fruit of the vine are unbiased, thus; they are neither good or bad. However, how we elect to consume, exploit, or manipulate the vineyard and its fruit is what determines whether the vineyard is good or evil. Which the same precept as the love of money (I Timothy 6:10) being the root of all evil. Money is just a tool, what you elect to do with the money creates the issue good or bad.

In verse twenty-one we learn that after Noah's vineyard began producing fruit that Noah began making a lot of wine and indulging in quantities of his strong drink and becoming intoxicated to the point of behaving inappropriately and creating the opportunity of being shamefully uncovered in the view of others within the community.

Contemplate some of the abominable behavior and the direct consequences of carnal excesses and drunkenness outlined throughout the inspired Holy Scriptures: Incest, perversion, torture, murder, assassinations, adultery, shame, loss of respect, strife, incontinence, lewdness, imprudence, and the like.

Here are but a fraction of the Scriptures on this subject matter. (Genesis 19:32-35, Judges 16:25, I Samuel 25:36, II Samuel 11:13, II Samuel 13:28, I Kings 16:9, I Kings 20:16, Psalm 107:27, Proverbs 20:1, Proverbs 23:19-21, Isaiah 19:14, Jeremiah 48:26, Daniel 5:1-4, Habakkuk 2:15-16, I Corinthians 6:9-11, Ephesians 5:18, I Peter 4:3)

Who has woe? Who has sorrow? Who has strife? Who has complaining? Who has wounds without cause? Who has redness and dimness of eyes? Those who tarry long at the wine, those who go to seek and try mixed wine. Do not look at wine when it is red, when it sparkles in the wineglass, when it goes down smoothly. At the last it bites like a serpent and stings like an adder. [Under the influence of wine] your eyes will behold strange things [and loose women] and your mind will utter things turned the wrong way [untrue, incorrect, and petulant]. Yes, you will be [as unsteady] as he who lies down in the midst of the sea, and [as open to disaster] as he who lies upon the top of a mast. You will say, They struck me, but I was not hurt! They beat me [as with a hammer], but I did not feel it! When shall I awake? I will crave and seek more wine again [and escape reality]. Proverbs 23:29-35 AMPC

May we be very candid here and declare that anyone that is not convinced that getting drunk or partaking of any mind-altering drug is a very bad idea and it is not for the Lord's overcomers, then the more than seventy other verses on this topic in the Bible will not correct that persons thinking either. So, let's move on.

In the first part of verse twenty-two, we learn that Ham, the progenitor of Canaan; saw the nakedness of his father. According to many other Scriptures, we know precisely what sort of conduct the Holy Spirit is identifying.

You shall not have relations with your father's wife, for this exposes your father's nakedness. Leviticus 18:8 MEV

If a man lies with his father's wife, he has exposed his father's nakedness. Both of them shall surely be put to death. Their blood guilt shall be upon them. Leviticus 20:11 MEV

Cursed is he who dishonors his father or his mother. All the people shall say, Amen. Deuteronomy 27:16 AMPC

Cursed is he who lies with his father's wife, because he uncovers what belongs to his father. All the people shall say, Amen. Deuteronomy 27:20 AMPC

In you they have uncovered their father's nakedness. In you they have humbled her who was unclean in her menstrual impurity. Ezekiel 22:10 MEV

It is actually reported that there is sexual immorality among you, and such immorality as is not even named among the Gentiles, that a man has his father's wife. I Corinthians 5:1 MEV

While Noah is getting passed-out drunk and embarrassing himself and his family, Ham is having sexual intercourse with Noah's wife. If that isn't bad enough, it is very possible that this woman is Ham's mother; and the consequence of this illicit behavior is the bastard child named Canaan.

In the last part of verse twenty-two we learn that after Ham had fornicated with his father's wife, he went and "told" his brothers. The English word told in this verse is the Hebrew word *Nagad,* which means to be conspicuous, to announce, to declare, to proclaim.

Behold, the self-ambitions of Ham. He did not carefully go and whisper this shameful news in his brother's ears in a private place, hoping for forgiveness. No, Ham proclaimed to his competition that he had in fact went in to Noah's wife and had sexual intercourse with her and he wanted them all to know it.

Why would Ham behave in such a shocking way and do such an abhorrent thing? Ham had succumbed to the influence of seducing spirits. He had opened the door to unclean spirits and was being oppressed by the post-flood disembodied demonic spirits. And because of his unrepentant belligerent behavior, this demonic oppression was passed along to the next generation as a *generational curse*, and every generation thereafter.

Noah was obviously the patriarch of the family, and the principal man on the planet at that time. As Noah aged, he began to become worldlier, even to the point of becoming drunken. This was shameful for the Chief leader and certainly inappropriate for (II Peter 2:5) the preacher of righteousness. Thus, Ham saw this as an opportunity for a new Chief and attempted to usurp Noah's authority, the authority given and ordained by God Almighty.

In the ancient eastern cultures, when the throne usurper attempted a coup to overthrow the established authority, he would blatantly and overtly go into the seated Chieftain's harem of wives and concubines, and he would then have sexual intercourse with these females as the ultimate act of contempt and rebellious defiance against the apparent authoritative position of the Chieftain. We can clearly see this tactic deployed in the attempted overthrow of King David by his son Absalom in Second Samuel chapters fifteen through eighteen.

Then Absalom said to Ahithophel, Give your counsel. What shall we do? And Ahithophel said to Absalom, Go in to your father's concubines whom he has left to keep the house; and all Israel will hear that you are abhorred by your father. Then the hands of all who are with you will be made strong. So they spread for Absalom a tent on the top of the [king's] house, and Absalom went in to his father's harem in the sight of all Israel. II Samuel 16:20-22 AMPC

Furthermore, we can see this widely known and practiced cultural norm in the ancient world manifested in Abram's behavior (Genesis 12:10-20, 20:1-18) when he was forced by famine to journey with his entire clan into the domain of another Chieftains or Kings.

Abraham knew these pagan Rulers would take his beautiful wife as an overt demonstration of their dominance. Yet, even among these heathens it was considered a grievous act to take another man's wife. However, they didn't have any issue or moral trepidation with murder, thus; to avoid this culturally undignified and shameful act, they would simply eliminate the husband and henceforth the woman was no longer anyone's wife. Hey, problem solved!

This is just what Ham the usurper did. He went in to the Chieftain's wife and had sexual intercourse with her and then went to the other possible heirs of the throne and declared to them exactly what he had done, thinking they would back his power play, or just passively allow him to assert himself and avoid conflict.

However; Shem and Japheth wisely chose not to participate or allow Ham to dishonor their father and mother, nor did they want any part of this insurgence against God's chosen and appointed voice and vessel in the earth.

We see in verse twenty-three that Shem and Japheth demonstrated that they did not want to support or approve of any part of brother Ham's plot, plans, or actions to humiliate and overthrow the leader of their family and of the known world.

Thus, in an act of obvious loyalty to their God ordained Chief they took upon themselves to shoulder the responsibility to protect their leader and to cover for their father's weaknesses and his indiscretion. Shem and Japheth deliberately chose not to contribute in this effort by their irreverent brother to seize their father's authority and dominion within the family, the community, and beyond.

So, what was the long-term impact and profound effects of their reverential fear of the Lord and of His delegated authority here in the earth? What about their demonstrated loyalty and continued honor for their mother and father?

In verse twenty-four we see that eventually Noah awoke from his stupor and weakened mental state of discernment to discover what his unrepentant youngest son had attempted to do to him personally and obviously what he had done physically to his wife, evidenced by this bastard child that was named *Lowland dweller,* or more commonly known to us as the equally unrepentant Canaan his son, who was expelled from the family and the territory of which they dwelled.

In verses twenty-five and twenty-six, Noah was prophesying the oracles of God and the future of all the inhabitants of the promised land when he proclaimed:

Canaan be cursed! He will be a servant of servants to his brothers. Blessed be the Lord God of Shem, and let Canaan be his servant. May God enlarge Japheth, and may he dwell in the tents of Shem, and may Canaan be his servant.

The English word "cursed" is transliterated from the Hebrew word *Arar,* which means to execrate, bitterly curse, or dedicated to destruction.

We must understand that the Lord God Almighty was speaking through His chosen voice in the earth – Noah. Therefore, it was the Lord Himself who prophesied what their destiny would be in the future when He declared that Canaan was cursed! And that unrepentant Canaan and his descendants would be slaves to his brothers, slaves to his brother's children, and slaves even to slaves. The lowest of the low, if they sustained this unrepentant sinful existence and behavior.

However, it was also the same Master and Creator of the universe that prophesied blessings over Shem, Japheth, and their offspring. Amen.

Behold, Father God did not "curse" Ham and Canaan – they did by their thoughts, choices, deeds, and unrepentant lifestyle. No, the Lord simply foretold what would be the ultimate consequences of their rebellious choices. Wow, don't you think that Shem, Ham, and Japheth would have and should have known exactly where the broad road of wickedness, pride, and rebellion ultimately leads to? Could they have possibly forgotten about the ark and the flood?

Next in our exposition, we will study these demonized, thus cursed Canaanite tribes by name, but; we must note here that Abraham sojourned in this same land and he remained faithful to the Lord and separated from the influences of these very same tribal groups, as an example to them and to every subsequent generation to come.

Father God never once commanded or suggested that Abraham should aggressively attack these people in any way, except to defend himself and those under his dominion and care. (Note: God supports the second amendment)

Why?

Because our loving heavenly Father is good, and His mercy endures forevermore. Our Lord and our God is full of great mercy, grace, love, and justice for all of His creation. The Lord God Almighty gave Canaan and his offspring that occupied the land of Canaan more than five hundred years to humble themselves and repent and turn from their wicked, rebellious, and sinful ways and return to Him and to walk in His ways, just as our awesome Lord has extended His great mercy and forgiveness to innumerable multitudes throughout the generations since the fall in the garden of Eden. We will expound on these great Truths in chapter twelve, which will focus on our Father God's goodness and His justice.

First, we need to consider the three tribes that were overcome and no longer existed in any meaningful numbers by the time Joshua crossed over. Thus, these three represent iniquities and issues that we each must learn to overcome also.

Kenites: Fabricator–liar, distorter, deceiver, partial truth.

Kenizzites: Possessor–possessive, selfish, covetous.

Kadmonites: Ancient easterner–ancient ways, traditions, religious spirit.

These three ancient tribal clans are representative of the typical manifested behaviors of the unclean spirits that had been overcome before crossing over the Jordan river and specifically these three were conquered and overcome without Father God specifically driving them out before His people.

Therefore, this is suggesting there are iniquities that the Lord will expect us to deal with as we separate and consecrate ourselves and continuously mature spiritually. To become like Jesus, we all must go through the sanctification process of self-denial and taking up our cross and being Spirit led as overcomers. There must be something to overcome to be overcomers.

However, according to the Holy Scriptures; there are seven tribes/oppressive spirits greater and stronger than us that we must have the Lord's help to drive out of our lives. Thus, these seven tribes are symbolic of seven unclean demonic spirits that we must have the help of the Lord to be delivered from.

And Joshua said, By this you will know that the living God is among you, and that He will thoroughly drive out the Canaanites, the Hittites, the Hivites, the Perizzites, the Girgashites, the Amorites, and the Jebusites from before you. Joshua 3:10 MEV

The first tribe in our list is the *Rephaites* that comes from the tribal list recorded in Genesis 15:20. All the tribes and clans recorded are generally known as and are many times simply referred to as the Canaanites, which are the occupiers of the land of Canaan.

Rephaites: *Giants* – the spirit of cowardice, quitter, run away, coward, deserter, fearful intimidation.

Canaanites: *Lowland dwellers* – the spirit of carnal excess, drug addiction, sexual psychopath, erotic perversion, traffickers, shameful merchants. They were the original, the most populous, and dominating tribe. Thus, the land was named after this clan of reprobates and corrupted carnal sexual deviants.

Hittites: *Terrors*–the spirit of suicide, deep emotional torment, despair, hopeless.

Hivites: *Showers of life* – the spirit of vanity, self-seeker of pleasure, sense of entitlement, narcissist, self-gratification, celebrate me.

<u>Perizzites</u>: *Villagers* – the spirit of victimization, unwalled, apathetic, squatter, spiritual cripple, self-deprecating, dependent, victim mind set.

<u>Girgashites</u>: *Clay dwellers* – the spirit focused on earthly gain, what do I want, greedy, workaholic, fear of man, man-pleaser.

<u>Amorites</u>: *Mountain dwellers* – the spirit of conceit, domineering, fame seeker, big talker, control others, superior, self-righteous.

<u>Jebusites</u>: *Trodden down* – the spirit of hatred, prejudice, thresher, rejection, blamer, racist, bigot, trample down others.

Joshua leading the sons and daughters of Israel into the land of promise provides for us yet another prophetic pattern of our consecration and separation from the carnality of this present world system. Our sanctification, spiritual growth, and the maturing process is our *training for reigning* with King Jesus when we enter the one-thousand-year Kingdom age.

We will now consider the crossing-over of the Jordan river with Israel after the Lord commissions Joshua with the overcomer's mandate:

Now after the death of Moses the servant of the Lord, the Lord spoke to Joshua son of Nun, the assistant of Moses: Moses My servant is dead, so now get up and cross over the Jordan – you and all this people – to the land that I am giving to the children of Israel.

I have given you every place that the sole of your foot shall tread, as I said to Moses. From the wilderness and this Lebanon, as far as the great river, the River Euphrates, all the land of the Hittites, and to the Mediterranean Sea toward the setting of the sun will be your territory. No man will be able to stand against you all the days of your life. As I was with Moses, I will be with you. I will not abandon you. I will not leave you.

Be strong and courageous, for you shall provide the land that I swore to their fathers to give them as an inheritance for this people. Be strong and very courageous, in order to act carefully in accordance with all the law that My servant Moses commanded you. Do not turn aside from it to the right or the left, so that you may succeed wherever you go. This Book of the Law must not depart from your mouth. Meditate on it day and night so that you may act carefully according to all that is written in it. For then you will make your way successful, and you will be wise. Have I not commanded you? Be strong and courageous. Do not be afraid or dismayed, for the Lord your God is with you wherever you go. Joshua 1:1-9 MEV

Oh, my brothers and sisters in the Lord, this is the clarion call of every child of the living God, so let's get up and be strong and very courageous overcomers and possess the land of promise.

As with most passages throughout the Bible, there are many, many lessons to be gleaned from these events we are about to discuss, but; for our study here, we will cover the highlights and provide a summary of the prophetic patterns within the details of the Jordan crossing and the fall of Jericho, and the problems that can hinder our walk with the Lord and the victorious overcoming life of the believer.

The year was 1451 BC and Moses had died (Deuteronomy 34:1-8) at the age of one hundred and twenty a month earlier and Joshua was about to lead the nation of Israel into the promised land. The manna was about to stop, (Joshua 5:12) therefore; the Shemitah years would be reckoned from this date.

Israel crossing the River Jordan at Passover: Joshua chapters three and four.

Joshua commanded the people to gather at the crossing location for three days. Then when they saw the Levites carrying the ark of the covenant, they are to follow behind, but; they must keep a distance of two thousand cubits between them and the ark of the covenant, so they will know the way they should go because they had never been this way before and wait till you see what the Lord's gonna do.

There must be a distance of two thousand cubits between you and it. Do not draw closer to it, in order that you may know the way you should go. For you have not passed this way before. Joshua said to the people, Consecrate yourselves, for tomorrow the Lord will perform wonderous deeds among you. Joshua 3:4-5 MEV

When the feet of the Levities carrying the ark stepped into the overflowing waters of the Jordan, then the floodwaters that flowed down from the spring melt coming off Mount Hermon stood still and rose up in a heap twenty miles upstream – all the way back to the place named Adam at Zarethan (which means *dwelling place*)

Then the water that flows down from upstream stood still and rose up in a heap very far away at Adam, the city beside Zarethan. The water that flows down toward the Sea of Arabah (the Dead Sea) stopped and was cut off. The people crossed over opposite Jericho. Joshua 3:16 MEV

The Levite priests carrying the ark stood on dry ground in the middle of the dry riverbed until all of Israel had crossed over to the other side. When the people had all crossed over, Joshua commanded twelve men to go into the riverbed to the very place where the Levites were standing and collect twelve smooth stones from the bottom of the river and carry them to the camp site on the west river bank and stack them to form a memorial of this day.

Then the children of Israel did as Joshua commanded and picked up twelve stones from the middle of the Jordan, one for each of the tribes of the children of Israel, as the Lord had spoken to Joshua. They crossed over with them to the settlement and set them there. Joshua 4:8 MEV

Then, they were to carry twelve rough field stones from the camp site on the west bank back down into the bottom of the river where the Levites were standing and place them and leave them there.

Joshua also set twelve stones in the middle of the Jordan at the place where the feet of the priests who carried the ark of the covenant were standing. The stones are there to this day. Joshua 4:9 MEV

When all the fighting men had crossed over and everything was completed as they were commanded then the Levites carrying the ark of the testimony were commanded by the Lord–Come up out of the

Jordan! Thus, when the Levites came up out of the bottom of the Jordan riverbed, the floodwaters returned to their place and overflowed all its banks as before.

About forty thousand battle-ready men crossed over before the Lord for battle on the plains of Jericho. On that day, the Lord honored Joshua in the sight of all Israel. They feared him as they had feared Moses, all the days of his life. Joshua 4:13-14 MEV

So Joshua commanded the priests, Come up out of the Jordan! Joshua 4:17 MEV

Now over one thousand four hundred and eighty years later, as John the Baptist was preaching the gospel of the kingdom and baptizing those that repented in the Jordan river at the very same place that Joshua crossed-over that day and the "twelve stones" placed in the riverbed were still there. Perhaps John was even standing on top of them as he preached!

Therefore, bear fruit worthy of repentance, and do not think to say within yourselves, We have Abraham as our father, for I say to you that God is able *from these stones* to raise up children for Abraham. Matthew 3:8-9 MEV

As we have discussed previously, the crossing-over is a type and shadow of the death, burial, and resurrection of Jesus and thus a prophetic picture of our death, burial, and spiritual resurrection, or *born-again* experience. Of course, the ark of the covenant two thousand cubits ahead is a picture of Jesus Christ.

It was two thousand years from Adam until Abraham, and two thousand years from Abraham until Jesus Christ came as the Son of Man and will be two thousand years until King Jesus comes again. Jesus came and crossed-over two thousand years ahead of us to show us the way we should go because He is the Way the Truth and the Life leading us into the Kingdom.

The floodwaters flowing into the Dead Sea are a type and shadow of being overwhelmed by the sin and iniquities of this world, nevertheless, when Jesus came two thousand years before us and died and was buried and rose again, all our sins were backed-up all the way back to the garden of Eden–Adams dwelling place!

The twelve rough field stones represent our old sin nature dying and being buried and the twelve water-washed smooth stones lifted from the bottom of the river represent our new born-again spirit man crossing-over into the new resurrection life. Oh, praise the Lord! These twelve stones were carried up from the river crossing to Mount Ebal and erected as a memorial to the renewal of the covenant. (see Deuteronomy 27)

Then Joshua built an altar to the Lord God of Israel on Mount Ebal, as Moses the servant of the Lord had commanded the children of Israel. As is written in the Book of the Law of Moses, it was an altar of uncut stones not shaped by iron tools. They sacrificed burnt offerings to the Lord on it, as well as peace offerings. There in the presence of the children of Israel he wrote a copy of the Law of Moses on the stones. Joshua 8:30-32 MEV

This place between Mount Ebal and Mount Gerizim is the village of Shechem, the first place Abraham built an altar (Genesis 12:6-7) when he in obedience entered the promised land. Father God does everything in patterns.

Now after crossing-over, the people are to wait on their marching orders from the Lord and His plan and purposes on what we must do to be overcomer's in the present world.

First, we must understand that Jericho prophetically represents the world system and the stronghold of the enemy, and we do not have the strength or the understanding to overcome the fortified world system and destroy the enemy's strongholds without the plan, the power, and the leadership of the Holy Spirit.

Just as Israel had to hear from heaven, we too must consecrate ourselves and wait to receive the battle plan and our specific marching orders from the Captain of the Angel Armies, Jesus Christ.

Okay, here is the Master's battle plan: Joshua chapter six.

All the fighting men of twenty years of age and up were to march from the camp at Gilgal and then around the walls of the city of Jericho one complete trip for six consecutive days.

Some of these men of war were to be the rear guard following the Levites carrying the ark of the covenant and they were to follow seven priests carrying and blowing seven shofars, and the other armed men of war were to go before the ark and the priests.

No one was to shout or make a sound. The only sound would be the continuous sound of the seven shofars. Then on the seventh day, the entire company was to encircle the city seven times, and on the seventh pass around the city wall, the men of war were to shout the battle cry when they heard the sound of the seven priests blowing the seven shofars and were commanded to shout the battle cry by Joshua.

Clearly the Holy Spirit is alerting us to the fact that these events are a prophetic pattern for us to discern because the number seven represents spiritual perfection and God was consecrating these events, actions, the place, and the things as His people were about to possess the promised land.

All the fighting men were instructed to simply obey the commands and not to be distracted or enticed by the things they would see inside Jericho. Specifically, they were instructed not to take anything from the city because it was all accursed and dedicated for destruction and all the valuable commodities and precious metals were to be set apart for the Lord.

But you, keep yourselves from the accursed and devoted things, lest when you have devoted it [to destruction], you take of the accursed thing, and so make the camp of Israel accursed and trouble it. But all the silver and gold and vessels of bronze and iron are consecrated to the Lord; they shall come into the treasury of the Lord. Joshua 6:18-19 AMPC

So they blew the seven trumpets and the men of war shouted the battle cry.

When the people heard the trumpet sound, they shouted a loud battle cry, and the wall fell down. So the people went up into the city, one man after the other, and they captured it. They destroyed all that was in the city: man and woman, young and old, and oxen, sheep, and donkey with the edge of the sword. Joshua 6:20-21 MEV

One detail about this awesome supernatural encounter that some might overlook is the fact that the battle plan of the Lord commanded all the fighting men, the priests, and the Levites to march around the city for seven successive days. That means no matter what day they started or what day the walls came down, one of those seven days was the Sabbath day. Clearly the Lord was doing a new thing. Amen.

Joshua learns his first leadership lesson the hard way – Joshua chapter seven.

But the Israelites committed a trespass in regard to the devoted things; for Achan son of Carmi, the son of Zabdi, the son of Zerah, of the tribe of Judah, took some of the things devoted [for destruction]. And the anger of the Lord burned against Israel. Joshua 7:1 AMPC

What message has the Holy Spirit encoded here for us to discover?

Achan: which means *Serpent.* Carmi: which means *My vineyard.* Zabdi: which means *The gift of Jehovah.* Zerah: which means *A rising.* Judah: which means *the Lord be praised.*

The *serpent* is in *My vineyard* which is *the gift of Jehovah* to bring *a rising praise to the Lord.*

After the absolute total overwhelming victory and annihilation at Jericho, Joshua sent spies to Ai and based on their report, Joshua then commanded a small band of fighting men of about three thousand to advance and take the town of Ai, however; something went terribly wrong. The men of Ai easily turned back the Israelites attack and the men of Ai killed thirty-six men as they fled towards Shabarim. (Ai means *heap of ruins* and Shebarim means *a fracture*)

This had never happened, and this was not supposed to happen. Perhaps Joshua should have waited until he had heard from the Lord before he proceeded with any offensive.

Then they returned to Joshua and said to him, All the people need not go up. Let about two or three thousand men go up and strike Ai. Since they are few, all the people need not weary themselves. So about three thousand men went up from among the people there, but they fled from before the men of Ai. The men of Ai struck down thirty-six men and pursued them from the gate to Shebarim. They struck them down on the mountainside, and the hearts of the people melted like water. Joshua 7:3-5 MEV

Joshua went before the ark and was desperately crying out before the Lord about this appalling situation that wasn't supposed to happen, thus Joshua was basically blaming God for his problems and this painful lost battle at Ai.

Then Joshua ripped his clothes. He and the Israelite elders fell on their faces to the ground in front of the ark of the Lord until evening and threw dirt upon their heads. Joshua said, O Lord God, why did You bring this people across the Jordan to give us into the hands of the Amorites to destroy us? If only we had been content to dwell on the other side of the Jordan! O my Lord, what should I say now that Israel has fled before its enemies? The Canaanites and all the inhabitants of the land may hear, turn on us, and cut off our name from the earth. What will You do for Your great name? Joshua 7:6-9 MEV

The Lord said to Joshua, Get up! Why do you lie thus upon your face? Israel has sinned; they have transgressed My covenant which I commanded them. They have taken some of the things devoted [for destruction]; they have stolen, and lied, and put them among their own baggage. That is why the Israelites could not stand before their enemies, but fled before them; they are accursed and have become devoted [for destruction]. I will cease to be with you unless you destroy the accursed [devoted] things among you. Joshua 7:10-12 AMPC

Up, sanctify (set apart for a holy purpose) the people, and say Sanctify yourselves for tomorrow; for thus says the Lord, the God of Israel: There are accursed things in the midst of you, O Israel. You can not stand before your enemies until you take away from among you the things devoted [to destruction]. Joshua 7:13 AMPC

God Almighty commanded Joshua to get up off his face and dry it up. Quit the whining and consecrate the people and sanctify yourself. There is sin in the camp! You will not be able to stand before your enemies until you perceive, locate, and remove the things that are cursed and dedicated for destruction that are in your camp because if you hold on to these things, you are defiled and have become cursed also, therefore; you too will be dedicated for destruction and you have allowed Satan access to steal, kill, and destroy within your life.

Behold, this is the exact same sin that fifteen hundred years later that Ananias and his wife Sapphira were guilty of (Acts 5:1-10) and the Lord hasn't changed His mind on how He views these things.

The sin and iniquity will hinder our faith, corrupt our walk, and shipwreck our spiritual victory, when we allow the devil access into our life by allowing things that God says is cursed to remain in our own camp, or misusing things that are dedicated unto the Lord.

Please remember and do not forget that the Lord God clearly says to His people: Get up. Sanctify yourself. Remove the accursed things from among you!

(1) Get up–It is time to get up and quit praying to God to fix the problem when the problem is you because you have left the door open to the devil and allowed and tolerated sin in your camp, home, family, business, health, or finances.

(2) Sanctify yourself–You must discern and identify all the accursed things that you have allowed in or the iniquities that you have tolerated to remain your heart and life.

(3) Remove the accursed things–We are responsible to remove the things that Jesus says is cursed. Things like ungodly thoughts,

attitudes, behaviors, habits, possessions, and toxic relationships. You must identify all things that are linked to the occult such as horror movies, ungodly music, books (like Harry Potter), idols, satanic images, Tarot cards, Ouija boards, occultic video games, horoscopes, pornography, etc.

Carnal, worldly believer's will never live the victorious Christian life until we have done these things because we have inadvertently left an open entrance and thus allowed the enemy of our soul access and permission to steal, kill, and destroy the precious things in our life and all that concerns us, and we have grieved the Holy Spirit.

The life of Joshua and these events are prophetic patterns of the overcomer's mandate.

CHAPTER ELEVEN

Overcomers: Zacharias, Elisabeth, & John.

Foundational Truth: Genuine overcomers keep standing on the Word and hold on to their faith, even when life does not go as planned or as we think it should.

Walking with Zacharias, Elisabeth, and John.

We are going to examine the family and the events surrounding the supernatural conception, birth, life, and ministry of the greatest prophet that Jesus Christ said ever lived, as recorded in Scriptures. For we believe these folks are true overcomers.

The voice of him that crieth in the wilderness, Prepare ye the way of the Lord, make straight in the desert a highway for our God. Isaiah 40:3 KJV

Behold, I will send My messenger, and he shall prepare the way before Me: and the Lord, whom ye seek shall suddenly come to His temple, even the messenger of the covenant, whom ye delight in: behold, He shall come, saith the Lord of hosts. Malachi 3:1 KJV

Behold, I will send you Elijah the prophet before the coming of the great and dreadful day of the Lord: And he shall turn the heart of the fathers to the children, and the heart of the children to their fathers, lest I come and smite the earth with a curse. Malachi 4:5-6 KJV

Isaiah prophesied in the eight century BC of the messenger from the wilderness that would prepare the way before the Messiah and Malachi did as well in the fifth century. After these final verses found in the book of Malachi from the last prophetic book of the canonized Old Testament, there was then no known revelation for four hundred years. That one single blank page in your Bible between the prophet Malachi and the gospel of Matthew represents four hundred years of no recorded prophetic revelation whatsoever from heaven.

Of course, we can glean much from reliable historical records from multiple sources about the many profound and inspired events that occurred during this time and especially the Maccabean revolt from 168-165 BC. These men who were outnumbered more than ten-to-one, were undeniably overcomers with God Almighty's help, as they battled against the Syrian king Antiochus Epiphanes, whom was prophesied to come by Daniel as recorded in the book of Daniel in chapters nine and eleven.

Antiochus Epiphanes, who was a type and shadow of the coming antichrist; is the story behind *Hanukkah* resulting in the feast of dedication, or as some prefer to call the Festival of lights; that was known by Jesus Christ and His disciples as distinguished in saint John's gospel account.

And it was at Jerusalem the feast of dedication, and it was winter. And Jesus walked in the temple in Solomon's porch. John 10:22-23 KJV

It is thought-provoking to note that although no one knows for sure the day or the hour of Jesus' birth; many Bible scholars believe that Jesus, who is *the Light of the world,* was conceived in Mary's womb by the Holy Spirit during this winter festival.

Then spake Jesus again unto them, saying, I am the light of the world: he that followeth Me shall not walk in darkness, but shall have the light of life. John 8:12 KJV

As long as I am in the world, I am the light of the world. John 9:5 KJV

There was no prophetic voice in the earth until the first manifestation and fulfillment of these prophetic revelations transcribed by Malachi prophesying the forerunner of the Messiah.

Who, what, where, and how did these prophetic utterances come to pass?

Then as these men went their way, Jesus began to speak to the crowds about John: What did you go out in the wilderness (desert) to see? A reed swayed by the wind? What did you go out to see then? A man clothed in soft garments? Behold, those who wear soft clothing are in the houses of kings. But what did you go out to see? A prophet? Yes, I tell you, and one [out of common, more eminent, more remarkable, and] superior to a prophet. This is the one of whom it is written, Behold, I send My messenger ahead of You, who shall make ready Your way before You. Matthew 11:7-10 AMPC

Truly I tell you, among those born of women there has not risen anyone greater than John the Baptist; yet he who is the least in the kingdom of heaven is greater than he. And from the days of John the Baptist until the present time, the kingdom of heaven has endured violent assault, and violent men seize it by force [as a precious prize – a share in the heavenly kingdom is sought with most ardent zeal and intense exertion]. Matthew 11:11-12 AMPC

For all the Prophets and the Law prophesied up until John. And if you are willing to receive and accept it, John himself is Elijah who was come [before the kingdom]. He who has ears to hear, let him be listening and let him consider and perceive and comprehend by hearing. Matthew 11:13-15 AMPC

We believe this mighty man of God is worthy of study, so; we shall begin at the events surrounding his elderly parents heavenly encounter and his supernatural pre-natal care.

The text for our study is found in Luke 1:1-80

The faithful priest of the 8th division of Abijah, per the priestly divisions established by king David and the prophet Samuel as outlined in I Chronicles 24, Zacharias (*the Lord remembers*), and his devout wife Elisabeth (*my God is my oath*), also a descendent of Aaron; have a child even though they are both well advanced in years.

According to early Jewish history, they were both more than seventy years old, and a few weeks or months after the supernatural birth and naming of baby John (which means *Jehovah has graciously given*), Elisabeth must flee with the child into the hills of the wilderness to save him from being murdered by king Herod the Great's paid assassins. Why would the king Herod want to kill a baby?

(Study text Matthew 2:1-12) King Herod (which means *anxious fleer*) was visited by these wise men traveling from the east, because they had seen His star in the east, (we believe it could have been the scepter shaped Comet Hale-Bopp?) and had come seeking in faith that this was the sign of the prophesied King of the Jews.

And now, behold, I am going to my people; come, I will tell you what this people [Israel] will do to your people [Moab] in the latter days. And he took up his [figurative] discourse, and said: Balaam son of Beor speaks, the man whose eye is opened speaks, he speaks, who heard the words of God and knew the knowledge of the Most High, who saw the vision of the Almighty, falling down, but having his eyes open and uncovered: I see Him, but not now; I behold Him, but He is not near. A star (Star) shall come forth out of Jacob, and a scepter (Scepter) shall rise out of Israel and shall crush all the corners of Moab and break down all the sons of Sheth [Moab's sons of tumult]. And Edom shall be [taken as] a possession, [Mount] Seir also shall be dispossessed, who were Israel's enemies, while Israel does valiantly. Out of Jacob shall one (One) come having dominion and shall destroy the remnant from the city. Numbers 24:14-19 AMPC

And the Gentiles shall come to thy light, and kings to the brightness of thy rising. Isaiah 60:3 KJV

But thou, Bethlehem Ephratah, though thou be little among the thousands of Judah, yet out of thee shall he come forth unto me that is to be ruler in Israel; whose goings forth have been from of old, from everlasting. Micah 5:2 KJV

After this initial meeting, Herod asked these intrepid and wise travelers that when they found this very special child, to return and tell him where this distinct little boy was, so; he could go and worship this newborn child too. Yeah, right!

That was not Herod the Great's plan. No, Herod who was a descendant of Esau, (per the first century AD Jewish historian Josephus) who still harbored the family feud and had great animosity against the sons of Jacob, was plotting to kill the helpless infant. Herod was extremely paranoid, being motivated by a demonic political spirit, would have anyone killed that he suspected didn't think he was so great; including his wife(s) and his own offspring.

Herod had every intension to destroy this child, and any other child; that might become a political rival to him or a threat to his legacy. The Greek word for *Edom* is Idumea and Herod's father was an Idumean and his mother was Arab, or a descendant of Ishmael.

Now these are the generations of Esau, who is Edom. Genesis 36:1 KJV

Thus dwelt Esau in mount Seir: Esau is Edom. Genesis 36:8 KJV

That old fox Herod was not going to take any chances and he would kill any perceived threat.

These *wise* men from the east, that began their journey by faith; traveled for more than eight hundred miles one way by camel to Jerusalem. These were obviously men that studied and knew the Word of God because there is absolutely no way the Holy Spirit, the Author of the Bible; would have called any man *wise* that did not have knowledge the Holy Scriptures. And as we all know:

So then faith cometh by hearing, and hearing by the word of God. Romans 10:17 KJV

These men were believed to have been trained as participants of the school of astrophysics and science of the Magi that Daniel, who also was a dream interpreter; was made chief over during his service to the various kings in Babylon. (Daniel 1:17-21, Daniel 2:46-49)

Then the king advanced Daniel and gave him many great gifts, and made him ruler over the whole providence of Babylon and chief of the governors over all the wise men of Babylon. Daniel 2:48 MEV

God Almighty saved these Gentile souls through Daniel. These wise men of Babylon were saved because God had a plan and purpose, and the Scriptures teach us that: The fruit of the righteous is a tree of life, and he that winneth souls is wise. Proverbs 11:30 KJV

And as recorded, Daniel is prophesying about the days we are living now and what we should be doing: And they that be wise shall shine as the brightness of the firmament; and they that turn many to righteousness as the stars for ever and ever. Daniel 12:3 KJV

And Jesus taught us in the parable of the wheat and tares: Then shall the righteous shine forth as the sun in the kingdom of their Father. Who hath ears to hear, let him hear. Matthew 13:43 KJV

According to Matthew 2:12 we know the *wise men* were warned supernaturally by God in a dream that they should not return to king Herod the Great, so; they departed another way into their own country.

Then Herod, when he saw that he had been tricked by the wise men, was utterly enraged and sent forth and killed all the male children who were in Bethlehem and the surrounding region, from two years old and under, based on the time which he had diligently inquired of the wise men. Then was fulfilled what was spoken by Jeremiah the prophet: Matthew 2:16-17 MEV

Herod then ordered the indiscriminate slaughter of all the male children of two years and younger they could find in the surrounding region. This event was prophesied by Jeremiah approximately six hundred years before it came to pass.

Thus says the Lord: A voice is heard in Ramah, lamentation and bitter weeping, Rachel weeping for her children, refusing to be comforted for her children, because they are no more. Jeremiah 31:15 MEV

Jacob, Rachel, and the rest of the family were on their way to Hebron, where Isaac was still living. And as they were travelling through what is now called Judah, Rachel went into hard labor and delivered Benjamin, and died. This was the 12th son of Jacob, now called Israel. He buried his beloved wife Rachel in Bethlehem (*house of bread*) and set a memorial pillar on Rachel's grave. So, the children from the hill country of Judah were all generally referred to as the children of the matriarch Rachel.

Rachel died and was buried on the way to Ephrath, which is Bethlehem. Jacob set a pillar on her grave. It is the pillar of Rachel's grave to this day. Genesis 35:19-20 MEV

With all the fuss and stir being made in Jerusalem and throughout the hill country about all the super-natural events and the wild stories being spread about baby John (the Baptist) being miraculously born to this old Priest and his old, barren wife, there is no doubt that paranoid, sadistic, and unhinged Herod would have sent his ruthless minions out to track down this extraordinarily special child.

Immediately his mouth was opened and his tongue was loosed, and he spoke and praised God. Fear came on all who lived around them. And all these facts were talked about throughout all the hill country of Judea. All those who heard them laid them up in their hearts, saying, What kind of child will he be? For the hand of the Lord was with him. Luke 1:64-66 MEV

Jewish history records that these ruthless men sent from Herod's private security team came to Zacharias seeking his young son, but; Elisabeth had fled with the child and she hid in the wilderness with her infant son. Herod's henchmen murdered Zacharias while serving in the temple because he would not tell them where his wife and child had gone.

Isn't it interesting that Satan is always after the children? From the child sacrifices to the Canaanite demigods such as Molech, to Pharaoh in Egypt drowning the male Hebrew children in the Nile river, to Herod's slaughter of the two-year-old toddlers in Judea, to our current culture sacrificing multiplied millions of children (approximately two billion world-wide since 1973) on the altar of convenience, plea-sure, and self-ambition.

Today we label this abominable sin and idolatry with more socially acceptable names like *Pro-choice* or *Reproductive rights*, or as some ignorantly or simply callously claim it's my health and my body!

No, it is not your body or your child if believe the Word! (I Corinthians 6:19-20, Psalm 139:13-15, I Peter 1:18-19, Romans 14:8) Nonetheless, it is still the work and the influence of our enemy and his evil, demonic horde that comes only to steal, kill, and destroy lives – young, old, or those in between.

We know John lived in the wilderness for thirty years, with animal hides for clothing and eating locusts and wild honey. John's message, mission, and purpose was prophesied by Isaiah more than seven hundred years before it came to pass. John remained in the wilderness until God called him to begin to preach to Israel. (Matthew 3:1-17, Luke1:13-17, Luke 1:76-80, Luke 3:1-22)

The voice of him that crieth in the wilderness, Prepare ye the way of the Lord, make straight in the desert a highway for our God. Every valley shall be exalted, and every mountain and hill shall be made low: and the crooked shall be made straight, and the rough places plain: And the glory of the Lord shall be revealed, and all flesh shall see it together: for the mouth of the Lord hath spoken it. Isaiah 40:3-5 KJV

And on the eighth day when Elisabeth and Zacharias brought their son to be circumcised, miraculously Zacharias was able to speak again, and he named his son John just as Gabriel had instructed him and then, being filled with the Holy Spirit, Zacharias prophesied over his infant son his destiny.

And you, child, will be called the prophet of the Highest; for you will go before the face of the Lord to prepare His ways, to give knowledge of salvation to His people by the remission of their sins, through the tender mercy of our God, whereby the sunrise from on high has visited us; to give light to those who sit in darkness and in the shadow of death, to guide our feet into the way of peace. Luke 1:76-79 MEV

And the child grew and become strong in spirit, and he remained in the wilderness until the day of his appearance to Israel. Luke 1:80 MEV

The rumors were still circulating about the possibility that John the baptizer was the Messiah. This was ended for the most part, when Jesus came to the Jordan river and was baptized/cleansed by John with water and Anointed/baptized with the Holy Spirit and fully commissioned by His Father. Jesus the Christ was thirty years old (the age of a priest) when he began His public ministry.

The Levites from thirty years old and up were counted, and their head count of men was thirty-eight thousand. I Chronicles 23:3 MEV

We do not know exactly how long John the Baptist's preaching ministry was, but; from the various accounts in the gospels it seems that it was less than one year before Jesus began His public ministry and shortly thereafter John was locked-up in prison by Herod Antipas (which means *likeness of his father*) the tetrarch.

Herod has sent and seized John and bound him in prison for the sake of Herodias, his brother Philip's wife, for he had married her. For John said to Herod, It is not lawful for you to have your brother's wife. So Herodias had a grudge against him and would have killed him, but she could not, for Herod feared John, knowing that he was a righteous and holy man, and protected him. When he heard him, he was greatly perplexed, but heard him gladly. Mark 6:17-20 MEV

This was the son of Herod the Great and John had rebuked him for his various sins, including adultery with his brother Herod Philips' wife. Herod Antipas had a fear of John and he feared not having the peoples' approval, and thus Herod was afraid that killing John would not be political expedient for him, so instead; he had John thrown in prison to placate his malicious, evil, and manipulating wife Herodias (which means *trembling fleer*), the granddaughter of Herod the Great.

After John had been in prison for some time, but; obviously before his death; John had heard of all the miraculous things that were happening in Jesus' ministry and sent two of his followers to Jesus. John was basically asking "I thought for sure you are the Messiah, but; why haven't you come to rescue me?"

Now when John had heard in prison the works of Christ, he sent two of his disciples, and said to Him, Are You He who should come, or should we look for another? Jesus answered them, Go and tell John what you hear and see: The blind receive their sight and the lame walk, the lepers are cleansed and the deaf hear, the dead are raised up, and the poor have the gospel preached to them. Blessed is he who does not fall away because of Me. Matthew 11:2-6 MEV

Jesus answered and sent His response back with the messengers to John that Yes, He is the Messiah, and that His miraculous works are the proof because it is the fulfillment of prophecy as recorded in Scripture.

Then the eyes of the blind shall be opened, and the deaf shall be unstopped. Then the lame man shall leap as a deer, and the tongue of the mute sing for joy. For in the wilderness waters shall break out and streams in the desert. Isaiah 35:5-6 MEV

The Spirit of the Lord God is upon me because the Lord has anointed me to preach good news to the poor; He has sent me to heal the broken-hearted, to proclaim liberty to the captives, and the opening of the prison to those who are bound; Isaiah 61:1 MEV

In Matthew 11:11 and in Luke 7:28 Jesus went on to tell those He was teaching that there has not been any man born that was a greater prophet than John the Baptist.

John 1:6-9 tells us that John the Baptist was sent from God as a witness, and it was prophesied in Malachi 3:1 that he was sent as God's messenger.

We also see in John 1:29-34, that John the Baptist was sent to bear witness to the fact that Jesus is Lamb of God to take away the sin of the world and that Jesus is the Son of God. It was also said of John the Baptist in John 10:41-42, that John the Baptist did no miracle, but everything he said about Jesus was true, and many believed in Jesus because of John's preaching.

Jesus also said in Mathew 11:11 and Luke 7:28 *but he that is least in the Kingdom of God is greater than he*. Selah. Jesus said that we (if you are born-again) are greater than John the Baptist, the last Old Testament prophet and the greatest prophet that ever lived! How could this be?

Romans 8:16-17 tells us we are joint-heirs with Christ and Galatians 4:7 says that we are no more a servant, but a son; and if a son, then an heir of God through Christ, and Ephesians 2:4-6 says But God, who is rich in mercy, for His great love wherewith He loved us, Even when we were dead in sins, quickened us together with Christ, (by grace ye are saved); And hath raised us up together, and made us sit together in heavenly places in Christ Jesus.

And in Titus 3:7 we see that being justified by His grace, we should be made heirs according to the hope of eternal life, and we also see in Revelation 21:7 Jesus says he that overcometh shall inherit all things; and I will be his God, and he shall be My son. Amen. This should be the goal of our lives: to become a sanctified overcomer.

That is why those in the Kingdom (born-again) are greater that John the Baptist. John was not born-again, and at the time, he couldn't be, however; we can be, glory to God! All of this means that if we are born-again, Spirit-filled, faithful followers of Jesus, we all have a much greater potential impact on this world as forerunners of our soon coming King than the blessed and beloved John the Baptist!

Not long after this, in a lust-filled, drunken stupor, as Herod Antipas was bloviating at his birthday party, (Matthew 14:1-12) he vowed to give his seductive step daughter anything she wanted. According to the Jewish historian Flavius Josephus, the step-daughters name was Salome (*very shady*). Her hateful and vindictive mother seized the opportunity and instructed her daughter to ask for the head of John the Baptist on a platter, so; bigmouth Herod had John murdered and his severed head was then presented to the girl. John's followers came and took his body and buried it and went to report to Jesus that His kinsman was deceased.

There is much more that could be said about this passage, but; let's stay focused on the life and ministry of John the Baptist, and his righteous and blameless parents.

Let us contemplate and consider John's father. Was Zacharias blessed?

As a descendent of Aaron, he spent his life as a servant to God as a priest at the Temple. In his old age he is visited by the angel Gabriel. He came to deliver a message from the throne room in heaven that God has heard his prayers and God Almighty was going to grant his request. After this, Zacharias can't talk for over nine months (because of his unbelief), and yet miraculously, he fathers a baby boy; praise God.

Zacharias was informed that his son shall be great in the sight of the Lord and won't drink strong drink and shall be filled with the Holy Spirit before he is even born, and he shall have the spirit and power of Elijah and he shall make ready a people prepared for the Messiah. Zacharias was promised his son would be a mighty man of God, and the prophesied forerunner of the long-promised Messiah!

Then a brief time after his birth, Zacharias seemingly must have sent his elderly wife and young son out into the wilderness to preserve their lives, and apparently, he had a deadly confrontation with the evil men sent by Herod to assassinate his one and only son.

According to the Jewish historical writings and oral tradition, Zacharias died a martyr defending his family to the death, being murdered in the temple because he would not disclose the hiding place of his wife and son.

Did Zacharias live a blessed life? What about his wife Elisabeth. Was she blessed?

They were both righteous before Go, walking in all the commandments and ordinances of the Lord blamelessly. But they had no child, because Elizabeth was barren, and they both were now well advanced in years. Luke 1:6-7 MEV

The Scriptures say that Elisabeth was righteous and blameless before God and barren. This was in absolute total contradiction to the accepted beliefs of the culture in those days for such righteous people to be childless, which was considered by all to be a curse from God.

She had longed and prayed for decades for a family of her own, yet; she remained barren. Many today associate difficult and undesirable circumstances on some hidden iniquity, unforgiveness, or some other unrepentant rebellion, but; this is not what this passage of Scripture is showing us.

Now, try to visualize her very old priest of a husband as he came home from his duty at the temple, with a wild tale to tell. Just one problem, he could not verbally communicate.

Can you just imagine how that discussion went? How long do you think it took old Zach to convince Elisabeth that they were going to have a son and that this son of theirs would be the messenger prophesied in the Scriptures over seven hundred years before, and that their son would be the forerunner of the Messiah!

He would have had to write all of this on parchment or slate for her, and then answer her hundreds of questions. You know she would have had to know every single detail! (yes, I too have a wife) This would take great faith.

Hey married men, how long do you think that might of took? Could it be possible that ole' Zacharias is the one who invented the game we now call *Charades*, or maybe God used him as the forerunner to reintroduce some ancient Semitic sign language? Or, maybe this explains why he was in his 70's? Because it took him this long to mature and learn the patience required to relate all the tender details of this encounter to his inquisitive bride?

[Oh, very sorry, please excuse the author's very weak attempt at humor]

But hey, obviously, our hero Zach was motivated enough to find a way to persuade Elisabeth that he had heard from the Lord and she becomes pregnant, glory to God! Oh, how our heavenly Father loves to see His children just simply trust Him and trust His Word. For we walk by faith, not by sight. II Corinthians 5:7 MEV

After approximately six months pass, Elisabeth gets a visit from her young teenage cousin Mary, who like Zacharias had a visit from the same heavenly messenger. Mary had received a visit from the heavenly envoy Gabriel and had her own wild story to tell. Other than Joseph her husband, there probably wasn't another person on the planet that would have believed this young teenager's incredible story except Elizabeth.

So, here we have these two pregnant women, one very old and one very young; prophesying to one another: The mother of the forerunner of the Messiah, and the mother of the Savior of the world. Oh hallelujah, glory to God; they were having what we would call today a Holy Ghost blow-out!

And Mary arose in those days, and went into the hill country with haste, into a city of Juda; and entered into the house of Zacharias, and saluted Elisabeth. And it came to pass, that, when Elisabeth heard the salutation of Mary, the babe leaped in her womb; and Elisabeth was filled with the Holy Ghost: And she spake out with a loud voice, and said, Blessed art thou among women, and blessed is the fruit of thy womb. And whence is this to me, that the mother of my Lord should come to me? For, lo, as soon as the voice of thy salutation sounded in mine ears, the babe leaped in my womb for joy. And blessed is she that believed: for there shall be a performance of those things which were told her from the Lord. Luke 1:39-45 KJV

And Mary said, My soul doth magnify the Lord, and my spirit hath rejoiced in God my Saviour. For He hath regarded the low estate of his handmaiden: for, behold, from henceforth all generations shall call me blessed. For He that is mighty hath done to me great things; and holy is His name. And His mercy is on them that fear Him from generation to generation. He hath shewed strength with His arm; He hath scattered the proud in the imagination of their hearts. He hath put down the mighty from their seats, and exalted them of low degree. He hath filled the hungry with good things; and the rich He hath sent empty away. He hath holpen His servant Israel, in remembrance of His mercy; As He spake to our fathers, to Abraham, and to his seed for ever. Luke 1:46-55 KJV

Both Elisabeth and Mary were speaking under the unction of the Holy Spirit and Elisabeth declared that the embryo in Mary's womb was her Lord. This could very well be the single strongest Word of Truth that an inseminated egg in the mother's womb is a child, and to destroy that embryo is murder.

Now, after Mary has a good long visit to build her faith and courage, she returns to her family home in Galilee and Elisabeth gives birth to John. We don't know how long afterwards, but; shortly after John's birth, Elisabeth flees into the wilderness with her son to preserve and protect his life.

Elisabeth probably never saw her husband, Zacharias alive again. She might not have ever returned home again either, but; we know from the Scriptures John did not ever return to his father's house.

So, was Elisabeth, the mother of the child called the *prophet of the Highest, that shall go before the face of the Lord to prepare His ways* (Luke 1:76) who spent her elderly years living like a wild animal to protect her son from being murdered, and without her husband or support. What do you think? Was Elisabeth blessed?

Which brings us to John the Baptizer.

John was on the run, living like a vagabond in the lonely wilderness for thirty years. After living in the backcountry and wearing camel skin clothing, and eating bugs, seeds, and honey, with the Spirit of God leading him. At the prescribed time the Spirit of the Lord led John in from the wilderness into the country around the Jordan river, to preach the true gospel of the Kingdom. John preached repentance and as the people responded, he begins baptizing the people in the Jordan.

John's ministry had continued for less than a year when Jesus came to John at the river on His thirtieth birthday thus asking John to baptize Him. Jesus wasn't being baptized for repentance because Jesus had nothing to repent for, instead Jesus was symbolically being cleansed and consecrated (as in a Mikvah) in accordance with the Torah requirements (Exodus 30:20, Leviticus 8:6,16:4,24) to enter the office and service of High Priest. We know that John does in-fact baptize the Lamb of God and hears the audible voice of God Almighty speak from heaven. He also witnesses the Holy Spirit come upon and abide on Jesus, the Son of God.

I have seen and borne witness that He is the Son of God. John 1:34 MEV

Not long after that, John is arrested and thrown in prison, kept there for about another year, and then murdered on the request of Herod's heathen step-daughter at a drunken birthday bash.

Was John the Baptist blessed? Do you think his life developed and ended the way he thought it would?

He probably didn't have any memory of his earthly father, nor did he receive his earthly inheritance.

Do you think he might have gotten tired of eating bugs every day and wearing the same camel hide outfit? He never had a girlfriend, or any chance of a family of his own. He lived like a desperado, living in caves and temporary shelters–Waiting on the Lord.

Perhaps John, the intrepid forerunner; meditated on this Psalm as he watched the sun disappear in the west, has he prepared for another cold and lonely night.

Be still, and know that I am God. I will be exalted among the heathen, I will be exalted in the earth. The Lord of hosts is with us; the God of Jacob is our refuge. Selah. Psalm 46:10-11 KJV

Do you think John ever had days that he wondered about these "promises" from God that his mother taught him about? What about his time in Herod's dungeon? John setting there day after day, month after month, wondering: Is Jesus gonna get me out of here? Do you think he ever had to struggle with his thoughts and fight to stay in faith?

Then after all these things, some of Herod's men come to his prison cell one day and announce that they have come to cut off his head today. Why? Because some carnal belly dancer asks for his life that day.

Was this the way it should have ended for John? Did he live a blessed life?

Jesus called John the greatest prophet ever born. He was filled with the Holy Spirit from his mother's womb. John lived a true Spirit led life. His father was murdered, and his mother probably died when he was still a youngster. He did not have brothers, sisters, or any other family to help or comfort him. I doubt that he had the opportunity to attend any formal school. His life was all about trusting God to survive one more day. I believe this is another out-standing example of: For we walk by faith, and not by sight. II Corinthians 5:7 MEV

How should we conduct our lives based on what we know about John and his parents' lives? Did Jesus promise that we wouldn't have troubles? Do you believe that Jesus stripped Himself of His divinity and came to this planet to be treated like a criminal and to be tortured and die nailed to a tree, just so we could live happy-happy-happy lives with lots of money?

No, matter of fact; Jesus said just the exact opposite:

These things I have spoken unto you, that in Me ye might have peace. In the world ye shall have tribulation: but be of good cheer; I have overcome the world. John 16:33 KJV

Jesus is the Overcomer, therefore; we too are all called to follow His footsteps and thus become overcomers just like our Lord Jesus Christ.

Has everything in your life worked out just the way you thought it would? What about the dreams that the Lord as given you? Or perhaps a prophetic word? Has everything worked out just perfectly and in accordance to your plan and your concept of how life should unfold?

Have you ever experienced any setbacks or disappointments? Have there been any bumps, curves, or detours in your road? Has anything taken much longer or been more difficult than you ever thought it could or would be? Has your heart ever been bruised or broken? Has life ever seemed unfair? Are you blessed?

Selah. (pause and carefully meditate deeply on these truths)

Jesus said: Verily, verily, I say unto you, except a corn of wheat fall into the ground and die, it abideth alone: but if it die, it bringeth forth much fruit. He that loveth his life shall lose it; and he that hateth his life in this world shall keep it unto life eternal. If any man serve Me, let him follow Me; and where I am, there shall also My servant be: if any man serve Me, him will My Father honour. John 12:24-26 KJV

And He said to them all, if any man will come after me, let him deny himself, and take up his cross daily, and follow Me. Luke 9:23 KJV

And in Jesus said: No man, having put his hand to the plough, and looking back, is fit for the Kingdom of God. Luke 9:62 KJV

In the second pastoral epistle of apostle Paul to Timothy, he teaches us all: Thou therefore endure hardness, as a good soldier of Christ Jesus. No man that warreth entangleth himself with the affairs of this life; that he may please Him who hath chosen him to be a soldier. II Timothy 2:3-4 KJV

Other Scriptures that are additional witnesses to the truth that we can't ever look back to the world system, which is Satan's kingdom.

Then the Lord rained upon Sodom and upon Gomorrah brimstone and fire from the Lord out of heaven; And He overthrew those cities, and all the plain, and all the inhabitants of the cities, and that which grew upon the ground. But his wife looked back from behind him, and she became a pillar of salt. Genesis 19:24-26 KJV

If any man come to Me, and hate not his father, and mother, and wife, and children, and brethren, and sisters, yea, and his own life also, he cannot be My disciple. And whosoever doth not bear his cross, and come after Me, cannot be My disciple. Luke 14:26-27 KJV

Cast not away therefore your confidence, which hath great recompense of reward. For ye have need of patience, that, after ye have done the will of God, ye might receive the promise. Hebrews 10:35-36 KJV

Many of us grew-up being told by parents and others that had influence in our lives that "You can be anything you want to be if you work hard enough" well folks, this is simply not the Truth, and it is entirely unscriptural. No, this is the wisdom of the world, not God's plan and purposes. The plan of our Lord is for all His bond-servants to be led by His Holy Spirit in all things, and to find and follow His plan and purposes.

Every believer's mandate is to surrender our life to follow Jesus. Following Jesus is a life of self-denial. We must lay down our selfish ambitions, pursuits, and desires, in complete submission of our will to our Master's will. The more we die to self-ambition; the more Jesus can live through us. This is what it means when we say, Jesus is Lord of all.

This is the overcomer's mandate.

This is precisely what John the Baptist meant when he said: He must increase, but I must decrease. John 3:30 KJV

Thy Word is a lamp unto my feet, and a light unto my path. Psalm 119:105 KJV teaching us that the Lord will light the next step or two, on the path of life for us, but; that's all. The Lord will not reveal to us His whole plan and purpose for our lives for some good and profound reasons.

The first reason is out of His great love and mercy for us. We simply can't handle it. Jesus said: I have many things to say to you, but ye cannot bear them now. John 16:12 KJV

The Lord's will for all of us to be totally yielded to Him and absolutely dependent on Him for everything. Jesus said: I AM the vine, ye are the branches: he that abideth in Me, and I in him, the same bringeth forth much fruit: for without Me ye can do nothing. John 15:5 KJV

Jesus said our #1 priority must be the Fathers business, first and foremost; above everything else in our lives: But seek ye first the kingdom of God, and His righteousness; and all these things shall be added unto you. Matthew 6:33 KJV

The Lord Jesus expects us to believe Him, trust Him, and to have absolute faith in Him; today, tomorrow, and the next day because: For we walk by faith, not by sight. II Corinthians 5:7 KJV

It is a very interesting observation that God prepared Moses for 80 years for his 40-year ministry. And John the Baptist was being prepared for nearly 30 years for about 1 year of ministry. And Jesus was trained for 30 years for His 3.5-year Anointed ministry. And Saul of Tarsus was trained and prepared for 40+ years before becoming apostle Paul and completing his 20-year ministry.

Or even consider the original twelve disciples that lived with Jesus and personally interacted with Him night and day for over three years before they were sent out, however; even then not before being baptized with the Holy Spirit and being clothed with power from on high.

Yet; we see some ministers today training for six months to a couple of years and then launching out into big-time ministry. Perhaps this could be why so many of these end-up on the spiritual junk heap, or preaching some weird hyper grace message, or falling into some carnal sin that takes them out.

Could there possibly be something wrong with this scenario? Could there be some in leadership positions within the Church today that are not really prepared to minister to others, or spiritually mature enough to stand? Just some thoughts to ponder.

Some final thoughts and questions to prayerfully consider: Must everything go perfectly in your life for you to believe you are blessed and highly favored?

Have you surrendered your will today? Is your faith in Jesus and Him alone?

Have you embraced the believer's mandate for your life?

Jesus said: For many are called, but few are chosen. Matthew 22:14 KJV

Who are the *called?* Who are the *chosen?*

The called and the chosen are those that have totally submitted their lives to the Lordship of Jesus Christ. This is every believer's mandate and the Rock foundation of doctrine that we are commanded to build our lives of service upon.

This basic foundational truth is the first requirement to becoming one of the faithful overcomers that are still standing when (not if) the storms of life come to rage against us all.

Please hear the words of our Lord as He gives us the synopsis of His longest and most famous discourse of all time, the sermon on the Mount.

Therefore whosoever heareth these sayings of mine, and doeth them, I will liken him unto a wise man, which built his house upon a rock: And the rain descended, and the floods came, and the winds blew, and beat upon that house; and it fell not: for it was founded upon a rock. And every one that heareth these sayings of Mine, and doeth them not, shall be likened unto a foolish man, which built his house upon the sand: And the rains descended, and the floods came, and the winds blew, and beat upon that house; and it fell: and great was the fall of it.

And it came to pass, when Jesus had ended these sayings, the people were astonished at His doctrine: For He taught them as one having authority, and not as the scribes. Matthew 7:24-29 KJV

The storms come to every house, but the only one left standing is built on the Rock.

The late Smith Wigglesworth, man of God (1859-1947) had brilliantly summed-up the faithful life of the overcomer this way–*Great faith is the product of great fights. Great testimonies are the outcome of great tests, and great triumphs can only come out of great trials.*

These shall make war with the Lamb, and the Lamb shall overcome them: for He is Lord of lords, and King of kings: and they that are with Him are called, and chosen, and faithful. Revelation 17:14 KJV

We can clearly see here that the only ones with King Jesus are the called, and the chosen, and the faithful.

The called, the chosen, and the faithful are the overcomer's.

Chapter twelve

God is Good and Just.

Foundational Truth: Our heavenly Father is good all the time, and He is also just all the time, therefore; there will be consequences for our poor choices and our sustained unrepentant disobedience and rebellious attitudes.

Folks, this foundation stone of Truth is not a new concept. This principle has been well established throughout the whole counsel of God, even beginning with the very first dysfunctional family.

And Adam knew Eve as his wife, and she became pregnant and bore Cain; and she said, I have gotten and gained a man with the help of the Lord. And [next] she gave birth to his brother Abel. Now Abel was a keeper of sheep, but Cain was a tiller of the ground. And in the course of time Cain brought to the Lord an offering of the fruit of the ground. And

Abel brought of the firstborn of his flock and of the fat portions. And the Lord had respect and regard for Abel and for his offering, but for Cain and his offering He had no respect or regard. So Cain was exceedingly angry and indignant, and he looked sad and depressed. And the Lord said to Cain, Why are you angry? And why do you look sad and depressed and dejected? If you do well, will you not be accepted? And if you do not do well, sin crouches at your door; its desire is for you, but you must master it. Genesis 4:1-7 AMPC

The Lord God Almighty spoke to Cain and said, why are you having this emotional meltdown as if you have been treated unjustly? I am God and you are not, therefore; I determine what is good and acceptable. If you chose to do what is right you will be accepted, but; if you choose to do what is not right you will be in sin. Sin is your enemy and that sin will overwhelm you and take you out unless you learn to master your emotions and overcome it.

It would have been wise for Cain to say, Yes Lord, Your ways are right, and You are good and just. Please teach me Your ways so I won't offend You. But, that is not what he did. Instead, Cain decided the obvious answer here was to kill his brother. Cain's pride and self-ambition controlled his actions and every one of us would do well to remember this Truth every time we are about to have a selfish emotional meltdown. Are we not behaving just like rebellious Cain?

Our heavenly Father's heart is always open to redemption and restoration of fellowship.

Come now, and let us reason together, says the Lord. Though your sins are like scarlet, they shall be as white as snow; though they are like red crimson, they shall be like wool. If you are willing and obedient, you shall eat the good of the land; but if you refuse and rebel, you will be devoured by the sword. For the mouth of the Lord has spoken it. Isaiah 1:18-20 AMPC

I, even I, am He who blots out your transgressions for My own sake, and will not remember your sins. Put Me in remembrance; let us plead together; state your cause, that you may be justified. Isaiah 43:25-26 MEV

The overcoming life is the narrow path. The narrow path leads to the narrow gate which is the entrance into real peace now and ultimately the Kingdom of God.

Behold then the kindness and severity of God; to those who fell, severity, but to you, God's kindness, if you continue in His kindness; otherwise you also will be cut off. Romans 11:22 NASB

We must always consider the balance between the kindness and the severity of God. The narrow path and gate that leads to the overcoming life is between these two ditches.

Many preachers and teachers today want to declare that we are in the age of grace and that we can live however we so choose, and God's amazing grace is sufficient to cover it all. Well, that is partially true. God's amazing grace was manifest in His Son on this earth and His sacrifice and shed blood is more than enough to wash away and atone for every sin – past, present, and future. Amen. However, we must also consider God's impartial justice.

One of the favorite verses in the Bible for these super-grace preachers is *"it's the goodness of God that leads men to repentance"* and that is a fraction of one verse of Scripture, however; they almost always quote this partial verse out of its context of defining the guilt of mankind and the righteous and impartial judgement of God. We have the entire verse within the context of the passage of Scripture where it is written, and we have included forthwith.

For I am not ashamed of the gospel, for it is the power of God for salvation to everyone who believes, to the Jew first and also the Greek. For in it the righteousness of God is revealed from faith to faith; as it is written, But the righteous man shall live by faith. For the wrath of God is revealed from heaven against all ungodliness and unrighteousness of men who suppress the truth in unrighteousness, because that which is known about God is evident within them; for God made it evident to them. For since the creation of the world His invisible attributes, His eternal power and divine nature, have been clearly seen, being understood through what has been made, so that they are without excuse. For even though they knew God, they did not honor Him as God or give thanks, but they became futile in their speculations, and their foolish heart was darkened. Professing to be wise, they became fools, and exchanging the glory of the incorruptible God for an image in the form of corruptible man and of birds and four-footed animals and crawling creatures.

Therefore God gave them over to the lusts of their hearts to impurity, so that their bodies would be dishonored among them. For they exchanged the truth of God for a lie, and worshiped and served the creature rather than the Creator, who is blessed forever. Amen. For this reason God gave them over to degrading passions; for their women exchanged the natural function for that which is unnatural, and in the same way also the men abandoned the natural function of the women and burned in their desire toward one another, men with men committing indecent acts and receiving in their own persons the due penalty of their error. And just as they did not see fit to acknowledge God any longer, God gave them over to a depraved mind, to do those things which are not proper, being filled with all unrighteousness, wickedness, greed, evil; full of envy, murder, strife, deceit, malice; they are gossips, slanderers, haters of God, insolent, arrogant, boastful, inventors of evil, disobedient to parents, without understanding, un trustworthy, unloving, unmerciful; and although they know the ordinance of God, that those who practice such things are worthy of death, they not only do the same, but also give hearty approval to those who practice them.

Therefore you have no excuse, everyone of you who passes judgement, for in that which you judge another, you condemn; for you who judge practice the same things. And we know that the judgement of God rightly falls upon those who practice such things. But do you suppose this, O man, when you pass judgement on those who practice such things and do the same yourself, that you will escape the judgement of God? Or do you think lightly of the riches of His kindness and tolerance and patience, not knowing that *the kindness of God leads you to repentance*? But because of your stubbornness and unrepentant heart you are storing up wrath for yourself in the day of wrath and revelation of the righteous judgement of God, who will render to each person according to his deeds: to those by perseverance in doing good seek for glory and honor and immortality, eternal life; but to those who are selfishly ambitious and do not obey the truth, but obey unrighteousness, wrath and indignation. There will be tribulation and distress for every soul of man who does evil, of the Jew first and also the Greek, but glory and honor and peace to everyone who does good, to the Jew first and also the Greek. For there is no partiality with God. Romans 1:16–2:11 NASB

We all were depraved sinners in desperate need of a Savior and we had no standing to judge anyone else, and it was the great grace, mercy, and sacrifice of Jesus Christ that caused us all to turn from our wicked ways and put our trust in Him, and by that amazing gift of grace we were all saved through faith in what Jesus did for mankind on the cross. But,

Jesus didn't save us, so we could then live any way that seems right to us. No, Jesus suffered and died to become both our Savior and Lord, and very soon He will be returning to this earth as Judge and King. We need to be clear on this—sin is not okay, and it will cost you.

Many pulpits in the churches today have preached and taught the grace message to the point that many people do not even know what sin and iniquity are anymore, thus; the Church is full of carnality, worldliness, and ungodliness.

The Holy Scriptures are a progressive revelation of God Almighty and His ways, so; let's now join Moses as he is leading God's people out from bondage to the promised land, and we will see that Father God's message is consistent and unwavering from Genesis to Revelation.

And the Lord descended in the cloud and stood with him there and proclaimed the name of the Lord. And the Lord passed by before him, and proclaimed, The Lord! The Lord! a God merciful and gracious, slow to anger, and abundant in loving-kindness and truth, keeping mercy and loving-kindness for thousands, forgiving iniquity and transgressions and sin, but Who will by no means clear the guilty, visiting the iniquity of the fathers upon the children and the children's children, to the third and fourth generation. Exodus 34:5-7 AMPC

You shall not bow down yourself to them or serve them; for I the Lord your God am a jealous God, visiting the iniquity of the fathers upon the children to the third and fourth generation of *those that hate Me*, but showing mercy and steadfast love to a thousand generations of those who love Me and keep My commandments. Exodus 20:5-6 AMPC

The Lord is long-suffering and slow to anger, and abundant in mercy and loving -kindness, forgiving iniquity and transgression; but He will by no means clear the guilty, visiting the iniquity of the fathers upon the children, upon the third and fourth generation. Numbers 14:18 AMPC

You shall have no other gods before Me or besides Me. You shall not make for yourself [to worship] a graven image or any likeness of anything that is in the heavens above of that is in the earth beneath or that is in the water under the earth. You shall not bow down to them or serve them; for I, the Lord your God, am a jealous God, visiting the iniquity of the fathers upon the children to the third and fourth generations of *those who hate Me*, and showing mercy and steadfast love to thousands and to a thousand generations of those who love Me and keep My commandments. Deuteronomy 5:7-10 AMPC

You shall perish among the nations; the land of your enemies shall eat you up. And those of you who are left shall pine away in their iniquity in your enemies' lands; also in the iniquities of their fathers shall they pine away like them. Leviticus 26:38-39 AMPC

Wow, God Almighty is making this principle quite clear that unrepented sins, transgressions, and iniquities will undoubtedly be a growing problem for each subsequent generation if it is not dealt with, but; eventually judgement will come to those that choose to hate God and His ways.

Let us be very clear, and please understand that our good, good Father is not saying that He is punishing each subsequent generation. Instead, the Lord is forewarning us of the consequences for our sin if it is not acknowledged and repented of, turned from, and put out of our lives.

But if they confess their own and their fathers' iniquity in their treachery which they committed against Me – and also that because they walked contrary to Me I also walked contrary to them and brought them into the land of their enemies – if then their uncircumcised hearts are humbled and they then accept the punishment for their iniquity, then will I [earnestly] remember My covenant with Jacob, My covenant with Isaac, and My covenant with Abraham, and [earnestly] remember the land. Leviticus 26:40-42 AMPC

The fathers shall not be put to death for the children, neither shall the children be put to death for the fathers; only for his own sin shall anyone be put to death. Deuteronomy 24:16 AMPC

As soon as the kingdom was established in Amaziah's hand, he slew his servants who had slain the king his father. But he did not slay the children of the murderers, in compliance with what is written in the Book of the Law of Moses, in which the Lord commanded, The fathers shall not be put to death for the children, nor the children for the fathers; but every man shall die for his own sin only. II Kings 14:5-6 AMPC

In those days they shall say no more, The fathers have eaten sour grapes, and the children's teeth are set on edge. But everyone shall die for his own iniquity [only]; every man who eats sour grapes – his [own] teeth shall be set on edge. Jeremiah 31:29-30 AMPC

Behold, all souls are Mine; as the soul of the father, so also the soul of the son is Mine; the soul that sins, it shall die. Ezekiel 18:4 AMPC

The soul that sins, it [is the one that] shall die. The son shall not bear and be punished for the iniquity of the father, neither shall the father bear and be punished for the iniquity of the son; the righteousness of the righteous shall be upon him only, and the wickedness of the wicked shall be upon the wicked only. Ezekiel 18:20 AMPC

Have I any pleasure in the death of the wicked? Says the Lord, and not rather that he should turn from his evil way and return [to his God] and live? Ezekiel 18:23 AMPC

Therefore I will judge you, O house of Israel, every one according to his ways, says the Lord God. Repent and turn from all your transgressions, lest iniquity be your ruin and so shall they not be a stumbling block to you. Cast away from you all your transgressions by which you have transgressed against Me, and make you a new mind and heart and a new spirit. For why will you die, O house of Israel? For I have no pleasure in the death of him who dies, says the Lord God. Therefore turn (be converted) and live! Ezekiel 18:30-32 AMPC

Father God's message has always been the same since Adam and Eve and Cain and Abel and shall never change. If you have sinned against the Lord, you must humble yourself and confess your sin, repent, and live.

But now since you have been set free from sin and have become slaves of God, you have your present reward in holiness and its end is eternal life. For the wages which sin pays is death, but the [bountiful] free gift of God is eternal life through (in union with) Jesus Christ our Lord. Romans 6:22-23 AMPC

Our astonishingly good heavenly Father has extended grace and mercy to literally multiplied millions of grumbling, complaining, fearful, faithless, obstinate, knot-heads – even after He performed some of the most incredibly awesome displays of His power, protection, and provision ever known in the history of mankind before these stiff-necked doubters.

Consider the interceding and meek Moses:

In Exodus chapter twenty-three the Hebrews were camped at Mount Horeb and God is giving the Torah to Moses. Father God tells Moses that He is going to send an angel with them into the wilderness to protect them and to lead them to the place God had prepared for Israel.

Indeed, I am going to send an angel before you to guard you along the way and to bring you into a place which I have prepared. Be on guard before him and obey his voice. Do not provoke him, for he will not pardon your transgressions, for My name is in him. But if you diligently obey his voice and do all that I say, then I will be an enemy to your enemies and an adversary to your adversaries. Exodus 23:20-22 MEV

Then while Moses and Joshua were meeting with God on the mountain, the people become restless and impatience and made themselves an idol demigod and were making plans to go backwards and return to Egypt. (Exodus 32) Moses intercedes on behalf of the people and God doesn't release His wrath on the multitude, however; three thousand leaders of the insurrection were killed.

Then God tells Moses again to depart for the promised land, but; He is not going to be dwelling with them, but; as God had said before He would send an angel to lead them and protect them.

Then the Lord said to Moses, Depart, go up from here, you and the people whom you have brought up from the land of Egypt, to the land which I swore to Abraham, Isaac, and Jacob, saying, To your descendants I will give it. I will send an angel before you, and I will drive out the Canaanite, the Amorite, the Hittite, the Perizzite, the Hivite, and the Jebusite. Go up to a land flowing with milk and honey. However, I will not go up in your midst, for you are a stiff-necked people, and I might destroy you on the way. Exodus 33:1-3 MEV

But you see, Moses believed everything God had told him because Moses was spending time with God and was building a relationship with the Lord.

The Lord spoke to Moses face to face, just as a man speaks to his friend.... Exodus 33:11a MEV

Moses knew that the only hope of survival was for the Holy Presence of Father God to go with them because God had told Moses that the angel that He would send *would not pardon their transgressions*, and Moses wisely had absolutely no faith in these people not to sin. Nevertheless; Moses did trust the Lord and he believed that the Lord is good, and His mercy endures forevermore.

Therefore, Moses said to the Lord, if You aren't going with us, I'm not going either because our only hope is in your Presence.

And He said, My Presence will go with you, and I will give you rest. Then he said to Him, If Your

Presence does not go with us, do not bring us up from here. Exodus 33:14-15 MEV

Then Moses said, I pray, show me Your glory. Then He said, I will make all My goodness pass before you, and I will proclaim the name of the Lord before you. I will be gracious to whom I will be gracious and will show mercy on whom I will show mercy. Exodus 33:18-19 MEV

The Lord God Almighty instructed His friend Moses to come to the top of the mountain the next morning and God would write on two new tablets of stone, replacing the first two that were broken, and then Almighty God would hide him in the cleft of the rock as He would allow all His glory and goodness to pass by as He covered Moses with His mighty hand, declaring Who He is! Wow!

The Lord passed by before him, and proclaimed, The Lord, the Lord God, merciful and gracious, slow to anger, and abounding in goodness and truth, keeping mercy for thousands, forgiving iniquity and transgression and sin, but who will by no means clear the guilty, visiting the iniquity of the fathers on the children and on the children's children, to the third and fourth generation. Exodus 34:6-7 MEV

Moses made haste and bowed to the ground and worshipped. He said, If now I have found favor in Your sight, O Lord, let my Lord, I pray, go among us, for we are a stiff-necked people. Pardon our iniquity and our sin, and take us for your inheritance. Exodus 34:8-9 MEV

Then He said: Indeed, I am going to make a covenant before all your people. I will do wonders such as have not been done in all the earth nor any nation. And all the people among whom you live will see the work of the Lord, for it is a fearful thing that I will do with you. Exodus 34:10 MEV

The Lord God Almighty caused all His goodness and glory to pass before Moses as he was there in a cave on Mount Horeb and the Lord allowed Moses to see Jesus Christ in His manifest glory, and Elijah was there too! (I Kings 19:1-12 same cave on the same mountain)

Now about eight days after these teachings, Jesus took with Him Peter and John and James and went up on the mountain to pray And as He was praying, the appearance of His countenance became altered (different), and His raiment became dazzling white [flashing with the brilliance of lighting]. And behold, two men were conversing with Him – Moses and Elijah,

He was about to bring to realization at Jerusalem.
Now Peter and those with him were weighted down
with sleep, but when they fully awoke, they saw His
glory (splendor and majesty and brightness) and the
two men who stood with Him. Luke 9:28-32 AMPC
(study II Peter 1:16-21)

Behold, we must grasp the revelation that the
glory and goodness and the grace of Father God is
Jesus Christ, the Lord of glory.

And the Word (Christ) became flesh (human,
incarnate) and tabernacled (fixed His tent of flesh,
lived awhile) among us; and we [actually] saw His
glory (His honor, His majesty), such glory as an only
begotten son receives from his father, full of grace
(favor, loving-kindness) and truth. John 1:14 AMPC

And now, O Father, glorify Me in Your own presence with the glory which I had with You before the
world existed. John 17:5 MEV

And he answered, Brethren and fathers, listen
to me! The God of glory appeared to our forefather
Abraham when he was still in Mesopotamia, before
he [went to] live in Haran, Acts 7:2 AMPC

None of the rulers of this age or world perceived and recognized and understood this, for if they had, they would never have crucified the Lord of glory. I Corinthians 2:8 AMPC

He is the sole expression of the glory of God (the Light-being, the out-raying or radiance of the divine], and He is the perfect imprint and very image of [God's] nature, upholding and maintaining and guiding and propelling the universe by His mighty word of power. When He had by offering Himself accomplished our cleansing of sins and riddance of guilt, He sat down at the right hand of the divine Majesty on high. Hebrews 1:3 AMPC

This event was one of the prophetic patterns foreshadowing the advent of Jesus Christ our Savior and Lord of glory coming to dwell in the midst of His people, and to establish a new covenant, thus; paying the ransom price to pardon our sin debt for all our iniquities, transgressions, and depravity – and to lead us to our promised land as overcomers. The goodness and grace of God is the Presence of God among His people.

Consider the Canaanite prostitute Rahab:

Going all the way back to Noah and his sons Shem, Ham, and Japheth and the prophetic proclamation that Noah declared over Canaan that he would be cursed, which means dedicated to destruction; and then consider the more than four generations (over five hundred years) that had followed all had the opportunity to repent of their evil ways and turn back to God, but; they did not.

Now these unrepentant descendants of Canaan, which are the occupiers of Jericho, are facing the judgement of God Almighty. We know that Joshua sends two spies (one from the tribe of Judah and one from the tribe of Ephraim) into the city and they encounter Rahab the Canaanite prostitute, and she literally risks her home, business, family and her life when she lies to the king of Jericho to protect the Hebrew spies hiding at her house. Why?

Faith in the God of Israel!

So then faith comes by hearing, and hearing by the word of God. Romans 10:17 MEV

Before the spies went to sleep, Rahab went up to them on the roof. She said to the men, I *know* that the Lord has given you the land, for dread from you has fallen upon us, and all the inhabitants of the land melt in terror before you. For we *heard* how the Lord dried up the waters of the Red Sea before you when you came out of Egypt, and what you did to Sihon and Og, the two kings of the Amorites who were on the other side of the Jordan, whom you completely destroyed. Our hearts melted when we *heard* these things, and no man had any breath in him because of you, for the Lord your God Is God in heaven above and on earth below. So now, since I have acted faithfully toward you, please swear to me by the Lord that you will also act faithfully toward my father's house. Joshua 2:8-12 MEV

Rahab (which means *to make courageous*) broke the Canaanite *generational curse* off her life and off her entire family that day by her genuine faith in the One true living and awesome God that she had *heard* about and put a stained blood-red scarlet cord out the window of her house and waited for their salvation from sure and utter destruction.

Every single person in the land from their progenitor Canaan forward had the very same opportunity to wake-up and realize their plan was not working and humble themselves and repent and turn from their evil ways and return to the Lord.

For, Everyone who calls on the name of the Lord shall be saved. Romans 10:13 MEV

Because of faith the walls of Jericho fell down after they had been encompassed for seven days [by

Israelites]. [Prompted] by faith Rahab the prostitute was not destroyed along with those who refused to believe and obey, because she had received the spies in peace [without enmity]. Hebrews 11:30-31 AMPC

Likewise, was not Rahab the prostitute justified by works when she received the messengers and sent them out another way? James 2:25 MEV

Bottom line: You can claim to love the Lord, but; your actions and how you live tell the real story of your faith life and your devotion to Jesus and His Word.

Wow, what is really incredible about this story is that Rahab ends-up married to one of the two spies that she protected that faithful night. (Joshua 6:17-25) Those same spies had given their word that she and her father's household would be saved from the forthcoming utter destruction and they went in and personally saved her and everyone that was within her household.

And the spy from the tribe of Judah named Salmon takes Rahab as his bride, who becomes the mother of Boaz, who no doubt must have been taught by his mother that it is okay to take a Gentile bride.

Salmon was the father of Boaz by Rahab, Boaz the father of Obed by Ruth, and Obed the father of Jesse. Jesse was the father of David the king. Matthew 1:5-6 MEV

Of course, we all know that the long-promised Messiah of the world would be the son of David from the tribe of Judah.

But the angel said to her, Do not be afraid, Mary, for you have found favor with God. Listen, you will conceive in your womb and bear a Son and shall call His name JESUS. He will be great, and will be called the Son of the Highest. And the Lord God will give Him the throne of His father David, and He will reign over the house of Jacob forever. And of His kingdom there will be no end. Luke 1:30-33 MEV

Rahab was from the accursed family of the sexual deviant Canaanites, but; by grace she was saved through faith, and now is forever known as the great-great grandmother of king David and of the linage of the Messiah. Wow, that is awesome.

We serve a good, good Father and you can trust Him.

Our loving and merciful heavenly Father has even forgiven many of the rebellious kings throughout the history of Israel and Judah. The rebellious kings that were forgiven were the ones that realized the error of their ways and they humbled themselves, repented of their sins, iniquities, omissions, and transgressions, and asked the Lord to forgive them.

Consider the enduring oracle that God Almighty spoke to King Solomon:

If My people, who are called by My name will humble themselves and pray, and seek My face and turn from their wicked ways, then I will hear from heaven, and will forgive their sin and will heal their land. II Chronicles 7:14 MEV

Here in the book of James is the New Testament version of these very same thoughts, precepts, and commands:

You adulterers and adulteresses, do you not know that friendship with the world is enmity with God? Whoever therefore will be a friend of the world is the enemy of God. Do you think the Scripture says in vain, He yearns jealously for the spirit that lives in us? But He gives more grace. For this reason it says: God resists the proud, but gives grace to the humble. Therefore *submit yourselves* to God. *Resist* the devil, and he will flee from you. Draw near to God, and He will draw near to you. *Cleanse your hands*, you sinners, and *purify your hearts*, you double-minded. Grieve and mourn and weep. Let your laughter be turned to mourning, and your joy to dejection. *Humble yourselves* in the sight of the Lord, and He will lift you up. James 4:4-10 MEV

Consider young and impetuous King Rehoboam:

Now when the reign of Rehoboam was established and strong, he, and all of Israel with him, abandoned the law of the Lord. And in the fifth year of King Rehoboam, Shishak king of Egypt went up against Jerusalem for they had acted unfaithfully against the Lord. II Chronicles 12:1-2 MEV

There's some good thinking Rehoboam. God has just divided the kingdom because of the unfaithfulness of your father Solomon and his lack of obedience to the Word, yet God Almighty establishes you and you think you did it, and you become lifted-up in haughty pride, and then you think you don't need God anymore.

And when he humbled himself, the anger of the Lord turned away from him so that there was not complete annihilation. Moreover, there were some good things in Judah during this time. II Chronicles 12:12 MEV

Consider old, arrogant, and angry King Asa:

Asa did what was good and right in the eyes of the Lord his God. He took down the foreign altars and high places, and he shattered the pillars and cut down the images of Asherah. Then he urged Judah to seek the Lord the God of their fathers and to keep the law and commandments. II Chronicles 14:2-4 MEV

But in the thirty-sixth year of the reign of Asa, Baasha king of Israel went up against Judah and built Ramah and did not allow anyone to come in or go out to Asa king of Judah. II Chronicles 16:1 MEV

Then Asa removed silver and gold from the storehouses of the house of the Lord and palace of the king, and he sent it to Ben-Hadad king of Aram in Syria, who lived in Damascus, saying, There is a covenant between me and you as between my father and your father. I am sending you silver and gold. Go and break your covenant with Baasha king of Israel so that he might leave me. II Chronicles 16:2-3 MEV

Then Asa took *all* the silver and the gold that were left in the treasures of the house of the Lord, as well as the treasures of the king's house, and delivered them into the hand of his servants, and sent them to Ben-Hadad, I Kings 15:18a MEV

Asa took all the money from God Almighty's temple treasury and from the royal treasury and bribed a nasty foreign king to corrupt himself and come against an aggressor that was threatening the sovereignty of Judah, and Asa's plan worked, so he thought.

However, Asa now had a much more momentous problem. Asa did not trust Father God to solve his problem, and instead; he put his trust in an unscrupulous foreign king that it's obvious his covenants are meaningless. If that wasn't stupid enough, he also wasted all the combined resources of the Lord's that was stored-up for future generations for the repair, maintenance, and operations of the temple and the palace.

Arrogant, self-ambitious, and faithless Asa had lived and reigned in peace for thirty-five years before this mess, and apparently, he must have begun to think and believe that it was his prowess, ingenuity, and extraordinary leadership strategies that had caused the kingdom of Judah to prosper, but; he didn't seem to recall the astounding victory the Lord had given him twenty-five years earlier over a world super-power.

It is difficult to imagine, but; the Lord had defeated the single largest recorded military operation in the Hebrew Scriptures for Asa and the people of Judah, when the Cushite's came against Asa and God's covenant people.

But Zerah the Ethiopian Cushite came out against them with an army of a million men and three hundred chariots. II Chronicles 14:9 MEV

And Asa cried out to the Lord his God, and said, Lord, it is nothing with You to help, whether with many or with those who have no power. Help us, O Lord our God; for we trust in You, and in Your name we come against this multitude. O Lord, You are our God. Let no man prevail against You. II Chronicles 14:11 MEV

Okay, so what do you think happened when Asa and these faith-filled people that had been living in obedience to the Lord and His Word put their complete confidence and trust in Him as their deliverer? What happened here is exactly what will happen now for you and me when we place our faith in our living Savior and Lord Jesus Christ and live in obedience to His Word and walk in His ways–Total victory! Amen.

So the Lord struck down the Ethiopian Cushites before Asa and Judah, and the Cushites fled. Then Asa and those with him pursued them until Gerar. And the Cushites fell till there was *not one left alive* because they were struck down before the Lord and His army. And those in Judah carried off a very great plunder. II Chronicles 14:12-13 MEV

One million armed Cushite combatants died in this one battle. Wow, that is incredible. This overwhelming victory on the battlefield is a larger number of combat deaths than all the collective total combat deaths of U.S. soldiers in every war fought by Americans including the Revolutionary War, Civil War, War of 1812, Mexican-American War, WW I, WW II, Korean War, Vietnam War, Iraq War, and the War in Afghanistan combined.

Please take notice here of the fact (Genesis 10:6-8) that Cush was the son of Ham thus the brother of Canaan and he was also the father of Nimrod.

Well, let's go back now to arrogant Asa. His situation had even grown worse because God Almighty sent His prophet to speak to Asa and to bring correction, nevertheless; king Asa wasn't receiving the man of God either.

And at that time Hanani the seer came to King Asa of Judah saying, Because you depended on the king of Aram and did not depend on the Lord your God, therefore the army of the king of Aram escaped from your hand. Were not the Cushites and the Libyans a very large army with chariots and horses, but when you depended on the Lord, He gave them to your hand. For the eyes of the Lord move about on all the earth to strengthen the heart that is completely toward Him. You have acted foolishly in this, and from this point forward you will have wars. II Chronicles 16:7-9 MEV

Then Asa was angry with the seer and placed him in prison stocks, for he was enraged by these words. Asa even oppressed some of the people during this time. II Chronicles 16:10 MEV

In the thirty-ninth year of the reign of Asa, he had a sickness in his feet until his sickness became grave. Even in his disease he did not seek after the Lord, but the physicians. So Asa slept with his fathers; he died in the forty-first year of his reign II Chronicles 16:12-13 MEV

Father God would have defended Asa and His people again and again. And based on the goodness and mercy of our God, we believe that if Asa would have humbled himself when the Lord sent His prophet to deliver this message of correction after Asa's foolishness, we believe our good God would have seen to it that Asa would have lived his last years in peace, and the Lord would have helped Asa in his illness and healed him. It didn't have to end this way for Asa.

Consider weak-willed and wicked King Ahab:

But there were none compared to Ahab, who sold himself to evil deeds in the sight of the Lord, which Jezebel his wife stirred up. I Kings 21:25 MEV

The word of the Lord came to Elijah the Tishbite, saying, See how Ahab humbles himself before Me? Because he humbles himself before Me, I will not bring the disaster during his lifetime, but during his son's lifetime I will bring the disaster on his household. I Kings 21:28-29 MEV

Our loving and merciful heavenly Father has even forgiven and restored some of the most extremely wicked people that has ever walked this earth when they humbled themselves and repented of their evil ways and professed that the Lord God Almighty is the Master and Creator of the universe and thus LORD of all.

Consider the pagan King of Babylon – wicked Nebuchadnezzar, the man that took nearly all of Judah into captivity and destroyed the Temple of God.

That very hour the thing was [in process of] being fulfilled upon Nebuchadnezzar. He was driven from among men and did eat grass like oxen [as Daniel had said he would], and his body was wet with the dew of the heavens until his hair grew like eagles' [feathers] and his nails [were] like birds' [claws]. Daniel 4:33 AMPC

And at the end of the days [seven years], I, Nebuchadnezzar, lifted my eyes to heaven, and my understanding and the right use of my mind returned to me; and I blessed the Most High [God] and I praised Him and honored and glorified Him Who lives forever, Whose dominion is an everlasting dominion; and His kingdom endures from generation to generation. And all the inhabitants of the earth are accounted as nothing. And He does according to His will in the host of heaven and among the inhabitants of the earth, and none can stay His hand or say to Him, What are You doing? Daniel 4:34-35 AMPC

But after seven years of this man living like a wild animal, he humbled himself and declared our Lord as the Most High God and praised, honored, and glorified our Lord. Our incredibly awesome heavenly Father restored this man to his position and place. Wow.

Now at the same time my reason and under-standing returned to me; and for the glory of my kingdom, my majesty and splendor returned to me, and my counselors and my lords sought me out; I was reestablished in my kingdom, and still more greatness [than before] was added to me. Now I,

Nebuchadnezzar, praise and extol and honor the King of heaven, Whose works are all faithful and right and Whose ways are just. And those who walk in pride He is able to abase and humble. Daniel 4:36-37 AMPC

Consider God's missionary Jonah and the Assyrians:

The single most successful evangelist in recorded history, and he also was probably the most unenthusiastic literally fleeing in the opposite direction from his God ordained assignment.

Now the word of the Lord came to Jonah son of Amittai, saying, Get up, go to Nineveh, the great city, and cry out against it, because their wickedness has come up before Me. Jonah 1:1-2 MEV

Nineveh was the capitol city of the Assyrian empire and they were the enemies of Israel. The Assyrians have the infamous reputation of being some of the most ruthless, violent, and utterly cruel people on the planet and the first know terrorist.

Their warfare terror tactics were widely known and their treatment of those they captured and conquered went way past sadistic, such as skinning people alive or cutting a captured combatants belly open and stuffing a live wildcat inside them and stitching them back up just for sport, or piercing a captives lips with fish hooks and tying them bound to the back of a cart as they marched them back to their new home to be sold into slavery, if they survived the trail.

Just imaging being called of God to leave your home and travel alone to modern day Syria or Iraq to preach repentance to a bunch of Al Qaeda terrorists or the Lord asked you to go confront the leader of the ISIS gang in their stronghold. This is basically what Jonah was facing in his day when the Lord spoke to him and told him to go and preach to Nineveh.

But Jonah went in the opposite direction away from Nineveh, nevertheless; we know that God had prepared a plan to adjust Jonah's thinking and to deliver Jonah there anyway, although the boat would have been much easier option for Jonah.

We do not believe Jonah was a coward, we believe Jonah knew that if God was sending him to preach repentance to these people that they would probably repent, and Jonah knew if they did in-fact sincerely humble themselves and turn from their wicked ways, that our incredibly gracious and merciful God would forgive them and not bring judgement against them.

We believe that is exactly what Jonah didn't want to happen because he did not like these people and he certainly wasn't alone in his contempt for the Assyrians.

Jonah probably would have been perfectly happy to see God wipe out these wicked enemies of his family, friends, and nation.

So, a very haggard and odoriferous Jonah went into the city of one hundred and twenty thousand people and preached the "Turn or Burn" message God gave him. Here is Jonah's message recorded in its entirety. It was very short, but; it was very anointed!

Jonah began to enter the city, going a day's walk. And he cried out, *In forty days' time, Nineveh will be overthrown!* Jonah 3:4 MEV

And from this one very curt message the entire city responded from the king down to the most common resident and all repented of their evil ways. That is incredible.

So the people of Nineveh believed God, and proclaimed a fast. And everyone, great and small, put on sackcloth. Jonah 3:5 MEV

When God saw their actions, that they turned from their evil ways, He changed His mind about the disaster that He had said He would bring upon them, and He did not do it. Jonah 3:10 MEV

This is exactly what Jonah knew about his Lord – God is good, and He is full of great mercy and grace, way beyond what we can even begin to comprehend.

The men of Nineveh will appear as witnesses at the judgement with this generation and will condemn it; for they repented at the preaching of Jonah, and behold, here is more than Jonah. Luke 11:32 AMPC

The Lord has expected every generation from the very first family to the youngest generation of today to seek Him and live right no matter where you are from or what your family history might be; no exceptions and no excuses.

Our God is a good God, however; we will not always understand everything He does.

Seek, inquire for, and require the Lord while He may be found [claiming Him by necessity and by right]; call upon Him while He is near. Let the wicked forsake his way and the unrighteous man his thoughts; and let him return to the Lord, and He will have love, pity, and mercy for him, and to our God, for He will multiply to him His abundant pardon. For My thoughts are not your thoughts, neither are your ways My ways, says the Lord. For as the heavens are higher than the earth, so are My ways higher than your ways and My thoughts than your thoughts. Isaiah 55:6-9 AMPC

What shall we conclude then? Is there injustice upon God's part? Certainly not! For He says to Moses,

I will have mercy on whom I will have mercy and I will have compassion (pity) on whom I will have compassion. Romans 9:14-15 AMPC

So, what is the end of the matter? Our God is a good God and we must trust Him. We must trust in the goodness of our heavenly Father God even when we do not comprehend or immediately appreciate everything we see, our everything we hear, or everything we have read in His Word. We simply must trust and obey as quickly as we can as completely as we can everything that is grounded in our understanding and the measure of revelatory light we are walking in at that time, place, and season of our life.

Walk in the light that you have, and our good, good Father will honor your faith in Him.

For with You is the fountain of life; in Your light we see light. Psalm 36:9 MEV

Oh, the depth of the riches and wisdom and knowledge of God! How unfathomable (inscrutable, unsearchable) are His judgements (His decisions)! And how untraceable (mysterious, undiscoverable) are His ways (His methods, His paths)! For who has known the mind of the Lord and who has understood His thoughts, or who has [ever] been His counselor? Or who has first given God anything that he might be paid back or that he could claim a recompense? For from Him and through Him and to Him are all things. [For all things originate with Him and come from Him; all things live through Him, and all things center in and tend to consummate and to end in Him.] To him be glory forever! Amen (so be it). Romans 11:33-36 AMPC

The late prophet and teacher Kenneth E. Hagin would have summed it up like this: *God said it, I believe it, and that settles it.* Which means you can have absolute faith in the goodness of God even when we don't fully understand everything that is going on around us.

The conclusion, when all has been heard, is: fear God and keep His commandments, because this applies to every person. For God will bring every act to judgement, everything which is hidden, whether it is good or evil. Ecclesiastes 12:13-14 NASB

Believe in and trust the goodness and justice of our God – This is the overcomer's mandate.

CHAPTER THIRTEEN

Enter or Possess and Inherit.

Foundational Truth: Our son or daughter status is sealed at our born from above salvation, however; our inheritance and rewards are conditional based on our walk of faith and obedience to the Word of the Lord now.

As we have said repeatedly and believe we have aptly demonstrated, our heavenly Father teaches us by types, shadows, similitudes, and patterns and this important Truth is no exception. So, let's begin with the similitudes.

The nation of Israel entering the promised land and then engaging and thus overcoming the various enemy combatants inhabiting the land before they could actually possess the land and inherit their tribal portion of the conquered territory and settle down in peace, is yet another prophetic pattern to teach us the ways of God. The inheritance in the promised land is a similitude of the faithful overcomers loving the Lord by their devotion to remain separated from the things of this world and fully follow and obey Him throughout their life here during the Church age and thus receiving their place and inheritance in the Kingdom age during the one-thousand-year millennial reign of King Jesus here on this earth.

When Moses led the Hebrew children out of Egypt and to the borders of the promised land the people did not have the faith or the spiritual maturity to go in and take the land, therefore; they wandered in the wilderness for nearly forty years until this generation that was full of fear, doubt, and unbelief all perished.

Yet you were not willing to go up, but rebelled against the commandment of the Lord your God. You murmured in your tents, and said, Because the Lord hates us, He has brought us out of the land of Egypt to deliver us into the hand of the Amorites to destroy us. Deuteronomy 1:26-27 MEV

The Lord heard the sound of your words, and was angry, and vowed, saying, Not one of these men of this evil generation will see the good land which I swore to give to your fathers. Deuteronomy 1:34-35 MEV

The exception will be Caleb the son of Jephunneh. He shall see it, and to him I will give the land upon which he has walked, and to his children, because he has wholly followed the Lord. Deuteronomy 1:36 MEV

Also the Lord was angry with me on your account, saying, You also shall not go in. But Joshua the son of Nun, who stands before you, he shall go in. Encourage him, for he will cause Israel to *inherit* it. Deuteronomy 1:37-38 MEV

Of all the Hebrew people who came out of Egypt the only two who got to cross over into the promised land were Caleb from the tribe of Judah because he fully followed the Lord, and Joshua from the tribe of Ephraim, the son of Joseph, because of his obedience to the Lord, he would cause the people to inherit the land. Of course, they are both overcomers, but Caleb is a type and shadow of us and Joshua is a type and shadow of Jesus. The English name Joshua is transliteration of the Hebrew name *Yeshua*.

As we know, the children of Israel were all under God Almighty's providential care and He absolutely provided for their basic needs every day of their life.

For the Lord your God has blessed you in all the works of your hands. He knows your wanderings through this great wilderness. These forty years the

Lord your God has been with you. You have lacked for nothing. Deuteronomy 2:7 MEV

Nonetheless, they could not obey and fully trust the Lord and cross over into the land and overcome the inhabitants there thus inheriting the land of promise and dwell in goodly homes they didn't build and enjoy vineyards, gardens, and fruit trees they did not plant.

The Lord spoke to Moses in the plains of Moab by Jordan near Jericho, saying: Speak to the children of Israel, and say to them: When you are crossing over the Jordan into the land of Canaan, then you will drive out all the inhabitants of the land from before you, and destroy all their carved images, and destroy all their molded images, and destroy all their high places, and you will drive out the inhabitants of the land and dwell in it, because I have given you the land to *inherit* it. You will possess the land by lot for an *inheritance* among your families, and to the larger you will give the larger *inheritance*, and to the smaller you will give the smaller *inheritance*. Every man's *inheritance* will be in the place where his lot falls. By the tribes of your fathers you will *inherit*. Numbers 33:50-54 MEV

But **if** you do not drive out the inhabitants of the land from before you, then those whom you let remain will be like thorns in your eyes and thorns in your sides. They will show hostility to you in the land in which you live. And what I had planned to do to them, I will do to you. Numbers 33:55-56 MEV

But God established requirements for them to cross over and enter (born-again) the promised land and then to overcome those dwelling there, to take possession of the land and therefore inherit the land. If Joshua and the children of Israel just remained in the camp at Gilgal and didn't break camp and did not go any further, do you think they would have been successful in overcoming, possessing, and inheriting the land beyond where they settled? Well of course not. They had to get up and go confront the Canaanite tribes and overcome them before they could take possession of and inherit any additional territory.

You must love the Lord your God and keep His charge, His statutes, His ordinances, and His com-mandments always. Deuteronomy 11:1 MEV

Therefore you must keep all the commandments which I am commanding you today, so that you may be strong and go in and possess the land which you are going to possess; and that you may prolong your days in the land which the Lord swore to your fathers to give to them and to their descendants, a land flowing with milk and honey. Deuteronomy 11:8-9 MEV

For **if** you diligently keep all these commandments which I am commanding you to do – to love the Lord your God, to walk in all His ways, and to hold fast to Him – then the Lord will drive out all these nations from before you, and you will dispossess nations greater and mightier than you. Deuteronomy 11:22-23 MEV

As we know the Book of Joshua is all about the children of Israel conquering and overcoming the giants and the various tribal clans inhabiting the promised land. It was God's command that they do this and fully possess and thus inherit all the land, however; they were not completely successful and not all the tribes of Israel were overcomers with the same level of zeal.

It is interesting that the three areas that Joshua and the Israelites did not overcome and take possession of are commonly known today by the names of Gaza Strip, West Bank, and the Golan Heights.

We hope that if you have gotten this far in our study that you have received the revelation of the fact that everyone that is born again is most definitely a child of God and they have entered Father God's family, but; that does not mean that all of God's children will automatically become overcomers, even though that would be the Father's will for all His children.

Jesus Christ received a visit one night from one of Israel's foremost authorities on the Scriptures and Jesus began their conversation with first things first.

Jesus answered him, Truly, truly I say to you, unless a man is born again, he cannot *see* the kingdom of God. Nicodemus said to Him, How can a man be born when he is old? Can he enter a second time into his mother's womb and be born? Jesus answered, Truly, truly I say to you, unless a man is born of water and the Spirit, he cannot *enter* the kingdom of God. John 3:3-5 MEV

When our spirit-man is renewed and born again, we then at that point enter the family of God, but; we do not possess our inheritance yet.

But when the fullness of time came, God sent forth His Son, born of a woman, born under the law, to redeem those who were under the law, that we might receive the adoption as sons. And because you are sons, God has sent forth into our hearts the Spirit of His Son, crying, Abba, Father! Therefore you are no longer a servant, but a son, and if a son, then an heir of God through Christ. Galatians 4:4-7 MEV

The day any one of us were born naturally we were a legal son or daughter and an heir of our parents and their property, assets, and liabilities. However, your parents did not transfer the possession of your inheritance of their estate to you.

No, what would ultimately be done with their estate would be determined at some future date based on what you did or did not do as you grew-up and matured. After you submitted to the process of being trained, taught, and prepared to be a good steward of the family business, then your faithfulness would be rewarded by granting you the right to then take your place as a leader in your family and receive possession of your inheritance.

But God, being rich in mercy, because of His great love with which He loved us, even when we were dead in sins, made us alive together with Christ (by grace you have been saved), and He raised us up and seated us together in the heavenly places in Christ Jesus, so that in the coming ages He might show the surpassing riches of His grace and kindness toward us in Christ Jesus. For by grace you have been saved through faith, and this is not of yourselves. It is the gift of God, not of works, so that no one should boast. For we are His workmanship, created in Christ Jesus for good works, which God prepared beforehand, so that we should walk in them. Ephesians 2:4-10 MEV

We know that we have absolutely nothing to do with our (past tense) justification which is described here in these two awesome passaged of Scripture. We are children of God and we are positionally seated with Christ and we have been saved by our faith in the free gift of grace that was made possible by Jesus' finished work on the cross.

All of this is the gift of God that we did not and could earn. It is true that we entered the family of God and became a legal heir and co-heir with Jesus Christ the very moment we were born from above, or saved, or born again; whatever expression you might prefer that describes the miracle performed by the Author of Life converting our old dying sin nature into our newly created spirit-man being resurrected from death, darkness, and sin.

We learned in *The Believer's Mandate* that it is the will of the Father that every one of His children would be fully transformed into the image of Jesus Christ, nevertheless; we know this is not a reality in the present world because Jesus Himself told us that only the few would walk the narrow path and ultimately go through the narrow gate.

Please take note of the fact that the inheritance and rewards being referred to here in the following Scriptures has been stored-up for the sanctified overcomers that have sincerely loved the Lord during the Church age.

And now [brethren], I commit you to God [I deposit you in His charge, entrusting you to His protection and care]. And I commend you to the Word of His grace [to the commands and counsels and promises of His unmerited favor]. It is able to build you up and to give you [your rightful] *inheritance* among all God's set-apart ones (those consecrated, purified, and transformed of soul). Acts 20:32 AMPC

The inheritance in the kingdom is for those genuine faithful overcomers that have yielded to the work of Holy Spirit as they become sanctified during this present age of grace. How did they become sanctified?

Sanctify them by Your truth. Your word is truth. As you sent Me into the world, so I sent them into the world. For their sakes I sanctify Myself, that they also may be sanctified by the truth. John 17:17-19 MEV

Listen, my beloved brethren: Has not God chosen those who are poor in the eyes of the world to be rich in faith and in their position as believers and to inherit the kingdom which He has promised to those who love Him? James 2:5 AMPC

And those that love the Lord Jesus will inherit the Kingdom, and Jesus told us who it is that truly loves Him.

Jesus answered him, If a man love Me, he will keep My word. My Father will love him, and We will come to him, and make Our home with him. He who does not love Me does not keep My words. The word which you hear is not Mine, but the Father's who sent Me. John 14:23-24 MEV

Those believer's that have become sanctified by being doers of the word and through their love for Jesus have become transformed into the overcomers that will possess and inherit the Kingdom. Simply stated those that trust, obey, and follow Jesus fully are the overcomers.

So, are these overcomers flawless super-saints? No, but when they have sinned they confess their sin and repent of their sin and get restored and back under the favor and grace of the Father. Some refer to this as "keeping short accounts" with the Lord. So, to say this another way when our conscience, which is the voice of our spirit, convicts us of our wrong-doing, we are quick to humble ourselves, confess it, repent, and get back in good graces with the Lord.

If we say that we have no sin, we deceive our-selves, and the truth is not in us. If we confess our sins, He is faithful and just to forgive us our sins and cleanse us from all unrighteousness. I John 1:8-9 MEV

By this we know that we know Him, if we keep His commandments. Whoever says, I know Him, and does not keep His commandments is a liar, and the truth is not in him. But whoever keeps His word truly has the love of God perfected in Him. Whoever says he remains in Him ought to walk as He walked. I John 2:3-6 MEV

Here is the bottom line, if you are *not* born again, you will *not* enter the Kingdom of God and your spirit and soul will be forever separated from the Lord because you are already judged and sentenced to eternal torment in the lake of fire forever, and you have made that free will choice.

Anyone whose name was not found written in the Book of Life was cast into the lake of fire. Revelation 20:15 MEV

Or, if you are born again (Your name is in the Book of Life) nevertheless you are *not* living in submission to the Lord and are living your life your way and thus living a lifestyle of unrepentant sin, then when your body dies, you will *enter* the Kingdom of God, however; you will not be ruling and reigning with Christ and you will not receive an inheritance or rewards in the Kingdom of God.

Do you not know that the unrighteous will not *inherit* the kingdom of God? Do not be deceived. Neither the sexually immoral, nor idolaters, nor adulterers, nor male prostitutes, nor homosexuals, nor thieves, nor covetous, nor drunkards, nor revilers, nor extortioners will *inherit* the kingdom of God. Such were some of you. But you were washed, you were sanctified, and you were justified in the name of the Lord Jesus by the Spirit of our God. I Corinthians 6:9-11 MEV

For be sure of this: that no person practicing sexual vice or impurity in thought or in life, or one who is covetous (who has lustful desire for the property of others and is greedy for gain] – for he [in effect] is an idolater – has any *inheritance* in the kingdom of Christ and of God. Ephesians 5:5 AMPC

Whatever may be your task, work at it heartily (from the soul), as [something done] for the Lord and not for men, knowing [with all certainty] that it is from the Lord [and not from men] that you will receive the *inheritance* which is your [real] reward. [The One Whom] you are actually serving [is] the Lord Christ (the Messiah). Colossians 3:23-24 AMPC

What we are firmly establishing here in the Word is the fact that all those who are born again will be allowed to *enter* the Kingdom, but; they won't be ruling and reining with King Jesus during the Kingdom age here on earth.

We believe this is the lesson that Jesus is teaching us within the parable of the Talents in chapter twenty-five of Matthew's gospel and the similar parable of the Ten Minas in chapter nineteen of Luke's gospel.

To place this parable in context, this portion of Scripture is commonly referred to as the Olivet Discourse. Jesus has been meeting with His disciples when they began asking about the end of the age and beyond:

As He sat in the Mount of Olives, the disciples came to Him privately, saying, Tell us, when will these things be, and what will be the sign of Your coming and of the end of the age? Jesus answers them, Take heed that no one deceives you. Matthew 24:3-4 MEV

Jesus commands them and us not to be deceived and then goes on to teach about the signs of the times leading up to the very last of the last days of the Church age and admonishes them to be ever watchful and to live ready because no one will know the day or the hour of His return.

Jesus then begins talking about the catching away of the faithful and wise five virgins that have prepared themselves (discussed in detail in chapter six) for the wedding supper in heaven, leading then to the next parable: The Parable of the Talents.

This parable is foreshadowing and describing the Day of the Lord, or Judgement day. Every born-again believer will participate in this event because it is at this time when we will receive our rewards based on our faithfulness.

So why do you judge your brother? Or why do you despise your brother? For we all shall stand before the judgement seat of Christ. For it is written: As I live, says the Lord, every knee shall bow to Me, and every tongue shall confess to God. So then each of us shall give an account of himself to God. Romans 14:10-12 MEV

For we must all appear before the Judgement seat of Christ, that each one may receive his recompence in the body, according to what he has done, whether it was good or bad. II Corinthians 5:10 MEV

The one whose name is found in the Book of Life will come before Jesus not to be judged for your destination because that is settled. This judgement is to determine whether you are simply allowed to *enter* the Kingdom or if you are an overcomer and thus receiving your inheritance, rewards, and establishing your commissioned place of authority in the Kingdom by the King.

The Parable of the Talents gives us an impression what judgement day will be as we each must give a reckoning for what we have done with the time, talent, and treasure that the Lord gave each of us to steward and an appraisal of our spiritual fruitfulness. Or simply stated how *Christ-like* have we become because the overcomer's mandate is to walk, talk, and act just like Jesus.

Again, the kingdom of heaven is like a man traveling into a far country, who called his own servants and entrusted his goods to them. To one he gave five talents, to another two, and to another one, to every man according to his ability. And immediately he took his journey. Matthew 25:14-15 MEV

The Master going away is Jesus calling all His own servants, that means everyone who is born-again; to Himself and giving us abilities and grace to do what He has asked of us.

He who had received the five talents went and traded with them and made another five talents. So also, he who had received two gained another two. But he who had received one went and dug in the ground and hid his master's money. Matthew 25:16-18 MEV

Obviously the five-talent guy and the two-talent guy had faith in their Master and went forth to do what He had ask of them. Equally clear, the one-talent guy didn't love his Master and went and put what the Master had given him into the world.

After a long time the master of those servants came and settled accounts with them. Matthew 25:19 MEV

This is the Judgement (*bema*) seat of Christ. This is the day when we all shall stand before our Lord and our God Jesus and give an open account for our lives.

He who had received five talents came and brought the other five talents, saying, Master, you entrusted to me five talents. Look, I have gained five more. His master said to him, Well done, you good and faithful servant. You have been faithful over a few things. I will make you ruler over many things. Enter the joy of your master. He who had received two talents also came and said, Master, you entrusted me with two talents. See, I have gained two more talents besides them. His master said to him, Well done you good and faithful servant. You have been faithful over a few things. I will make you ruler over many things. Enter the joy of your master. Matthew 25:20-23 MEV

Again, we see the five-talent guy and the two-talent guy hearing precisely what we all long to hear on that day – Well done faithful servant, come and I will make you a ruler in My Kingdom. They were given different amounts to steward now but the response from the Master was exactly the same for both because they did their best (100% increase) with what the Master had ask of them individually.

Then he who had received the one talent came and said, Master, I knew that you are a hard man, reaping where you did not sow, and gathering where you did not winnow. So I was afraid, and went and hid your talent in the ground. Here you have what is yours. His master answered, You wicked and slothful servant! You knew that I reap where I have not sown, and gather where I have not winnowed. Then you ought to have given my money to the bankers, and at my coming I should have received what was my own with interest. Matthew 25:24-27 MEV

The one-talent guy did not do well, and he will enter the Kingdom, but at a significantly lesser place in the Kingdom. This guy was a man-pleaser and surely didn't want anybody to think he was some sort of super-righteous Jesus freak, and was attempting to justify his actions. The Master also told him that even if he would have given His talent to someone who would have produced a modest gain, that would have been better than basically going and doing whatever he chose to do, thus producing nothing good and absolutely nothing of eternal significance or worth.

So take the talent from him, and give it to him who has ten talents. For to everyone who has will more be given, and he will have an abundance. But from him who has nothing, even what he has will be taken away. And throw the unprofitable servant into outer darkness, where there will be weeping and gnashing of teeth. Matthew 25:28-30 MEV

To those faithful servants that have done their best to love the Lord Jesus through their faithful obedience while here on this earth, the Lord will bless those overcomers with overflowing abundance and joy beyond what we can even think or imagine. Please take notice of the fact that the Master let the faithful servants (now overcomers in the Kingdom) keep everything he had given them to steward plus he gave them all the increase too! However, those that have chosen to be the lord of their own life during these last days, will not be blessed in the Kingdom age to come and beyond into our final eternal state.

None of us know precisely what that means or what all of this will look like, nevertheless; we believe there will be many one-talent people weeping in deep regret that day when they get a glimpse at what they could have received in the coming Kingdom age and forever if they would have made the choice to trust and obey the Lord instead of chasing their own hopes, dreams, desires, and self-ambitions. Selah.

And He charged us to preach to the people and to bear solemn testimony that He is the God-appointed and God-ordained Judge of the living and the dead. Acts 10:42 AMPC

According to the grace (the special endowment for my task) of God bestowed on me, like a skillful architect and master builder I laid [the] foundation, and now another [man] is building upon it. But let each [man] be careful how he builds upon it, because no other foundation can anyone lay than that which is [already] laid, which is Jesus Christ (the Messiah, the Anointed One). But if anyone builds upon the Foundation, whether it be with gold, silver, precious stones, wood, hay, straw, The work of [each] one will become [plainly, openly] known (shown for what it is); for the day [of Christ] will disclose and declare it, because it will be revealed with fire, and the fire will test and critically appraise the character and worth of the work each person has done. If the work which any person has built on this Foundation [any product of his efforts whatever] survives [this test], he will get his reward. But if any person's work is burned up [under the test], he will suffer the loss [of it all, losing his reward], though he himself will be saved, but only as [one who has passed] through fire. I Corinthians 3:10-15 AMPC

For we must all appear and be revealed as we are before the judgment seat of Christ, so that each one may receive [his pay] according to what he has done in the body, whether good or evil [considering what his purpose and motive have been, and what he has achieved, been busy with, and given himself and his attention to accomplishing]. II Corinthians 5:10 AMPC

And whosoever gives even a cup of cold water to one of these little ones in the name of a disciple, truly I tell you, he shall in no way lose his reward. Matthew 10:42 MEV

Then He said also to the one who invited Him, When you prepare a dinner or a supper, do not call your friends or your brothers or your kinsmen or your rich neighbors, lest they also invite you in return, and you be repaid. But call the poor, the maimed, the lame, the blind, and you will be blessed, for they cannot repay you. You shall be repaid at the resurrection of the just. Luke 14:12-14 MEV

As we can clearly see, when Jesus returns to gather His Church, we will then stand before Him and our life's efforts and activities will be measured and weighed, and assuming we have something more than a pile of ashes remaining after His examination; we will receive our eternal rewards, glory, and future assignments in the Kingdom. These rewards are greater and beyond what we see described in the Scriptures, however; we shall look at what is defined in the text regarding our future potential rewards.

The Crown of Life: The reward for martyr's and those that have suffered for their life of faith and witness for Jesus. Matthew 5:10-12, James 1:12, Revelation 2:10

The Crown of Righteousness: Those that live the believer's mandate of sanctification and faithfully follow Jesus. II Timothy 4:7-8, Titus 2:11-14, I John 3:2-3

The Crown of Glory: The reward for elders and teachers of the family of God that shepherd and feed the people. I Peter 5:1-4, II Timothy 2:15, Matthew 5:19

The Incorruptible Crown: The reward for spiritual self-discipline and crucifying our flesh. I Corinthians 9:25-27, Colossians 3:23-24, Hebrews 12:1

The Crown of Rejoicing: This is the soul-winners crown. I Thessalonians 2:19, Daniel 12:3, Matthew 28:19-20

Our rewards and crowns must be diligently guarded because Jesus warned us it is possible for us to be led astray and thus deceived and our rewards or our crown(s) could be lost or taken.

Therefore do not throw away your confidence, which will be greatly rewarded. For you need patience, so that after you have done the will of God, you will receive the promise. Hebrews 10:35-36 MEV

For many deceivers, who do not confess that Jesus Christ have come in the flesh, have gone out into the world. Each one is a deceiver and an antichrist. Watch yourselves, so that we do not lose those things for which we have worked, but that we receive a full reward. II John 1:7-8 MEV

Look, I am coming quickly. Hold firm what you have, so that no one may take your crown. Revelation 3:11 MEV

The synopsis—This is the genuine Gospel of the Kingdom.

As we have said before, Jesus speaks about *He who overcomes* several times in the Scriptures. Why would Jesus admonish His Church repeatedly to be overcomers if there wasn't something substantial and very important to overcome or forfeit or lose?

He who has an ear, let him hear what the Spirit says to the churches. To him who overcomes I will give permission to eat of the tree of life, which is in the midst of the Paradise of God. Revelation 2:7 MEV

He who has an ear, let him hear what the Spirit says to the churches. He who overcomes shall not be hurt by the second death. Revelation 2:11 MEV

He who has an ear, let him hear what the Spirit says to the churches. To him who overcomes I will give the hidden manna to eat. And I will give him a white stone and on the stone a new name written, which no one knows except he who receives it. Revelation 2:17 MEV

To him who overcomes and keeps My works to the end, I will give authority over the nations- He shall rule them with a rod of iron; like the vessels of a potter they shall be broken in pieces- even as I Myself have received authority from My Father. And I will give him the morning star. He who has an ear, let him hear what the Spirit says to the churches. Revelation 2:26-29 MEV

He who overcomes shall be clothed in white garments. I will not blot his name out of the Book of Life, but I will confess his name before My Father and before His angels. He who has an ear, let him hear what the Spirit says to the churches. Revelation 3:5-6 MEV

He who overcomes will I make a pillar in the temple of My God, and he shall go out no more. I will write on him the name of My God and the name of the city of My God, the New Jerusalem, which comes down out of heaven from My God, and My own new name.

He who has an ear, let him hear what the Spirit says to the churches. Revelation 3:12-13 MEV

To him who overcomes will I grant to sit with Me on My throne, as I also overcame and sat down with My Father on His throne. He who has an ear, let him hear what the Spirit says to the churches. Revelation 3:21-22 MEV

They overcame him by the blood of the Lamb and by the word of their testimony, and they loved not their lives unto the death. Revelation 12:11 MEV

Heaven will not be equivalent for every person. Heaven has many diverse levels, positions, places, rewards, and crowns. Heaven will be different for each of us, depending on the outcome of our final exam before King Jesus at the *bema* judgement at the end of the Church age and at the beginning of the one-thousand-year Kingdom age.

Within this volume of work in Chapter seven – *In Training for Reining*, we have included the Scriptures from the seven letters that Jesus Christ dictated to apostle John on the isle of Patmos to transcribe and give to you and me, and within those seven letters are an awesome representation of promised blessings, rewards, and astounding honors for those that are faithful overcomers. We have repeated those promises here for your convenience and because they bear repeating and reviewing the promises again now as you contemplate where you are and where you want to be. Whatever possession, activity, relationship, job, etc. that has your time, attention, and your devotion here and now worthy of you trading your eternal inheritance and rewards for?

Within Chapter eight – *Christ is our Plumb Line*, we attempted to highlight and demonstrate the areas of our lives that shall be measured, weighed, and judged. Jesus shall examine our spiritual fruit and our love walk. The Lord will measure our faithfulness compared to what He has commanded of all His disciples and His Church (that means you and me).

Jesus has gifted and equipped each of us individually and given us the grace to accomplish and walk-out these assigned tasks for His coming Kingdom. This is our personal ministry to the body of Christ, and this is the cost of discipleship, and this will be one of the things weighed that day when we stand before our Lord and the books are opened.

Friend, it really does matter how we choose to live our lives here on this planet as we watch and pray for our soon coming King. We sincerely hope that this discourse will encourage and inspire you to do some very solemn soul-searching of the priorities in your own life.

And if you are not living for the Lord today, we pray that you wake-up and realize that you have seen and heard the Truth and will repent and turn around now. It is never too late for anyone if we have breath in our lungs to say–*Here I am Lord, use me.*

He who overcomes shall inherit all things, and I will be his God and he shall be My son. Revelation 21:7 MEV

Oh, faithful believers and transforming overcomers of our Lord; won't it be awesome to be ruling and reigning with our King and sharing in the restoration of this earth while living free from Satan and his corruption and tormenting influences here on earth. Hallelujah.

We truly have great and glorious things ahead of us because the end of the age of grace is very near, and the Kingdom age is about to begin.

The grace of our Lord Jesus Christ be with you all. Amen. Revelation 22:21 MEV

This is the genuine Gospel of the Kingdom!

CHAPTER FOURTEEN

God's Plan for Earth and Man.

Foundational Truth: The Lord God Almighty's master plan for the earth and humanity are encoded within the seven days of creation and the seven Feasts of the Lord.

Thus the heavens and the earth were completed, and all their hosts. By the seventh day God completed His work which He had done, and He rested on the seventh day from all His work which He had done. Then God blessed the seventh day and sanctified it, because in it He rested from all His work which God had created and made. Genesis 2:1-3 NASB

For a thousand years in Your sight Are like yesterday when it passes by, Or as a watch in the night. Psalm 90:4 NASB

Know this first of all, that in the last days mockers will come with their mocking, following after their own lusts, and saying, Where is the promise of His coming? For ever since the fathers fell asleep, all continues just as it was from the beginning of creation. For when they maintain this, it escapes their notice that by the word of God the heavens existed long ago and the earth was formed out of water and by water, through which the world at that time was destroyed, being flooded with water. But by His word the present heavens and earth are being reserved for fire, kept for the day of judgement and destruction of ungodly men. But do not let this one fact escape your notice, beloved, that with the Lord one day is like a thousand years, and a thousand years like one day. The Lord is not slow about His promise, as some count slowness, but is patient toward you, not wishing for any to perish but for all to come to repentance. II Peter 3:3-9 NASB

The seven days of creation are a prophetic pattern of man and earth being in existence for seven thousand years, and at the end of the seventh day or the seven thousand years on this earth, life as we know it will end at the dawning of the eighth day. The eighth day is the new life beginning and the new heaven and the new earth and the New Jerusalem. This is the end of time as we know it and the emergence of eternity.

Two thousand years from Adam to Abraham, and then it was two thousand years from Abraham to Jesus, and now we are at the end of the last two thousand years from the first advent of Christ until Jesus comes again. Adam was the first perfect man ruling and reigning in the perfect garden of Eden and Jesus is the last Adam (I Corinthians 15:45) that will come to rule and reign reversing the curse and restoring garden of God on earth.

This will complete the six thousand years of man on earth before the seventh day or the one-thousand-year millennial reign of King Jesus here on earth when all those that enter His Kingdom will all be at rest. Human beings will be at rest because the Antichrist and the False Prophet have both been cast into the lake of fire and the destroyer Satan who is our enemy is bound in chains in the bottomless pit prison until the very last days of the millennium when he is released for a short time.

There are many different prophetic patterns that we could discuss, however; we intend to briefly summarize what we have already studied up to this point and close with a synopsis of the significant events of the last days and the end time teachings to help us all grasp the complexities and the chronology of the horrendous events soon to manifest and come to pass on this current diabolical world system here on earth.

We also studied how the seven Feasts of the Lord represent Father God's plan of redemption and restoration for man and earth with the three spring harvest feasts of Passover, Unleavened bread, and First fruits representing Jesus' death as our Passover Lamb and how Jesus is the sinless Bread of life from heaven broken for us and how Jesus is the First fruit of many that will be resurrected from spiritual death unto spiritual life forevermore.

The final spring harvest feast being seven weeks later, the feast of Pentecost, which is the inauguration day of the Church and the beginning of the age of grace because the Spirit of grace had been given to those that will receive Him. This is the day that the gift of the Father, the Holy Spirit; was sent to the true born-again believers and devoted disciples of Jesus to empower them to live their lives as faithful overcomers here on this earth. As we yield to the sanctifying work of Holy Spirit, He will lead each of us to discover and walk in the divine calling and plan our heavenly Father has ordained and purposed for each of His children's individual lives. This amazing gift is still very much available to all born-again believers that sincerely desire the Father's gift of the baptism of the Holy Spirit and seek Him.

We looked at many of the prophetic patterns throughout the Word that the first four feasts pointed to and how all four of these spring harvest feasts have all been perfectly fulfilled through the first advent of Jesus Christ.

We studied the last three fall harvest feasts that have yet to be fulfilled: Trumpets, Atonement, and Tabernacles. We have discussed how the last three fall feasts covered the harpazo of the faithful over-comers at the two-day feast of Trumpets followed by the seven days of awe representing the seven-year Tribulation followed by the tenth day being the one-day solemn feast of Atonement representing judgement day when Jesus returns with His heavenly army following Him to this earth to defeat His enemies at the battle of Armageddon. Then concluding with the seventh and final appointed time, the feast of Tabernacles, which represents the seventh one-thousand-year period of time which is the millennial reign of King Jesus and the commencement of the Kingdom age here on earth.

The feast of Tabernacles is a seven-day feast with a final day or an eighth day, or as the participants over the centuries have called it the great day of the feast which represents the completion of the annual daily Torah reading cycle of the Holy Scriptures and the beginning of the new daily reading cycle of the Word of God. This is pointing to the conclusion of time and the Kingdom age and the commencement of eternal life in the new heaven and the new earth and the holy city, New Jerusalem.

We have also demonstrated that in accordance with Bible prophecy we are in-fact living in the *last* of the last days at the very end of the age of grace. We have covered the prophesied apostasy within the Church and how we are living in the days of the manifestation of the seventh Church of the seven churches in the Book of Revelation, which is the Laodicean Church now. We confirmed that this Church is thus controlled by the people and not the Head of the Church, which is Jesus Christ. We have illuminated the sad fact that Jesus is standing outside this apostate Church right now knocking to see if anyone will trust Him to be their Lord and accept His personal invitation to submit to Him and thus join Him at the marriage supper of the Lamb that is coming very soon.

Behold, I stand at the door and knock; if anyone hears My voice and opens the door, I will come in to him and will dine with him, and he with Me. Revelation 3:20 NASB

The last days at the very end of the age of grace:

The apostacy of the Church is followed by the harpazo of the faithful remnant of bond-servants which are the genuine overcomers of the Lord. The rapture of the overcomers is imminent, meaning it is a "signless" event. Or to say this another way, absolutely nothing must occur before the harpazo event. Our Lord Jesus could literally come to harpazo His faithful bond-servants before you finish reading this chapter of the book.

This is also the time of the resurrection of the bodies of those that have died in Christ and these shall be joined by those that remain alive to be caught up to meet the Lord in the clouds and receive their glorified bodies. All these faithful ones will soon be standing before the bema judgement seat of Jesus Christ in heaven and will then receive their recompence as we have covered within this study. These faithful saints will also be enjoying the marriage supper of the Lamb before they return with King Jesus to take up their ordained positions to rule and reign with Jesus here on earth in His Kingdom. This is our *blessed hope* as overcomers.

For the grace of God (His unmerited favor and blessing) has come forward (appeared) for the deliverance from sin and the eternal salvation for all mankind. It has trained us to reject and renounce all ungodliness (irreligion) and worldly (passionate) desires, to live discreet (temperate, self-controlled), upright, devout (spiritually whole) lives in this present world, awaiting and looking for the [fulfillment, the realization of our] blessed hope, even the glorious appearing of our great God and Savior Christ Jesus (the Messiah, the Anointed One), Who gave Himself on our behalf that He might redeem us (purchase our freedom) from all iniquity and purify for Himself a people [to be peculiarly His own, people who are] eager and enthusiastic about [living a life that is good and filled with] beneficial deeds. Titus 2:11-14 AMPC

For the Lord Himself will descend from heaven with a shout, with the voice of the archangel and with the trumpet of God, and the dead in Christ will rise first. Then we who are alive and remain will be caught up together with them in the clouds to meet the Lord in the air, and so we shall always be with the Lord. Therefore comfort one another with these words. I Thessalonians 4:16-18 NSAB

Now I say this, brethren, that flesh and blood cannot inherit the kingdom of God; nor does the perishable inherit the imperishable. Behold, I tell you a mystery; we will not all sleep, but we will all be changed, in a moment, in the twinkling of an eye, at the last trumpet; for the trumpet will sound, and the dead will be raised imperishable, and we will be changed. I Corinthians 15:50-52 NASB

The seven-year Tribulation will then commence after the harpazo/rapture of the Church which will end the age of grace on earth. Those that have not been living their life for the Lord will be left behind to endure, if at all possible, the absolutely undisputed worst time in human history on this planet we call earth. We implore you friends, you do not want to be left behind.

Now we request you, brethren, with regard to the coming of our Lord Jesus Christ and our gathering together to Him, that you not be quickly shaken from your composure or be disturbed either by a spirit or a message or a letter as if from us, to the effect that the day of the Lord has come. Let no in any way deceive you, for it will not come unless the apostasy comes first, and the man of lawlessness is revealed, the son of destruction, who opposes and exalts himself above every so-called god or object of worship, so that he takes his seat in the temple of God, displaying himself as being God. Do you not remember that while I was still with you, I was telling you these things? And you know what restrains him now, so that in his time he will be revealed. For the mystery of lawlessness is already at work; only he who now restrains will do so until he is taken out of the way. Then the lawless one will be revealed whom the Lord will slay with the breath of His mouth and bring to an end by appearance of His coming; that is, the one whose coming is in accord with the activity of Satan, with all power and signs and false wonders, and with all the deception of wickedness for those who perish, because they did not receive the love of the truth so as to be saved. II Thessalonians 2:1-10 NASB

As soon as the restrainer has been removed from the earth, which is the Holy Spirit within the bond-servants of Jesus Christ, the Antichrist will be revealed and known, and as the apparent geopolitical leader of the emerging one world governmental system he will broker (Daniel 9:27) the peace accord with the many that will commit to a seven-year peace treaty with Israel. This will mark the inauguration of the fulfillment of Daniel's seventieth week prophecy or the beginning of the seven-year Tribulation and the release of seal and trumpet judgements.

This is the start of the first conventional war during the Tribulation when one fourth of the world population will be killed (Revelation 6:8) and following this war will be yet another escalation in the fighting with the probable introduction of more powerful and efficient means of mass destruction including nuclear weapons and the subsequent contamination and devastation of the trees and vegetation on the earth, (Revelation 8:7) and the destruction of another third of the world population. (Revelation 9:15) Now at this point, more than fifty percent of the entire world population has perished in World War III during the first three and half years of the Tribulation. If we use todays estimated world population numbers that would be nearly four billion human deaths so far and the daily death toll would average exceeding three million people dying every single day.

At this same time, the one hundred forty-four thousand selected and sealed Israeli evangelists are sent out by the Lord and additionally the two witnesses (Elijah and Moses) will be preaching in Jerusalem until the end of the first forty-two months of the Tribulation. Then the Antichrist will kill the two witnesses and he will break the seven-year peace covenant with Israel and he will stop the sacrifices at the Temple in Jerusalem and he will then proclaim that he is god and the real savior of the world and the environment. He will demand and enforce the support of one world religion and one world government and one world economic system. The Antichrist will require that every one of every nation to praise, worship, and obey him.

Everyone living at that time will be required to prove their allegiance to the Antichrist by receiving his mark on their right hand or on their forehead or perish. Behold, all those that receive this mark are swearing their loyalty to the Antichrist and thus choosing to become the sworn enemy of Father God. We must be very clear here; all of the Lord's unrepentant enemies will ultimately be destroyed and judged and cast into the lake of fire forever. We believe many Jews and Gentiles will come to faith during this extraordinary stressful time. Once again, the people shall have the choice to believe the talking snake or to believe the Word of God.

After these things, the world will enter to the last half or more commonly known as the great Tribulation and it shall indeed become very, very bad here on this planet. Literally all hell has broken loose on earth for the final forty-two months of the Tribulation leading up to the battle of Armageddon (the Jezreel valley) when Jesus Christ returns with His army of overcomers.

At this time King Jesus shall come against His enemies with extreme prejudice and He annihilates the Antichrist and the kings of this earth and his two hundred-million-man army (Revelation 9:16) that the Antichrist has marshalled to come against Jesus and Israel and the Lord's capital city of Jerusalem.

Folks let's not misunderstand the realities of the so-called battle at the Mount of Megiddo (Revelation 16:16), this will be the most one-sided military offensive to ever come to pass on the earth. King Jesus shall utterly decimate His enemies with a spoken Word from His mouth. (Zechariah 14:12, Revelation 19:19-21) Wow. You do not want to be found as an enemy of the Lord Jesus.

The dawning of the Kingdom age:

The angel said to her, Do not be afraid, Mary; for you have found favor with God. And behold, you will conceive in your womb and bear a son, and you shall name Him Jesus. He will be great and will be called the Son of the Most High; and the Lord God will give Him the throne of His father David; and He will reign over the house of Jacob forever, and His kingdom will have no end. Luke 1:30-33 NASB

Next to come to pass is the long-awaited emergence of a new age, the seventh day and the dawn of the Kingdom of God being established on earth when King Jesus shall rule with all authority and in absolute righteousness all the nations of the earth from His throne in Jerusalem. Everyone from the nations of the world that survived the Tribulation will then stand before their Judge, and those judged righteous will be allowed to *enter* the King's domain, and those that He finds lacking will not enter His Kingdom. King Jesus will during this time be judging and separating the goat nations and the sheep nations of the world. The righteous sheep nations will be allowed into His kingdom, but the cursed goat nations will not be allowed to come in.

When the Son of Man comes in His glory, and all the holy angels with Him, then He will sit on the throne of His glory. Before Him will be gathered all nations, and He will separate them one from another as a shepherd separates his sheep from the goats. He will set the sheep at His right hand, but the goats at the left. Then the King will say to those at His right hand, Come, you blessed of My Father, inherit the kingdom prepared for you since the foundation of the world. Then He will say to those at the left hand, Depart from Me, you cursed, into the eternal fire, prepared for the devil and his angels. Matthew 25:31-34,41 MEV

Following these events will be a time of the restoration of all things on this earth. Of special interest of our blessed Lord is the wholeness of Israel and His holy city Jerusalem, and thus the answer to the innumerable multitudes that have faithfully prayed this prayer over the thousands of years since it was transcribed by king David as he was inspired by the Holy Spirit:

Pray for the peace of Jerusalem: May they prosper who love you. May peace be within your walls, And prosperity with in your palaces. For the sake of my brothers and my friends, I will now say, May peace be within you. For the sake of the house of the Lord our God, I will seek your good. Psalm 122:6-9 NASB

Jesus said to then, Truly I say to you, in the new age [the Messianic rebirth of the world], when the Son of Man shall sit down on the throne of His glory, you who have [become My disciples, sided with My party and] followed Me will also sit on twelve thrones and judge the twelve tribes of Israel. And anyone and everyone who has left houses or brothers or sisters of father or mother or children or lands for My name's sake will receive many [even a hundred] times more and will inherit eternal life. But many who [now] are first will be last [then], and many who [now] are last will be first [then]. Matthew 19:28-30 AMPC

The Lord spoke through His prophet Isaiah about the Messiah and His first and second coming when the prophet scribed these words thus prophesying of our Savior's first advent and His mission and then His second advent as our King.

The Spirit of the Lord God is upon me, Because the Lord has anointed me To bring good news to the afflicted; He has sent me to bind up the broken-hearted, To proclaim liberty to captives And freedom to prisoners; To proclaim the favorable year of the Lord (first advent) And the day of vengeance of our

God; To comfort all who mourn, To grant those who mourn in Zion, Giving them a garland instead of ashes, The oil of gladness instead of mourning, The mantle of praise instead of a spirit of fainting. So they will be called oaks of righteousness, The planting of the Lord, that He might be glorified. Then they will rebuild the ancient ruins, They will raise up the former devastations; And they will repair the ruined cities, The desolations of many generations. Strangers will stand and pasture your flocks, And foreigners will be your vinedressers. But you will be called the priests of the Lord; You will be spoken of as ministers of our God. You will eat the wealth of nations, And in their riches you will boast. Instead of your shame you will have a double portion, And instead of humiliation they will shout for joy over their portion. Therefore they will possess a double portion in their land, Everlasting joy will be theirs. (second advent) Isaiah 61:1-2a, 2b-7 NASB

All the surviving earth dwellers that are admitted into King's domain shall all celebrate the feast of Tabernacles and the Lord's harvest each year in Jerusalem as all things are being restored.

Then it will be that all the nations who have come against Jerusalem and survived will go up each year

to worship the King, the Lord of Hosts, and to celebrate the Feast of Tabernacles. Zechariah 14:16 MEV

On the seven days of the Feast of Tabernacles, the
burnt offering was sacrificed each day as outlined
in Numbers chapter twenty-nine. The first offering
sacrificed each day was: day one – thirteen bulls,
day two – twelve bulls, day three – eleven bulls, day
four – ten bulls, day five – nine bulls, day six – eight
bulls, and day seven – seven bulls. The total offering
of bulls during the seven days are a total of seventy bulls, or one bull for the seventy nations of the
world. Just as after Jesus selected and sent forth His
twelve apostles, Jesus then selected seventy additional apostles and sent them forth also. The twelve
represent (Luke 6:12-16) Israel and the seventy
represent (Luke 10:1) the nations of the world. The
twelve and the seventy were sent forth as laborers
into the harvest as the beginning of the Lord's harvest of souls from the harvest fields throughout all
nations of the earth.

On that day "Holy To The Lord" will be engraved
on the bells of the horses. And the pots in the house
of the Lord will be as the basins before the altar. And
every pot in Jerusalem and Judah will be holy to the
Lord of Hosts so that all who come to sacrifice will

take from those pots and boil the meat in them. And on that day there will no longer be a Canaanite in the house of the Lord of Hosts. Zechariah 14:20-21 MEV

Now it will come about that in the last days The mountain of the house of the Lord Will be established as the chief of the mountains, And will be raised above the hills; And all the nations will stream to it. And many peoples will come And say, Come, let us go up to the mountain of the Lord, To the house of the God of Jacob; That He may teach us concerning His ways And that we may walk in His paths. For the law will go forth from Zion And the word of the Lord from Jerusalem. And He will judge between the nations, And render decisions for many peoples; And they will hammer their swords into plowshares and their spears into pruning hooks. Nation will not lift up sword against nation, And never again will they learn war. Isaiah 2:2-4 NASB

But with righteousness He will judge the poor, And decide with fairness for the afflicted of the earth; And He will strike the earth with the rod of His mouth, And with the breath of His lips He will slay the wicked. And righteousness will be the belt about His loins, And faithfulness the belt about His waist. And the wolf will dwell with the lamb, And the leopard will lie down with the young goat, And the calf and the young lion and the fatling together; And a little boy will lead them. Also the cow and the bear will graze, Their young will lie down together, And the loin will eat straw like the ox. The nursing child will play by the hole of the cobra, And the weaned child will put his hand on the viper's den. They will not hurt or destroy in all My holy mountain, For the earth will be full of the knowledge of the Lord As the waters cover the sea. Isaiah 11:4-9 NASB

Behold, the days are coming, declares the Lord, When the plowman will overtake the reaper And the treader of grapes him who sows seed; When the mountains will drip sweet wine And all the hills will be dissolved. Also I will restore the captivity of My people Israel, And they will rebuild the ruined cities and live in them; They will plant vineyards and drink their wine, And make gardens and eat their fruit. I will also plant them on their land, And they will not again be rooted out from their land Which I have given them, Says the Lord your God. Amos 9:13-15 NASB

Each of them will sit under his vine And under his fig tree, With no one to make them afraid, For the mouth of the Lord of hosts has spoken. Micah 4:4 NASB

No longer will there be in it an infant who lives but a few days, Or an old man who does not live out his days; For the youth will die at the age of one hundred Will be thought accursed. Isaiah 65:20 NASB

At the very end of the Kingdom age, Satan will be released one last time to go forth on the earth and attempt to deceive the people to join his rebellion against the King. Once and for all time those living on earth at the very end of the millennium must choose between believing the talking snake or the Lord God Almighty. There will be many in that day that foolishly choose to follow their own lusts of the flesh and their self-ambitions. These that are deceived will listen to Satan and join his final insurgence against the Lord God Almighty, nevertheless; he and the multitude with him from the nations of the earth are all consumed by fire sent from heaven.

When the thousand years are completed, Satan will be released from his prison, and will come out to deceive the nations which are in the four corners of the earth, Gog and Magog, to gather them together for the war; the number of them is like the sand of the seashore. And they came up on the broad plain of the earth and surrounded the camp of the saints and the beloved city, and fire came down from heaven and devoured them. And the devil who deceived them was thrown into the lake of fire and brimstone, where the beast and the false prophet are also; and they will be tormented day and night forever and ever. Revelation 20:7-10 NSAB

Now the dramatic conclusion of the Kingdom age, which is marked by the second resurrection of the dead of all the unrighteous individuals that have ever lived in ages past will be brought up before the great white throne judgement. The books that have recorded in them the details of their lives are opened and reviewed. Just as the prophet spoke (Isaiah 45:23, Philippians 2:9-11) that every knee shall bow, and every tongue confess that Jesus is Lord of all.

Therefore, every person will be reminded of their choices and thus each one will know exactly why they are now being judged and cast into the lake of fire to receive eternal torment forever and ever. No one will be sent to eternal damnation by our King and Judge because just like you and me, each and every person was given multiple opportunities during their life to choose who they would harken to and obey; the talking snake or the Lord Jesus.

Then I saw a great white throne and Him who sat upon it, from whose presence earth and heaven fled away, and no place was found for them. And I saw the dead, the great and the small, standing before the throne, and the books were opened; and another book was opened, which is the book of life; and the dead were judged from the things which were written in the books, according to their deeds. And the sea gave up the dead which were in it, and death and Hades gave up the dead which were in them; and they were judged, every one of them according to their deeds. Then death and Hades were thrown into the lake of fire. This is the second death, the lake of fire. And if anyone's name was not found written in the book of life, he was thrown into the lake of fire. Revelation 20:11-15 NASB

The story of this earth and of fallen humanity will end just as it began with people living in the perfect place and the perfect environment, nevertheless; the vast majority of those individuals shall make the very same decision that the first two humans made and thus choosing to rebel against the Master and Creator of the universe. Even after all of these things most of the people will choose to listen to the talking snake instead of Father God, thus attesting forevermore that mankind is an absolute mess and is in desperate need of a Savior and Lord.

When will we learn that our plan does not work? The sad answer for most people is–*Never*.

The new heaven and the new earth and the New Jerusalem:

In the beginning God created the heavens and the earth. Genesis 1:1 NASB

Then I saw a new heaven and a new earth; for the first heaven and the first earth passed away, and there is no longer any sea. And I saw the holy city, new Jerusalem, coming down out of heaven from God, made ready as a bride adorned for her husband. Revelation 21:1-2 NASB

Our blessed Lord God Almighty does everything in types, shadows, similitudes, and prophetic patterns and He ends at the beginning and begins at the ending.

The thing that has been – it is what will be again, and that which has been done is that which will be done again; and there is nothing new under the sun. Ecclesiastes 1:9 AMPC

That which is now already has been, and that which is to be already has been; and God seeks that which has passed by [so that history repeats itself]. Ecclesiastes 3:15 AMPC

Just like the eighth day of the great day of the feast of Tabernacles that represents the annual Torah reading cycle. We shall begin with the Word and we shall end with the Word and everything is about the Word because the Word is King Jesus in print.

In the beginning was the Word, and the Word was with God, and the Word was God. He was in the beginning with God. All things came into being through Him, and apart from Him nothing came into being that has come into being. John 1:1-3 NASB

As our Lord and our King completes the Master's plan, time as we know it has ceased because as we have our departure from the Kingdom age the Lord God Almighty brings us into our eternal home, and we shall never again have need of time! Oh, hallelujah and glory to God and praise His Holy Name forever and ever! Amen.

For from the days of old they have not heard or perceived by ear, Nor has the eye seen a God besides You, Who acts in the behalf of the one who waits for Him. Isaiah 64:4 NASB

The apostle Paul was quoting this prophetic Scripture when he scribed by inspiration: but just as it is written, Things which eye has not seen and ear has not heard, and which have not entered the heart of man, all that God has prepared for those who love Him. I Corinthians 2:9 NASB

Thus says the Lord, Heaven is My throne and the earth is My footstool. Where then is a house you could build for Me? And where is a place that I may rest? For My hand made all these things, Thus all these things came into being, declares the Lord. But to this one I will look, To him who is humble and contrite of spirit, and who trembles at My word. Isaiah 66:1-2 NASB

He who overcomes will inherit these things, and I will be his God and he will be My son. Revelation 21:7 NASB

The city is laid out as a square, and its length is as great as he width; and he measured the city with the rod, fifteen hundred miles; its length and width and height are equal. Revelation 21:16 NASB

Do you believe that it is conceivable to reckon just how spacious this New Jerusalem the glorious capital city of our Lord and our God is? And should we even attempt to stretch our imaginations?

1500 miles x 1500 miles x 1500 miles equals three billion three hundred seventy-five million cubic miles

(5,280-foot cube) of volume within the parameters given in the Scriptures for this incredible city.

The largest known residence in the world is the Windsor Castle located in Berkshire, England and has about one thousand rooms totaling four hundred eighty-four thousand square feet, therefore; we will use that as our average mansion size in heaven.

Each floor or level would then be sixty-two trillion seven hundred twenty-six billion four hundred million square feet. We will continue to speculate that each mansion would be five hundred thousand square feet each. Thus the net yield would be one hundred twenty-five million four hundred fifty-two thousand eight hundred homes per each successive level having the common height of each being established at five miles.

However the most difficult to imagine is this issue of height. How many levels does this city have that is one thousand five hundred miles high? We would like to have our very own atmosphere in our mansion, so we will assume each home would have its own sky too. Therefore, we shall assume a ceiling height of twenty-six thousand four hundred feet or five miles high, thus; allowing more than twice the height for an eagle to soar.

This would then allow for three hundred levels for a total mansion home count within the city of thirty-seven billion six hundred thirty-five million eight hundred forty thousand individual homes of a half a million square feet each.

Considering the estimated total number of persons that have ever lived here at something under one hundred billion and using Jesus Christ's parable of the Sower estimation of 25% of all people being good soil and therefore believers, we come up with a housing need in just this one city of twenty-five billion, thus; our assumed calculations will accommodate the total estimated need for us all to have a very spacious home in New Jerusalem and enough acreage left over to have one hundred forty four billion acres total of common space within the city which would then allow a park of four hundred eighty million acres of common recreation space per each level. The size of each park on each level would be nearly ten times larger than all the combined acres of all the national parks within the United States of America.

What will it be like living in heaven?

No more war. No more sickness. No more pain. No more sorrows or tears. No sin or strife or stress or heartache or regrets.

We all shall have absolutely perfect glorified bodies. No more sun or moon because we don't need them because there is no more time keeping. No more darkness or night.

Streets made of solid pure gold. Enormous gates made of solid pearl and foundations of priceless gem-stones. Incredible colors and scents and sound we do not know and an abundance of flora and fauna of all sorts. Pure rivers of crystal-clear water and the tree of life bearing its twelve varieties of fruit.

And the glory of the Lord is its light. We will have unbroken fellowship. Praise and worship will go on endlessly and we get to study the Word of God forever.

None of us can really grasp, imagine, or even begin to comprehend everything our good, good Father has planned for His family, however; we unquestionably know this – it's gonna be awesome and forever!

I am the Alpha and the Omega, the first and the last, the beginning and the end. Revelation 22:13 NASB

We beseech you to please search your heart and carefully consider your relationship and your walk with Jesus Christ as you seek to fulfill the overcom-er's mandate.

Amen.

Epilogue

***B**lame Me Not.* As I contemplate the general condition of the worldwide Church that my Lord and my God came here to suffer and die for, my heart is heavy; and I am deeply and profoundly grieved. One evening as I was researching some study materials for this book, I happened across these inspired words that were composed anonymously and carved upon a Lutheran cathedral door in Lubeck, Germany in AD 1173. Please take a few moments to ponder the simple yet profound wisdom found within these words, as you reflect upon the sincere intentions of your heart.

You call Me Eternal, *then do not seek Me.*

You call Me Fair, *then do not love Me.*

You call Me Gracious, *then do not trust Me.*

You call Me Just, *then do not fear Me.*

You call Me Life, *then do not choose Me.*

You call Me Light, *then do not see Me.*

You call Me Lord, *then do not respect Me.*

You call Me Master, *then do not obey Me.*

You call Me Merciful, *then do not thank Me.*

You call Me Almighty, *then do not honor Me.*

You call Me Noble, *then do not serve Me.*

You call Me Rich, *then do not ask Me.*

You call Me Savior, *then do not praise Me.*

You call Me Good Shepherd, *then do not follow Me.*

You call Me the Way, *then do not walk with Me.*

You call Me Wisdom, *then do not heed Me.*

You call Me Faithful, *then do not believe Me.*

You call Me the Son of God, *then do not worship Me.*

At the end if I condemn you, *then blame Me not.*

Let the words of my mouth, and the meditation of my heart, be acceptable in thy sight, O Lord, my strength, and my redeemer. Psalm 19:14 KJV

Amen.

CPSIA information can be obtained
at www.ICGtesting.com
Printed in the USA
BVHW032136061022
648910BV00008B/48